Image in the Mirror

11-9-2019

To Cheryl

"Keep soaring with the eagles"

Homer S. Sewell III
A. Lincoln

Image in the Mirror

*A Man's Personal Life's Journey
Whilst Portraying Abe Lincoln*

HOMER S. SEWELL III

Tate Publishing & Enterprises

Image in the Mirror
Copyright © 2010 by Homer S. Sewell III. All rights reserved.

No part of this publication may be reproduced, stored in a retrieval system or transmitted in any way by any means, electronic, mechanical, photocopy, recording or otherwise without the prior permission of the author except as provided by USA copyright law.

The opinions expressed by the author are not necessarily those of Tate Publishing, LLC.

Published by Tate Publishing & Enterprises, LLC
127 E. Trade Center Terrace | Mustang, Oklahoma 73064 USA
1.888.361.9473 | www.tatepublishing.com

Tate Publishing is committed to excellence in the publishing industry. The company reflects the philosophy established by the founders, based on Psalm 68:11,
"The Lord gave the word and great was the company of those who published it."

Book design copyright © 2010 by Tate Publishing, LLC. All rights reserved.
Cover design by Amber Gulilat
Interior design by Nathan Harmony

Published in the United States of America
ISBN: 978-1-61739-015-9
Biography & Autobiography
10.08.02

Dedication

This book is dedicated to God, who has given me the strength to never give up ... and to a lot of very special people in my life. There have been so many people who have meant so much to me these past sixty-seven years.

To my new wife, Marti, and all the special qualities she brings to our life together.

To my three children: Homer IV (Chip) forty-two, Jason Leon and his twin sister, Kimberly Irene, thirty-three, and my two grandchildren, Rylan, five, and his sister, Addie, two.

To my mother and father who raised me: Homer, Jr. and Dorothy.

To my newly-found birth-mother and father: Millie Levitz Ferency Franklin and Alex Ferency.

To my brother and sister with whom I grew up—Michael and Dottie Ann (D.A.) and to my three newly found brothers: Barry, Stuart, and Gershon, and to my half-sister Jennifer, and to all my nieces, nephews, and cousins scattered around the world from Massachusetts to Florida, California, Washington, and all the way to Israel.

For cover picture a special thanks to Martha A. Smith and Maggie Hall.

For proofreading, Kenneth Hall

To my friend, Jacque B. Waller who needle pointed my favorite motto.

To my favorite people all over the world: my teachers, principals, librarians, nurses, counselors, custodians, cafeteria workers, and all the others who work so hard (for so little money!) in our schools to see that our next generation of leaders is properly trained in reading, writing, and arithmetic. Thank you for all you do for students everywhere! I know God has a very special place waiting for you.

To senior citizens everywhere!

To all the people who took me into their lives and their homes and fed me great meals, visited with me, and gave me warm places to sleep as I traveled all over this great, big, beautiful country I so lovingly call *Abe Lincoln's America*.

A very special thank you to these people for editing and editorial assistance: Becky James, Tracey Clark

And last, but certainly not least, my Masonic friends all over the world. Masons throughout the world do so much good to help children and all mankind. I am very proud to be a small part of this great fraternity.

Contents

The Birth of this Abe and Early Years	13
Early Years Continued	17
Growing Up and the Diary of a Sixteen-Year-Old	23
Storms in Life	41
Moving, Jobs, and Love	51
Jobs, Jobs, Jobs	67
More Jobs	73
Even More Jobs	95
Off to Washington	105
Gettysburg	109
Mom, Look Who's Here!	111
Importance of Letter Writing	119
Taking a Trip	131
Search for Family	135
A Bad Experience at the Theater	143
Life Happenings and Travel Log	155
Romance and Marriage	203
Coincidences and Travel List	213
P.S. My Suggestions for Change	299
And in Conclusion	303
Photo Gallery	307

PREFACE

Once upon a time, near Mickey Mouse town in Altamonte Springs, Florida (about twenty-five miles from Walt Disney World, Orlando), there lived a man by the name of Homer S. Sewell III.

No, this is not a real fairy tale, but the story about how one man became "Abe," as in Lincoln!

One day in 1975, as I was driving along I-4 in Orlando, I heard a public service announcement from the local school district. They were looking for volunteers to talk to students about any subject of interest. I wondered how many students had never had the opportunity to talk to and visit with someone who had actually worked in the White House. I called and volunteered to speak to the students about my experiences during the Johnson Administration.

At that same time, I had started growing a beard just as the real Abe had done right before his first election, at the suggestion of an eleven-year-old girl from Westfield, New York, by the name of Grace Bedell (11-4-1848 to 11-2-1936). Local people started telling me how much I looked like "Abe." That suggestion made me think perhaps I should study and do more research into the life and times of our sixteenth president.

The first few schools I visited, I delivered the Gettysburg Address and spent the other fifty minutes of my program talking to the students about my activities at the White House and on the road with the president and first family. We will go into a lot more details about these past thirty-five years of being Abe, but let me say it has been a rewarding experience to see the looks on students' faces when Abe walks into their schools. I will show you copies of letters from students, teachers, and principals about how I have, as Abe, touched their lives for the better.

And now the rest is history!

For those of you who have not had the opportunity to witness first-hand this one-hour program, I will at least give you *some* of the wording of what we use in the show. (The words in italics in the beginning of each chapter are from my show.)

You may want to get in touch with Abe to have an in-person visit to your school, church, synagogue, temple, Masonic Lodge, civic group, sales meeting, or gathering. Please call the number listed in this book to arrange for a visit from Abe.

I started out calling my book *Abe Lincoln's America*, because that is what I call my show. I have now changed the title to *The Image in the Mirror* because I feel it is a more appropriate title.

My show is a look into the life of Abe Lincoln from the log cabin to the White House. Excerpts from the show will be woven into the story of my life.

What this book will try to do for you, the reader, is take you on a journey through the life and times of the man who, since 1975, has been portraying Abe in front of over two million people in more than forty-six states and at hundreds of locations. And how, in his pursuit of Abe Lincoln's America, he has discovered Homer S. Sewell III's America and how *The Image in the Mirror* has transformed his life. It is a story about never giving up in the pursuit of your goals; how one man's dream of being a full-time Abe Lincoln has finally materialized, and of the many lessons in life I have learned through trial and error.

This book is also about a man who was raised by an adoptive family and after forty-nine years finally found his birth parents. It tells the story of his search for his birth parents and gives you suggestions and help in case you, too, might be looking for long-lost loved ones. It is the story about a man who was raised in Protestant Churches and found out in 1992 he was born Jewish, has a Rabbi for a step-brother, and eighteen generations of Rabbis in the family.

Even though I will address many of my messages to students in this book; it is indeed a book written for people of *all* ages. We *all* need to be inspired to do greater things with our lives!

This book is a story of love, caring about others, and of teaching our youth (the students who *are* the future of our great country!) to stay off drugs, do what they can to stop youth violence in America, read lots of good books, and have more respect for parents, teachers, and everyone they come in contact with each day.

If the author accomplishes what he wants to with this book, *you* will have more self-esteem, will want to continue to read more good books, and will learn what it means to be, "A dreamer, a stargazer, a rainbow chaser, and to soar with the eagles!"

I believe that in our society today our children are innocent victims of senseless violence, and if we had more hugging, we would have less mugging! Give someone a hug today!

Thank you for your interest and may God continue to bless you, your family, and our country.

—Homer S. Sewell III, aka
Abraham Lincoln

The Birth of this Abe and Early Years

I was born on Sunday morning, February 12, 1809 in Hardin County, Kentucky, in a dirt-floored log cabin with no running water and only one window. My sister, Sarah, was already two years old when I came bouncing into this world...just exactly like all of you did...crying!

I was born on Wednesday, August 4, 1943, at 8:20 a.m., in a doctor's office in Hinesville, Georgia. My dad, Alex Ferency, twenty-one, was in the U.S. Army stationed at Ft. Stewart, near Savannah. My mom, Millie Levitz Ferency, was only nineteen years old. The thought of raising a baby during the war and with a husband away in the army was more than she could handle.

They decided to give me up for adoption and went in search of a good family who might be interested in adopting a baby boy. My mother somehow ended up in a dress shop run by Madeline Simpson. She indicated that her sister-in-law, Dorothy Simpson Sewell, might be interested in adopting. She was, and the adoption took place in an attorney's office in Hinesville on October 13, 1943, when I was only ten weeks old.

I was fortunate enough to be adopted by a very loving couple who had been married for six years and had not been able to have any children. My new mom, Dorothy, was a legal secretary and my new dad, Homer S. Sewell, Jr., was a salesman.

I have a few memories from my early childhood growing up in South Florida. Two years after they adopted me, Mom gave birth to my sister, Dottie Ann, and two years later to my brother, Mike.

I attended my first year of school in Belle Glade. I really enjoyed going to school and learning how to read and write.

Once, when I was very little, maybe about six or so, I was playing below an outside porch in a large, empty refrigerator box. My brother Mike and I were building a playhouse in that big box. I asked him for a hammer and he tossed it down to me. I was hit in the head. Mother had to rush me to the hospital for stitches. I still have a scar on my head from that blow.

One scary time was during a bad hurricane. Dad was downtown at the Royal's Department Store, where he worked, boarding up windows and the water was already waist deep from Lake Okeechobee overflowing. They did not have the dikes and levees in place back then to keep it from overflowing. The whole town of Belle Glade was under about three or four feet of water for several days and there was a lot of damage everywhere.

Mom and Dad both worked hard to support us. We were very fortunate and I don't ever remember our family having any shortage of food to eat or a place to live. There were several times as I was growing up in Belle Glade when men stopped by the house looking for something to eat. My mother always had the makings for an extra sandwich and something cold to drink for those less fortunate people.

Most people think Florida is all beaches and sand, but some of the richest, most fertile land anywhere is found in the Belle Glade area of South Florida. There are a lot of vegetables grown there, which are shipped all over the country. Consequently, a lot of migrant workers live in the area.

The plight of these folks is still the same as it was in my youth, and even in the 1990s and 2000s these people are sometimes treated like slaves were in Abe's time. Those of us who care about people need to investigate migrant workers' camps all over this great, big, beautiful country of ours and do whatever we can to improve their conditions.

I learned at an early age that there were people in our world who didn't have a roof over their heads or a meal to eat. I also learned that those of us who did have the basic essentials of life should share with others.

Lesson to be learned here is: When God blesses us enough to have a little extra, share it with those in need. Our world will become a better place to live when we all care more about each other.

Early Years Continued

When I was seven years old, Dad heard the land was better in Indiana, so we packed up our belongings and moved. Two years later, my mom died. A year later, Pa went back down to Kentucky and married a widow-lady by the name of Sarah Bush Johnston. She had three children from her previous marriage: John, Elizabeth, and Matilda.

We moved to Savannah and I attended second and half of third grade there. We then moved to Central Florida and lived in Altamonte Springs. My grandfather, Homer S. Sewell, Sr. had moved into the area back in 1929 and there are still streets named after him.

When I was in third grade, our family attended the Methodist Church on Highway 17–92 in Casselberry. The pastor, Reverend Darwin Shea, was a pilot and told the young people that if we would come to Sunday school for six months without missing a Sunday he would take us for a ride in his airplane. I attended at least six months without missing a single Sunday and couldn't wait for my first airplane ride.

The date for the big flight was finally arranged and we flew out of a small grass-strip landing field called Slade Field. This is where the Woodlands Subdivision on Highway 436 in Longwood is now located. That first airplane ride was a thrill for me and is probably when I got the notion that some day I wanted to be able to fly my own airplane. There is nothing to compare to the feeling of flying in a small airplane.

My dad sold ladies' shoes at a large department store in Orlando, and when I was in sixth grade, he was asked to transfer to a store in Ocala, Florida.

While living in Ocala, we took a class trip to St. Augustine, the oldest city in the United States, and visited Fort Castillo de San Marcos. That was a wonderful trip back into history and may have been one of the first things that got me started on my interest in history.

That same school year, I was asked to deliver the Gettysburg Address on a radio talk show in Ocala. I know I didn't have a beard then, but perhaps I was already tall and skinny and someone thought I looked enough like Abe that I should be the one to do his most famous speech. *A bit of history crosses my path!* After six months, we moved back to Altamonte Springs.

One day, when I was only eleven or twelve years old, my brother and I got into a fight about something. When Mom came home from work, she found out about the fight we had and proceeded to give me a well-deserved spanking. When she finished punishing me, I turned to her and said, "You're just picking on me because I'm not really your child!" Well, I want to tell you the next statement that came out of her mouth I will never forget. Mom said to me, "Son, we picked you out! Your brother and sister just came along!" Boy, did that straighten out my thinking about being adopted. Those of you who are adopted, please be sure to let your adoptive parents know how much you really do appreciate what they did for you.

I've known I was adopted for as long as I can remember. My parents told me as soon as I was old enough to know what it meant. For you parents who either already have or are considering adopting, please *always* let your adoptive children know they are adopted and that you love them and respect them just as much as your biological children.

One morning in 1955 I woke up to find out the old Altamonte Hotel had burned down during the night. It was at the intersection of Highway 436 and Maitland Avenue and less than a mile from our house. A lot of famous people had stayed in the hotel and it was sad to see it burned to the ground. One of those who had stayed there was Ulysses S. Grant, Commander of the Union Forces during the Civil War and our eighteenth president. *Another bit of history crosses my path!*

I loved school, and during my twelve years there, I didn't miss very many days. I always wanted to be there to learn and to be with my friends.

I remember those days in the "Friendly City" of Ocala. I made a lot of friends and still have the autograph book I started at that school. In fact, I have included some of the more interesting poems from that book in this one.

These things were written in my autograph book during the years I was in sixth through twelfth grades:

> Just to be naughty. Just to be nice. I'll be naughty and write my name twice. EARL CLARKSON EARL CLARKSON

> Best of luck this summer in your job. It has been my pleasure knowing you all these years. God bless you. CHRISTENA RITCHISON

> Remember the girl from the country, Remember the girl from the town, Remember the girl who ruined your book, By writing her name upside down! VIRGINIA HUME

May you have the best of luck and may the girl you like (whoever it is) like you. Love, PAT MORGAN

There may be Golden Ships or Silver Ships but there is no ship like FRIENDSHIP. Yours truly, MIKKIE DELANEY

If you see a monkey up in a tree, don't throw a stick. It might be me. Your pal, PAT DELANEY

When you get married and live in the south, Remember me and my big mouth. PRISCILLA NIXON

The higher the mountain, the cooler the breeze, the younger the couple, the tighter they squeeze. JUDY HARDWICKE

Make it a rule as long as you live, no matter who's wrong, you always forgive. Yours 'till Alaska drinks Canada Dry. Your friend always, JOYCE

The best of luck to a swell guy. Yours truly, ALICE ANN HULL

If you get to heaven before I do, Pinch a little hole and pull me through. A friend, SHIRLEY LARGENT

I wish you the best of everything in anything you do. Keep up the good work. EILEEN MARSH

To a sweet boy. Success will come your way. Let me know…where you'll be a chef and I'll come and try it. Love and best wishes, JANET ELGIN

When you get married and live in a tree, send me a coconut C.O.D. KAYE CLARK

Image in the Mirror

When you get married and think you are sweet, pull off your shoes and smell your feet. A very nice, well behaved young man. Sincerely, CHI-CHI HALLETT

Roses are red, violets are blue, I have found a friend in you. Lots of luck and happiness in the future. Love ya, FRAN

Fall in a barrel, fall in a tub, But whatever you fall in, don't fall in love! Lots of luck and best wishes, PAT MCNEIL

You are a nice boy and I like you (as a friend) very much. I wish you the best of luck in the years ahead. 2-young 2-go 4 girls. 2-sweet 2-be 4-gotten Your friend, DIANE WHARTON

To a guy who will go places in this world. Lots of luck in the future with a special girl. PAUL MAE LEMONS

Any time you need any help just remind me that I owe you a couple of favors. You're a swell pal. Thanks a lot and good luck. ADRIAN WAHLBERG

You're one of the nicest boys I've ever known. Please stay that way and I know you'll go far if you do. I'll always remember your jokes. Keep telling them. Best wishes. CAMILLA KIRKLAND

To a very sweet and cute boy who asked me to the Prom and made me very, very happy. May you always find success in everything you do. Thank you for the very pretty flowers and I'll always remember you. When the sun has set its last and the earth no longer stands, may the good Lord bless and keep you 'till you reach the Promised Land. Thank you again. Good luck always, PATRICIA MORENE

The very best of everything. Sincerely, J.G. PAYNE (My Science teacher and coach)

It is a joy to teach one who is so conscientious in his work. I know that you will be successful in all that you undertake. Sincerely, ALDIA MILWEE (My English teacher grades nine through twelve. If it weren't for her, this book would not be written! Another really great teacher!)

That is the end of my little autograph book. Do any of those sound familiar to you older folks? Remember how much fun it was signing all those annuals and autograph books for your friends?

Lesson to be learned here is:

For Students: Have fun in school. Whether you know it or not, these are the best years of your life. You will never again have as much fun as you are having in school. You will also never learn as much in any other twelve or sixteen-year period as you will while still in school. Please pay attention to your teachers and let your minds become a sponge to soak up knowledge. Make sure you hug (for those older students, a handshake will suffice) a teacher every day and tell them how much you appreciate them.

Lesson to be learned here is:

For Adults: Take time to remember the good times you had while you were in school: the fads, music, movies, etc. As you deal with our youth of today, remember the times when you were young. Were the fads from *your* days any stranger to *your* parents than the fads of today are to *you?* Take time to stop and smell the roses.

Growing Up and the Diary of a Sixteen-Year-Old

I remember chopping down a lot of trees while growing up in Indiana. I was always helping my pa building fences, barns, cabins, and working in the garden.

The Diary of 1959

This is the only year I ever kept a diary, and I thought it might be interesting for you to see what we teenagers did back then. This is also the year I turned sixteen.

Looking back while I write this book, I don't know why I chose to keep a diary in 1959. But sixteen is a good age with lots of exciting things happening all around us and within our bodies. For those of you guys and gals who aren't already doing so, you might want to consider keeping a diary or journal of what you do each day. It will make interesting reading later in life. Don't worry, I have deleted the more boring days. Were those of us who are now "Over Fifty" so different than today's teens?

January

Thursday, 1–1: We ate New Year's dinner at my grandmother's house.

Monday; 1–5: Started first day of school after Christmas vacation. I started the first day of a church study course.

Tuesday: I went to second day of study course and then went to Boy Scout meeting.

Saturday: Boy Scout Troop 38 went on a hike to Sweetwater Hills from 10 a.m. to 5:30 p.m.

Wednesday: I got exempted from World History and English semester tests. I ran the 220-yard-dash in thirty-six.

Friday: Frank Loeser and I took a bouquet of flowers to Janet Elgin.

Monday; 1–19: I cut some oak logs for the fireplace. A man gave me a dollar for taking his boat to him.

Tuesday: Boy Scout meeting. I cut some firewood and then went to Allen's house.

Wednesday: I mopped and waxed the kitchen and bathroom floors.

Saturday: Mike and I left at 1:00 p.m. to go camping at Bear Island on the south side of Orlando.

Monday; 1–26: We went to see the movie, *The Light in the Forest*. My uncle, Bob Anderson, was in it.

Wednesday: Barry brought me a pound of Plaster of Paris so I could take castings of animal tracks. I went to Paul's house and then rode my bike to church.

Thursday: I raked the front yard and then went skating with the church choir.

Friday: Barry brought me another pound of Plaster of Paris. Harry, Barry, Greg, Allen, Teddy, and I spent the night at the clay pit and went frog-gigging.

Saturday: Barry and I came home and we cooked the frog legs along with toast, coffee, and spuds. Mom didn't like the frog legs jumping all over the pan! I then cleaned the kitchen and around the back door for grandmother. Pop Sewell (my grandfather) took Barry and me into Winter Park and later we went frogging.

February

Monday, 2–2: Mother had to work tonight. I called Elizabeth Banks about going to the Sweetheart Banquet with me.

Thursday: Allie gave me a quarter. I now have a total of $1.71.

Friday: I vacuumed the living room for Mother. Allen, Barry, Mike, and I camped out at the clay pit.

Sunday: Mr. Bradford gave me an usher's job at church. Mom cut my hair and talked to Mrs. Banks about the banquet.

Monday, 2–9: I did some work for Mrs. Douglas. She paid me $1.50.

Tuesday: Barry didn't come to scouts so I took over. Elizabeth called.

Thursday: I went back to work for Mrs. Douglas. She paid me $2.00. I called Elizabeth.

Friday: I mopped the kitchen and the bathroom. We went to get Dad in Orlando and ate at Morrison's Cafeteria. Mike, Allen, Gregory, and Teddy went camping. I had a patrol meeting. I washed Mrs. Spain's Cadillac for a dollar.

Saturday: I took Elizabeth to the Sweetheart Banquet and to the school dance. (I didn't know how to dance and would only attempt the slow stuff!) Her first date! What a ball!

Tuesday: I got a letter from Margy Ryder (I met her last summer while she was visiting her grandparents, the Watsons, who live in Altamonte Springs) from Massachusetts. We had a Board of Review meeting at scouts. I received my Second Class rank. We started track today at school. I ran the thirty-yard dash in 3.2 and the fifty-yard dash in 6.8.

Friday: I went to Orlando to get Dad and put a roll of film in a drug store to get developed.

Monday, 2–23: We went to the Prairie Lake Drive-in Theater to see "Houseboat." I vacuumed the living room rug. Dixon gave me a C+ for my fourth six-week's Biology notebook.

Tuesday: I went to scouts. Dad brought my pictures and all twelve were good. I pulled some more moss down. I ran the 440 in 1:13 and the fifty in 6.8.

Wednesday: Mom cut my hair. Allen and I got some crawfish for Biology class. I got a "C" on my English notebook. I took three pictures of Victor and Smoky, our dog and cat.

Friday: I didn't have a patrol meeting. There was a tornado warning. No tornado!

March

Sunday: I went to church and then I put up a fence for Mother. I took a negative to get duplicated and enlarged at Keyser's Drug Store.

Monday, 3–2: I went to Barry's house for a Patrol Leader's Council. I cut some kindling for Pop Sewell.

Tuesday: Mike and I walked to scouts. I mopped the floor for Mother.

Thursday: Elizabeth called me. Mike, D.A., and I went to Martha Wahlberg's birthday party.

Saturday: Mr. Kopp brought the hut out to the cow pasture. I did some work for Mrs. Douglas and she paid me $1.25 for the one hour I worked. Mike, Allen, and I went skating at the Coliseum in Orlando.

Monday, 3–9: I worked two hours mowing part of Mr. Hoberg's backyard. He gave me a $1.50. I dissected a frog for Biology. Barry and I caught him in the cow pasture and operated on him at Barry's house. I went to my first night of typing class at school. I don't feel so good. Mr. Payne gave me some formaldehyde for the frog, but I didn't use it. He didn't tell me that the stuff could kill me. I feel like it is going to.

Tuesday: Dad had me up at 6:30 this morning planting azaleas. I walked with Barry to scouts.

Saturday: I got a new pair of shoes in Orlando. Mother took me to Elizabeth's house to give her some pictures. Mike, Allen, and I slept in the hut.

Sunday: Mike, Allen, and I cooked pancakes for breakfast at the hut. We had our first Scout Court of Honor at the church. It was a candlelight service. I finished a roll of film tonight.

Monday, 3-16: I went to typing class again. I have a bad cold. I gave my roll of film to Dad this morning to get developed.

Tuesday: It is still raining. I went to Scout meeting. Mike slammed the car door on three fingers of my right hand. Dad brought home my pictures and all twelve were good.

Wednesday: Barry and I went down to the cow pasture. It is overflowing again. I called Elizabeth. We planted some castor bean seeds in the backyard.

Thursday: The cow pasture is a lake again like it was last year.

Friday: We didn't have to go to school because of a teachers' convention. I mopped the kitchen. Barry and I went frogging in the boat, but we didn't get any.

Monday, 3-23: I went to typing class at school. Barry, Teddy, and I went down to the cow pasture and set out a trout line. Mike caught eight bass in the lake.

Saturday: I helped Mr. Kopp take the dirt from around his orange trees. Mother, grandmother, D.A., and I went out to Colonial Plaza and got a banana split for thirty-seven cents.

Sunday: I got up at 5:30 to go direct traffic for the Easter sunrise service. It rained, so we had the service in the church. I just finished writing a 361-word essay on mental health for English. All I had to write was 250 words! Went to six hours of church today.

Monday, 3–30: I ate supper at the hut. Then I went to typing class. I rode home with Connie. I wrote a four-page essay on political parties for English.

Tuesday: There was a baseball game at school during fifth and sixth periods. I didn't go. We went to Prairie Lake Drive-In Theater to see "Tom Sawyer" and "Gulliver's Travels."

April

Thursday: There was a tornado in Orlando. Mr. Dixon gave me a C+ on my biology notebook.

Saturday: I mopped the front porch. I cut Mrs. Spain's lawn for a dollar an hour. I earned $2.25. I cleaned the rug on the front porch. Dicky Moore came over and he, Mike, and I went swimming in the lake.

Sunday: We caught thirty-one catfish on the trout line. We started building a three-story hut and look-out tower in the clay pit.

Saturday: I left about 7:30 a.m. to go with the Bradfords to Sanibel Island. We went to Thomas Edison's home in Fort Myers and ate at the Edison Cafeteria. *Another bit of history crosses my path.* We spent the night at the Hurricane House on the island. We gathered lots of sea shells.

Sunday: We left Sanibel Island and stopped at the Shell Factory and a wildlife farm.

Monday, 4–13: I mowed the Hoberg's yard for $3.00. I went to typing class. Mrs. Douglas told me to mow her yard in about a week and a half.

Tuesday: I went to typing class. I pulled some weeds at Mrs. Douglas's sister's house on Forest Avenue. It took me about thirty minutes and she gave me seventy-five cents.

Thursday: I mowed Mrs. Spain's yard for one and a half hours for $1.65. I went to Scouts. I have $9.56 toward a scooter in my savings account.

Friday: We got out of school at noon to go to a Boy Scout camporee.

Saturday: I camped with Greg, Jerry, and Allen in Greg's tent. We had campsite number twenty-five. About 4:30 p.m. the camporee was called off because of rain. Our troop decided to stay, but about 10:00 p.m. the rain was so bad we had to leave too.

Sunday: I helped Mother and Dad paint the living room.

Monday, 4–20: I put on the second coat of paint in the living room. I went to typing class. It is raining, thundering, and lightning like mad. Mom mailed a letter for me for some Write-Right Presidential coins.

Tuesday: It is raining hard again. I went to typing class and a PTA meeting. Mr. Metts made me do fifty push-ups for talking in study hall.

Wednesday: I mopped and waxed the kitchen floor. I played the chimes at the church.

Thursday: I went to Scouts. I worked two hours from 3:45 to 5:45 at Mrs. Spains's today. She is going to pay me Saturday. I still ache all over from doing those pushups.

Friday: I put ten dollars in my savings account.

Saturday: I worked at Mrs. Douglass's house from about nine to ten. She is going to pay me when she gets home tomorrow. I've got a steady job at the Halls,' Hobergs,' Douglas,' and Spains.' I bought a can of oil and some gas. I mowed Mrs. Spain's yard. She gave me $3.25. I mowed our yard.

Monday, 4–27: I went to typing class. I can type sixteen words per minute. I have $16.02 in my savings account. I mowed Mr. Hall's yard. He gave me $1.50. It took me one hour. Mrs. Douglas paid me $1.60.

Tuesday: I washed Mr. Hoberg's car for a dollar. I went to Barry's house. I went to typing class, but the lights wouldn't work so we came home at 8:00 p.m. I now have $17.02.

May

Sunday: I got up this morning and made a coffee cake. I served Mother and Dad breakfast in bed: eggs, bacon, toast, coffee, juice, and coffee cake. Mother cut my hair. I got my presidential coins.

Thursday: I went to Scouts but Jabo didn't come, so we played games. I made a flower garden for Mother outside of our window. I worked from 4:30 to 5:30 for Mrs. Spain hauling some leaves and mowing her backyard. She paid me a dollar. I made a seven-layer casserole for supper.

Friday: I got the ground inside the fence by the back door ready to plant some beans.

Saturday: I mowed the Douglas' and Bryants' lake front. They didn't pay me yet. We went to Orlando and I mailed some more coupons for presidential coins.

Sunday: I got up at 7 a.m., baked a coffee cake, and served Mother and Dad breakfast in bed. Dad, Mike, and I have been hauling some bricks all day. Mother saw an ad in the paper for 1,000 free bricks at the Sweeney's house, so we made four trips to the south side of Orlando.

Tuesday: I typed some biology and world history homework. I went to typing class and can type twenty-two words per minute.

Wednesday: It rained all afternoon. I have ten dollars in the bank and $14.75 here. I went swimming.

Thursday: I went swimming. I stayed at Robby Bradford's house from 6:30 to 10:00 p.m. while his mother and father went to a Garden Club meeting. Mrs. Bradford gave me two dollars and I now have $16.77.

Friday: I went swimming. I got five more presidential coins.

Saturday: I raked the Stewart's yard from 8:30 to 10:30 and got paid three dollars. I bought a new spark plug for the lawn mower at a cost of $1.06. I went to Barry's house from 7:30 to 11:00 p.m. We played four games of Parcheesi. We each won two games.

Monday, 5–18: I mowed Mrs. Spain's yard from 3:30 to 5:15 and got paid two dollars. I now have $29.50. I went to typing class but the lights didn't work again, so I came home at 8 p.m. I sent off for five more presidential coins.

Thursday: I started mowing the Hoberg's yard and got about half way through when the starter rope broke on the mower. Mr. Hoberg gave me a dollar and I went to Scouts.

Friday: Mother put twenty dollars in the bank for me. I got five more presidential coins.

Saturday: I worked two and one-half hours at Mrs. Hall's for three dollars. I mowed Pop Sewell's yard. It took me three hours and I earned $3.65. Barry and I went camping in the hut. I started mowing our yard.

June

Monday, 6–1: D.A. and I cleaned up the house. I got up at 6:30 this morning and baked a coffee cake. Mr. Harp called and told me he got some information for me about the C.I.A. (Culinary Institute of America). It has rained all afternoon.

Wednesday: I worked three and one-half hours mowing a yard for Pop Sewell. I went swimming. I went to Scouts at the firehouse. I went to school to see Mr. Harp about the C.I.A. info.

Thursday: I worked three and one-half hours mowing a yard for Pop Sewell. He still hasn't paid me.

Friday: I went to school again. Pop Sewell gave me a check for seven dollars. D.A. and I spent all afternoon in Orlando. We went to the Beecham Theater and saw the "Shaggy Dog."

Saturday: I got up at 6 a.m. and went swimming with Bob and his brother. Then I finished mowing our yard. I am getting ready to go on a Boy Scout camp to wilderness.

Tuesday: I started working in Pop Sewell's real estate office. I worked from 8:30 to noon and from 2:00 to 6:00 p.m. We got a female hamster.

Thursday: We got a canary. I worked for Pop Sewell 8:30 to 1:15 and from 2:00 to 7:00 p.m.

Friday: I worked from 9:45 to 12:30 and from 2:00 to 7:00 p.m. Barry, Mike, and I went camping. I mailed a story to *Reader's Digest*.

Saturday: I worked from 8:30 to 12:30. Bob, Bill, and I went swimming. Pop Sewell gave me a check for fifteen dollars for working for him this week. I went over to Barry's house. We played Monopoly and I won.

Wednesday: I called Elizabeth.

Thursday: Bob, Mike, D.A., and I went swimming this morning at 7:00 a.m. I then worked for eight hours. I went to Barry's and won two games of Monopoly. Bob left with his family to go back to Pennsylvania.

Friday: I worked a total of forty hours this week. I went camping with Mike, Allen, Harry, Barry, Doug, and Jerry.

Saturday: I worked from 8:45 to noon. Pop Sewell paid me fifteen dollars. I mowed our yard.

July

Friday: I worked forty hours this week for Pop Sewell.

Monday, 7–6: The canaries now have five eggs. I worked eight hours and then went to typing class. Allen and I went swimming tonight. Pop Sewell finally paid me $12.50 from last week.

Friday: I worked thirty-eight hours this week.

Saturday: I worked for three and one-half hours. Mike and I went swimming. Allen came over tonight.

Sunday: I went to church this morning. Dad and I mowed the yard. Mom cut my hair. It has rained all afternoon. I bought some pants, a belt, and socks for $5.68.

Monday, 7–13: I worked for eight hours and then went to typing. Dad bought me some shoes that cost me ten dollars.

Friday: I worked forty hours again this week. Mom, Grandmother, and I went to get Dad in town. We went to J.P. Morgan's Army Store. I spent two dollars on a belt and a flashlight.

Saturday: I worked three and one-half hours. I spent $6.50 for food for camping.

Sunday: Dad and I went swimming this afternoon. I bought some hair wax at Keyser's Drug Store.

Monday; 7–20: I worked eight hours and then went to typing. We went down to Allen's tonight.

Tuesday: I worked eight hours and then went to typing. We are leaving tomorrow to go on a camping trip.

Wednesday: Pop Sewell gave me five dollars for Monday and Tuesday's work. We left at 10:00 a.m. to go camping.

Thursday, Friday, and Saturday: Camping at Bear Island.

Monday, 7–27: I mowed our yard and Mike and I went swimming.

Tuesday: I worked with Harry Brown on Mrs. Spain's yard for five hours. She gave me $5.25.

Wednesday: Harry and I worked five hours at Mrs. Knudsen's house and each earned $6.25. Mother cut my hair and Dad made me shave. I went to a DeMolay meeting in Winter Park.

Thursday: We got a new 1959 green Brookwood Chevrolet. I got a card from Bob Sands.

Friday: I worked two hours mowing Mrs. Kain's yard.

August

Saturday: I mopped and waxed the bathroom. Mrs. Kain gave me $2.50. A woman gave me a dollar for changing a flat tire for her.

Sunday: We went to Cypress Gardens. I took eleven pictures. We stopped at Gatorland.

Monday, 8–3: Allen, Nancy Blackmer, and I went to the cow pasture and rowed around in a boat. I went to the Highway Patrol station in Orlando and passed the test for my restricted driving license.

I went to typing. I got a swimming mask, watch, shirt, pencils, stapler, and memo pad for my birthday. I still have a bad ear ache.

Tuesday: Today is my birthday! Big sixteen! Allie and Pop Sewell gave me five dollars. Allen, Steve Gillespie, and I went to the cow pasture and then went swimming. I went to typing. Marilyn Baker called me twice.

Wednesday: Allen and I worked two hours mowing Mrs. Harris's yard. We each made $2.50. Allen, Steve, and I went swimming. I walked to Scouts.

Monday, 8–10: It has rained all day. I went to typing. I did thirty words per minute.

Tuesday: D.A. and I were in Orlando all afternoon. I paid five dollars on a $8.22 pair of pants. I went to typing. I went frogging with Harry and Barry. We slept in the hut. Mom cut my hair.

Wednesday: I finished mowing the yard. I mopped and waxed the kitchen. I was initiated into DeMolay tonight.

Tuesday: I went swimming this afternoon. Teddy, Harry, Greg, Allen, Steve, and I went to the Prairie Lake Drive-in to see "The Girl in the Bikini" and "Bravado."

Wednesday: I worked for three hours at Mrs. Spain's. She paid me $3.25. I mowed our yard.

Thursday: I worked for Pop Sewell for two hours. I went swimming at Allen's beach. I mowed the Douglas' yard. It took me forty-five minutes and I got paid $1.75.

Friday: I worked at Mrs. Spain's for three hours. Got a check for three dollars. I worked for Pop Sewell for one and one-half hours. The Woodcocks (our rich relatives from Gainesville, Georgia) sent Mike, D.A., and I each a box of candy.

Saturday: We went to Sanford. I bought a hasp and lock for $1.50. Then we went to Winter Park and I bought four shirts for a dollar each, a notebook for a dollar, a painting for two dollars, and ice cream for a dollar. Greg and I went swimming.

Sunday: We went to New Smyrna Beach. Uncle John, Aunt Faye, and Cousin Harriet Woodcock came down from Georgia. I went to church.

Monday, 8–24: We went to school to get registered. I went swimming. We went to Prairie Lake Drive-in to see the "Ten Commandments."

Thursday: Allen and I worked for two hours at the Harris's and then we went on a twenty-mile hike to Sweetwater and other places.

Saturday: I went to a Troop and District Boy Scout swim meet in Orlando. I swam 175 yards.

Sunday: Mike and I went to work with Dad from 7:30 to 12:15 p.m. His boss, Mr. Holbrook, gave us each a dollar. Mother cut my hair.

Monday, 8–31: We started school. I have physical science first; health second; English-third; American history-fourth; algebra II-fifth, and study hall seventh. I went to typing class.

September

Tuesday: I fixed spaghetti supper. I built a badminton court across the street and went to typing class.

Wednesday: I mowed the yard and went to Scouts.

Monday, 9–7: We went to the fort in St. Augustine.

Tuesday: Allen and I built a bicycle for two.

Wednesday: We rode the bicycle to school. I went to DeMolay and received my second degree.

Thursday: Mother had to work late, so I fixed supper.

Saturday: DeMolay meeting at Dad Lehman's house.

Monday, 9–14: I went to typing class.

Friday: I mowed the yard in one and one-half hours. We left to go to the beach. The Moons' let us use their beach house.

Monday, 9–21: Allen and I worked on the hut and I went to typing class.

Wednesday: I went to a DeMolay meeting.

Saturday: I mowed Mrs. Spain's yard from 4:00 to 5:45 and she paid me $2.25. Allen, Mike, and I went skating.

Monday, 9–28: I went down to Allen's and to typing class.

Tuesday: Allen and I cut wood and I went to typing.

Wednesday: I worked in the yard and went to Scouts.

October

Friday: Allen and I cut down a tree in Pop Sewell's yard. He paid us $2.50 each. Mike, Allen, and I went camping.

Saturday: I worked at Mrs. Spain's. She gave me two dollars. I bought a pair of pants and a belt.

Tuesday: I baked a cherry pie.

Wednesday: I mowed Mrs. Douglas's yard for two dollars.

Thursday: I baked three nut cakes.

Saturday: Mike and I mopped and waxed the front porch. I bought myself a radio-phonograph.

Sunday: I went with the DeMolay to the Winter Park Methodist Church. I baked another cherry pie.

Monday, 10–12: I went to typing class. I came in second in the cherry pie baking contest.

Wednesday: I fixed supper. DeMolay meeting.

Thursday: I mowed Mrs. Spain's yard for $2.25.

Friday: I mopped and waxed the kitchen and bathroom.

Thursday: I sold some magazine subscriptions.

Friday: I earned $1.75 at Mrs. Douglas's.

Saturday: At 9:00 a.m. I took the SAT at school. It lasted until noon. I babysat for the Gerhardts from 7:30 to 12:15 and earned three dollars.

Monday, 10–26: Allen and I worked at Mrs. Douglas's house. She gave us seventy-five cents each.

Tuesday: I sold thirty-seven dollars worth of magazine subscriptions.

Wednesday: I mowed the yard with Allen's mower. I went to a DeMolay meeting.

Thursday: I babysat for Mrs. Gerhardt from 7:30 to midnight.

Friday: I have sold $42.29 worth of subscriptions. I drove a car during halftime at the homecoming game.

November

Sunday: Allen and I went fishing in the cow pasture. I have now sold $65.07 in magazine subscriptions.

Monday: 11–2: I got $1.25 from Mrs. Gerhardt. I have sold $73.37.

Tuesday: Got another silver dollar. I have sold $103.

Wednesday: I mopped and waxed the kitchen.

Thursday: I have sold $113.96.

Friday: I came in second in the magazine contest and won a stuffed dog.

Wednesday: I went to DeMolay. I mopped and waxed the bathroom.

Thursday: I have been hauling leaves all afternoon. I got five more silver dollars for magazines. I loaned one to Bill Franklin.

Saturday: I hauled leaves this afternoon. Pop Sewell gave us a check for fifty dollars.

Sunday: I got up at 7:30. Dad took me to a DeMolay practice. I came home and went to church. At 1:00 we (DeMolay) left for Sanford. We did some initiation work. I was a guard. We ate supper at S&S Cafeteria and I spoke to the manager about a job. He told me to come back in two weeks. I went to church.

Tuesday: I baked a cherry pie. I gave Mother a hair dryer for her birthday tomorrow.

Wednesday: We took a cake to Allie and Pop Sewell for their fifty-second anniversary. I am studying for two tests.

Thursday: I have $112 in the bank.

Monday, 11–23: Mike and I worked in the yard. I went to Barry's. Bill Franklin paid me the dollar he owed.

Sunday: Dad and I helped take inventory at his shoe store in Orlando from 8:30 to 1:30 and from 2:30 to 5:45. I got paid two dollars.

Monday, 11–30: I went to DeMolay. We are going to have a dinner December 9 and a hayride on December 19.

December

Thursday: I went to see a play at school. I mopped and waxed the kitchen.

Thursday: I made three 100s on tests at school.

Friday: I made an eighty-six on a health test. We got out of school for Christmas holidays.

Monday, 12–21: We went to town and I bought the rest of my Christmas presents. I took thirty-two dollars out of the bank.

Tuesday: Mike and I raked the yard.

Friday: I got a .22 rifle, shirts, clock, socks, and clothes for Christmas.

Monday, 12–28: I cut some kindling for Pop Sewell.

Wednesday: We caught nine flying squirrels. I did some typing for Mrs. Bradford and went to a party at Sharon Taylor's house.

Thursday: I worked for Mrs. Bradford. She gave me five dollars.

That is the end of my one and only *Diary of 1959*. I hope you have enjoyed reading it as much as I enjoyed living it.

Even in my teen years, I was already doing whatever I could to help with chores around the house. I didn't expect my parents to give me an allowance for doing what needed to be done. I did it because I appreciated having a house to live in and wanted to do my share. Teenagers of today think their parents should give them an allowance to do things like keeping their rooms picked up, helping with the dishes, taking the garbage out, etc. I say to them, "Do it because you care; not just for the money!"

As you can see from my diary, I started earning my own spending money at an early age. The quickest way for teenagers to learn respect for money is to do some jobs around the neighborhood to earn their own money. Do some babysitting, mow yards, rake leaves, or run errands for a neighbor. You will very quickly develop a new understanding of the value of money!

My dad used to tell me all the time, "Son, if it's worth doing at all, do it right the first time!" An important message for all of us, regardless of age.

This would be a good place for me to say something of importance to teenagers. Today's morality is a lot different than it was in my teen years, or in the teen years of Abe. You are under a lot of pressure to do drugs, have sex, smoke, drink and lots of other things I didn't do at that age.

Please don't let peer pressure cause you to do something you will live to regret. I was under a lot of pressure to do all of the same things you are/will be asked to do. I had made my mind up early that I had too much respect for girls and for myself to give in to peer pressure. You will always be a lot happier with yourself if you wait to have sex until after you are married and *never* smoke, drink, or do drugs at any age!

Lesson to be learned here is: Have fun during your teen years, but don't ever let anyone talk you into doing anything you will be sorry for later. Respect your bodies and respect all those you come in contact with; particularly those of the opposite sex.

Storms in Life

I was asked by James Gentry to build a flatboat and take some goods downriver 1,000 miles to New Orleans and sell them for him. His son, Alan, and I built that boat, sixteen feet wide and eighty feet long. Let me tell you what happened on that trip...

Do you think we were able to get to New Orleans without having any trouble of any kind? No sir're, bubba roo, we did not! I am here today to tell you life's not going to always deal you a straight, narrow road to walk down! Sometimes in your life you might have to do a little zig-zagging, just like that old river did for a 1,000 miles, to get where you want to go. But do you ever give up? No! Don't you ever give up in the pursuit of whatever you want out of life.

I never gave up and I don't want you to ever give up either. No matter how bad it gets today, just remember tomorrow will always be a better day. Don't ever give up! I want all of you to learn to do something starting today that I learned at an early age. I promise if you do, you will be big successes in your lives.

Starting today, I want you to learn to, "Be dreamers, stargazers, rainbow chasers, and to soar with the eagles." You can be-

come whatever you want. Just don't ever give up! And there is one more thing very essential to being able to obtain your goals in life. Someday, someone might come up to you and try to talk you into doing drugs, alcohol, or tobacco. When that happens, I want you to look them in the eye and say "No!"

I want all of you to raise your hands right now and repeat after me. "I promise... I will always... say 'No' to drugs." And I'll tell you something else. If someone ever does try to talk you into doing drugs and you get real serious, look them in the eye, and tell them you promised Abe Lincoln you would always say "No" to drugs, they will think you're already "high" and leave you alone anyway!

God gave each and every one of you a brain to become something very special and important, and you can't do that if you ever mess it up with drugs. Please, always say "No" to drugs!

Even at an early age, I was already being creative, experimenting with electricity and taking on all kinds of projects around the house. I installed a doorbell system and driveway lights for our house and was always tinkering and fixing anything that was broken or needed fixing.

In 1959, when I was in tenth grade, we were studying all about the United States: maps, capitals, locations, etc. I decided there needed to be a fun way to learn all of these things, so I designed and built a board game I called "StaCapilMap" for State-Capital-Map. It was approximately four feet by three feet with a map of the United States, a light, a buzzer, and two wires hanging from the middle of the board. If you stuck one of the wires into the hole beside Georgia, and stuck the other wire either into the map location for Georgia, or into the hole beside Atlanta, you would complete a circuit and the buzzer-light would come on.

I had a lot of wire I'd gotten from the phone company's scrap pile, so I used it to wire the back of the board. I took it to school and everyone had fun playing the game and learning at the same time.

In the middle of February, 1960, Harry Brown, Allen Hardwicke, and I were on the Wekiwa River and discovered what we at first thought was a log sticking out of the water. Upon closer investigation, we realized it was the remains of a fourteen foot long Indian dugout canoe estimated to be about 500 years old. We donated it to the Anthropology Department at Rollins College in Winter Park. *Another bit of history crosses my path.*

I've enjoyed writing stories since I was a teenager, and one of the first I wrote was during a hurricane.

Hurricane Donna

Today is Saturday, September 10, 1960. Hurricane Donna is almost here!

It all started about a week ago when we heard there was a hurricane forming in the Caribbean Sea. Central Florida has not had a hurricane since about 1950.

Yesterday afternoon, radio reports indicated the hurricane was about 350 miles southeast of Key West and was moving at nine miles per hour in a northwesterly course. It was then everyone started worrying about it and began to ready themselves for the storm.

This morning when I woke up at about 7:30 a.m. and turned on the radio, I heard Donna had hit Key West with full force and was moving up the Keys slowly but surely. The hurricane had done tremendous property damage to the Keys, but there had been very few casualties. Winds up to 166 miles per hour were recorded on some Keys!

The radio reported 80% of the 4,000 people on the second largest island in the Keys, Marathon, were evacuated to the mainland. Some of the people who did stay on Marathon went through a night of terror. Water reached a level of three feet in some of the houses. Most of the houses and buildings on this island have been blown down and completely demolished. Small outboard boats and large cabin cruisers have been snatched from their places and thrown onto the land. A UPI reporter gave an eye-witness report from the island that thousands of blue-shelled crabs are covering the roads and dodging automobiles. The main water line from the mainland to the Keys has been broken and communication lines are down everywhere.

At 8:30 this morning, our family went to our neighborhood grocery store to do our last-minute shopping. Everyone else had the same idea we did, and the store was crammed full of shoppers. The shelves were emptying fast! We did our shopping and running around and came home to prepare ourselves for the storm.

In an 11:00 a.m. report, the "eye" of the hurricane was located between Everglades City and Naples and still moving northwesterly at about nine miles per hour.

The wind has been blowing about twenty miles per hour with gusts up to thirty miles per hour. It is expected to get as high as seventy-five miles per hour today and tomorrow.

All stores in Orlando were closed by noon, but some had closed earlier because of the danger of the storm. People are warned to stay at home and stay off the streets in Winter Park because of the many large, old oak trees that might fall. Emergency shelters have been set up all over this area.

Small limbs and moss have been blowing out of the trees all day and a large oak tree has just fallen into our yard from our neighbor's yard.

In a radio report at 3:15 p.m., the "eye" of the hurricane is expected to be near Fort Myers in South Florida. The "eye" is expected to be in the Tampa area tonight by midnight.

It is about 4:00 p.m. now and the hurricane is about 140 miles from Orlando. The temperature is seventy-six degrees. The storm is still moving at about nine miles per hour in a northwesterly direction.

It is 5:00 p.m. now and I just noticed a very tall pine tree at the edge of our lot looks like it might be blown over because it is top-heavy. I have just heard Hurricane Donna's main intensity will reach this area at about midnight tonight. Right now in Orlando it is still seventy-six degrees with the winds at twenty miles per hour and gusts up to thirty miles per hour. The barometric pressure is 29.55 and falling. It has been requested by city police and safety officials that the streets in Orlando be cleared for safety's sake.

It is 5:35 p.m. and the hurricane's forward movement has increased to eleven miles per hour within the last half hour. It is a few miles north of Fort Myers and is carrying winds up to 125 miles per hour in a small area. The sky is a foggy-looking gray color and it is beginning to get dark. It is seventy-six degrees outside and the wind gusts are increasing to thirty-five miles per hour.

It is now 7:30 p.m. and I am writing by candlelight. All electricity in this area went off at exactly 6:30 p.m. Fortunately, we were able to prepare our supper before the power went off. We have no portable radio, so the only way we can get news of Donna's progress is for one of us to make a run for the car every hour or so and use the car radio. It is extremely dark outside and the wind has died down some for now. It is still raining "moss and limbs" continuously.

It is 8:10 p.m. The electricity just came back on. I have no idea how the lines were repaired so fast in this bad weather and I doubt the power will last for long. The latest radio bulletin said the "eye" of the storm was ninety-five miles south of Orlando with a forward speed of ten miles per hour and by 10:00 p.m. tonight there would be winds up to seventy-five miles per hour. The temperature still stands at seventy-six degrees with winds from the east at twenty-seven miles per hour and gusts up to thirty-five miles per hour. The barometric pressure is 29.49.

It is 8:55 p.m. I tried to take a short catnap, but I couldn't sleep because of the weather. In the 8:50 bulletin, the wind had increased to twenty-eight miles per hour with gusts up to forty-four miles per hour and the barometric pressure had dropped to 29.43 inches.

It is 2:00 a.m. The winds must be as high as 100 miles per hour and are blowing constantly.

It must be between 2:30 and 3:00 a.m. and the winds that were blowing so hard from the east-northeast have changed to the west-southwest. The "eye" has just passed us.

It is 3:00 a.m. Sunday morning. The electricity went off again at about 11:45 p.m. I was asleep when it did go off, but Mother just told me the power went off just before Miss America was crowned. I think the worst of the storm has already passed, but the wind is still blowing considerably. It is too dark outside to investigate for damage, but there are probably trees and limbs all over our yard.

It is 3:15 a.m. and I am going back to bed to try to get some sleep.

The time is 7:15 a.m. I ventured outside in the high winds to check for damage. Besides the one oak tree I have already mentioned, no trees have fallen in our yard. Every square inch of ground is covered with moss, limbs, pine needles, or other debris. It is really a big mess! Yesterday morning I looked on top of our house at the large television antenna there. It is now broken in the middle and laying on the ground. In our neighbors' yards, whole pine trees are down, palm trees bent double, and the top is completely blown out of a large ear tree. In the woods across the street I can see big limbs and trees down everywhere.

It is almost 9:00 a.m. I just got back from a trip around town. There are trees all over the roads everywhere in town. One of our friends across Lake Florida from us has eight big pine trees down in his yard and one of them is on his house. There is water across one of the main roads in town and the lake is beyond its banks. It is the worst mess I have ever seen in Altamonte Springs.

On one street in town, all the neighbors have gotten together and are trying to move some of the larger debris out of their yards. The wrecker from the Altamonte Garage is helping to move the larger trees out of the streets.

The time is 1:00 p.m. Sunday afternoon and the weather is getting considerably better all the time. My brother, Mike, and I have been trying to clean up around here and I tried to fix the broken TV antenna.

It is 5:00 p.m. We have been cleaning up all afternoon. The streets are finally being cleared for traffic and the wind is dying down. We still don't have electricity and won't have until tomorrow.

One of the bad things that came of the storm is we don't have school tomorrow. I will miss seeing my friends and teachers. I would have it a whole lot easier at school instead of helping with all the cleanup here at home. All of us survived Hurricane Donna and all her fury! It is time to go back to school and I am ready.

In high school, I was not the athletic type; didn't go out for many sports. The only sports I was interested in were baseball, track, swimming, and girls. I do remember running some pretty fast 100-yard-dashes and playing some pretty good baseball.

I was one of the few people at school who knew how to run the old sixteen-millimeter projectors, so I was always getting out of class to show movies to other classes. That was something I enjoyed being able to do.

Back then, boys were not allowed to take home economics. I really wanted to, so my parents got special permission from the principal, Mr. E.S. Douglas, who was a personal friend of my grandparents. We affectionately called him "Chrome Dome" because he was bald-headed and the top of his head always shone in the sun.

I wanted to be an Executive Chef when I graduated, so I really needed that home economics training. My plans were to attend the Culinary Institute of America (CIA) in New Haven, Connecticut, to learn how to be a great chef.

Florida Power Corporation each year sponsored a cherry pie baking contest for high schools all over the state. In my first year of home economics class, I entered the contest, and with my very first cherry pie I came in second at my school. Darlene Shea, our pastor's daughter, had been winning it for years. I entered the contest again in my senior year and I won at the school level.

My pie had a solid top-crust and I decorated it by using toothpicks dipped in red and green food coloring to make a big cherry with a green stem as the vents.

I then went on to a district contest in Winter Park. When the judging was all over, I went in to pick up my pie plate and saw that only a small piece had been cut out of my pie. The filling was running all over the place! I had either over-cooked or under-cooked the filling. Needless to say, I didn't win anything at district level. Just to have been able to win at the school level and go on to district level was an achievement though. The guys were always teasing me after that about baking them a cherry pie.

Drawing of Homer as a chef by classmate Honora Ciszewski

I was asked to escort the homecoming queen in my senior year. We rode in a nice convertible and I enjoyed being part of the festivities.

I was on the annual staff as the chief photographer and manager for ad sales and had my name printed in a Curtis Publishing book for being one of the top magazine subscription salesmen for my school fundraising event. I was already on my way to becoming a good salesman!

During school years, I had several part-time jobs to earn spending money. I pumped gas at Newell's Gas Station and bagged groceries at the Super Value Store on Highway 436. I also did a lot of yard mowing, leaf raking, and baby-sitting for neighbors.

One of my neighbors, who lived right behind our house, was Mr. William Wrigley, who had retired from Martha's Vineyard, Massachusetts. I enjoyed visiting with him and listening to stories from his youth. He was always telling me, "Homer, you're a gentleman and a scholar."

One of my best friends was Bob Sands from Pittsburgh, Pennsylvania. He came down each summer to visit his grandparents, Mr. and Mrs. Cliff Sands. Bob and I had some great times running around together all summer. We did a lot of swimming and boating on Lake Florida. Every time I would say, "Dad gum it… such and such." Bob would reply, "Well, mom glue it…"

Those were the good ole days! There was nothing to worry about except chasing girls and playing the pinball machines at Sergeant Bilko's Restaurant on Highway 436.

I dated a lot of different girls during my high school days. A few of the girls were not necessarily the most beautiful ones available, but we had some great times going to movies or to the beach. I believed then as I do now, that "beauty is only skin deep." There were a lot of girls who were very beautiful on the inside, but no one was asking them out. Guys, you can't always judge a book by its cover!

As you can see, I had a lot of fun during my school years. I paid attention to my teachers, did whatever homework needed to be done in a timely fashion, and helped around the house. I didn't need to be told what chores to do. I just did, without being asked, what I knew needed to be done!

Lesson to be learned here is: Work hard! Play hard! Don't ever let the "storms" in your life get you down. Good or bad, make the best of everything!

Moving, Jobs and Love

When I turned twenty-one, my pa decided to move up to the Decatur-Springfield area of Illinois. At twenty-one, a young man is supposed to move out on his own, but Pa said times were kinda hard and wanted me to stick around for another year to help support the family. I agreed to do that. A year later it was definitely time for me to move out on my own. I had had enough wood chopping to last a lifetime. I packed up my few belongings and moved about thirty miles out of Springfield to a new little village growing up there on the river called New Salem.

When I first arrived in New Salem, I stayed at the Rutledge Tavern and Inn. Mr. Rutledge had some rooms to rent. Well, fellows, he also had something else of interest to me. He had a beautiful daughter named Anne, with long brown hair and beautiful green eyes. She was a sight to behold!

My first job after I graduated from Lyman High School in 1961 was in a management training program with S & S Cafeteria in Winter Park, Florida.

I would go in about 3:00 a.m. and start getting vegetables and meats ready for the cooks. I soon became Storeroom Manager. I could de-bone a fifty-pound beef rump roast in ten minutes and have it standing tall like a Christmas tree, ready for the oven. I learned how to quarter a case of whole chickens in less than fifteen minutes and how to filet a fifty-pound box of Spanish mackerel in twenty minutes. If we left the skin on and broiled it, we sold it as Broiled Spanish Mackerel. If we skinned it, pounded it with crackers and almonds, and deep-fried it, we sold it as Trout Almondine. Same fish, different name! What a deception that was!

I put in some long hours in the cafeteria business for about seventy-five cents an hour. I also learned a lot about preparing food for hundreds of people. After I had run the storeroom for a while, I then worked in the bakery. Have you ever made fifty apple or custard pies at a time? From scratch? Lots of fun!

As part of my management training program, I also worked on the serving line. It was a challenge to see how thin I could carve those roast beef slices and to serve food to as many as 100 people an hour.

The cafeteria was a good learning experience, and with this first full-time job, I started doing something all teenagers still living at home should do. I started paying my mom and dad twenty-five dollars a week. Any teenager who thinks he/she can live cheaper on their own should go try it after they graduate from high school. I felt it was the least I could do to pay back my parents for all they had done for me over the years.

For those of you still living at home, as soon as you are able to get a job, start giving your parents something each week. They will appreciate it and you will feel better as a person.

I saved my money and bought my first car. A 1951 Pontiac, I believe it was. I only paid $300 for it and then had it painted, installed new Fingerhut seat covers, new tires, and had *no payments*. To newly licensed students, you will have more respect for your first car if you save your own money to buy it instead of having your parents give it to you. *Do not put yourself in debt for a car while you are still in school!* You will become a slave to your car payments!

After a year in the food business I decided it wasn't for me, so I went to work for Florida Gas Company in Orlando. One of my first assignments was to paint 600 gas lights and posts in front of everyone's houses in the Sky Lake Subdivision in South Orlando. It took me all summer to do it. What an experience!

Later, I went to work in the accounting department in the home office in Winter Park. I processed invoices, worked in the print shop, and then became station clerk at the Orlo Vista compressor station. I handled payroll, all shipping and receiving, answered phones, did TWX (teletype) operations, and whatever else needed to be done, including being a gopher!

As I have been going through my files and doing research for this book, I have come across a lot of interesting letters, pictures, etc. I will share some of them with you throughout the book. I found the following poem written by my grandfather, Homer Sewell, Sr. (Pop Sewell, we called him) for my birthday in 1962. I hope you enjoy it as much as I did.

> Nineteen years ago today
> Out of the sky like a cosmic ray
> A baby boy came hurtling down
> and after a while he hit the ground.
> His parents were very overjoyed
> to know they had a baby boy.
> He finally grew up and went to school,
> Learned everything by the rule.
> Physically active and very mature,
> He was to the girls quite allure.
> After going to school, early till late,

> this fine young man did graduate.
> Then he went to work in the Super Value store
> to learn all he could of grocery lore.
> Now he is working for Florida Gas
> And looking for a likely lass
> That he can marry and some fine day,
> Out of the sky comes a cosmic ray.
> Not a cosmic ray but a fine young boy
> That will be his parent's pride and joy.

My dad was on the town council for Altamonte Springs for several years and we both belonged to the volunteer fire department. Each year, the old Prairie Lake Drive-in Theater (currently the site of a Circuit City Store) would give all of the councilmen a free annual pass. Dad and Mom didn't care much for movies, so Dad would give me the pass. I could have a cheap date with another couple. We could load up a car and all get in *free*. All we had to pay for was the drinks and popcorn. Mrs. Hansen, the town clerk, was one of the ticket-takers at the drive-in and she was always very friendly as I would come through with another carload of my friends.

In 1963, I sold my '51 Pontiac and bought an old '54 Chevy. I had a small reel-to-reel tape recorder rigged up under the seat with a hidden microphone and start/stop switch. When my buddy and I would leave the car to go get drinks and popcorn for the girls, we would secretly turn on the tape recorder so we could tape what the girls had to say while we were gone.

When we came back to the car and the girls would go up to the bathroom, we could then play back the tape. It was interesting to hear what they had to say. Perhaps an early version of Watergate! Those were the nights alright!

I had my Chevy all painted up nice and even installed my own seat belts. They were not standard equipment back then like they are now. I was always tinkering around with electricity and building and installing various things around the house or in my car. I decided I would put a warning system into my Chevy, which would remind me and my passengers to fasten our seat belts.

Please be sure you and everyone who rides with you in any vehicle always fasten their belts. Seat belts do save lives.

I had an engineer draw up everything for me and had it all ready to send to the US Patent Office in Washington, D.C. Back then a Patent Application cost $300 and I just didn't have it.

In 1963 there were *no* buzzer/light indicators to remind you to fasten seat belts. In fact, most cars didn't even come with seat belts. If I had been able to get that patent, I would be getting royalties from every car, truck, and van that rolls off the assembly line now! So, for the lack of $300, I lost out on the possibility of a lot of money!

Always be on the lookout for a way to improve something that's already been built or to make something that will make life easier or safer for others. When you do, get your invention protected, and then find a way to get it marketed.

In 1964 we still had the draft and the Vietnam War was going strong. I was about to be drafted and knew I would not get any choice about my enlistment training. I decided to enlist in the Army instead of waiting to be drafted. I was officially sworn in on May 14, 1964, and was placed in charge of a group of soldiers being taken by train from Orlando to Jacksonville for testing and other induction activities.

I ended up in Ft. Gordon, Georgia, for my eight weeks of Basic Training. During one particularly hot summer day a couple of weeks after we had started training, I was called out of the exercises we were doing and told to report to the CO's (Commanding Officer) office—dirty green fatigues and all.

When I arrived in the CO's office, I was introduced to five distinguished-looking men dressed in shirts, ties, and coats. They said they were from the White House and that I should take a seat. I did! I wondered aloud what I had done that was so bad it required people from the White House to come looking for me. I was told my "201-file" (my military personnel file) had been selected from a couple of thousand files. Because of my test scores, work experience, etc., I had been chosen for a potential assignment to the White House Communications Agency (WHCA). This is the agency that takes care of all types of communications requirements for the president and the first family and the vice president and his family in the White House and on the road.

I was told they did not need anyone in computers, which was what I had signed up for, but they did need people to operate the switchboard. If I was interested, I would have to waive my enlistment assignment and agree to go to Switchboard School for eight weeks at Ft. Gordon. I would be required to pass a background investigation for a Top Secret Clearance (TSC) and also pass the required training classes in the top 5% of my class.

Knowing my other options might be going to the front lines in Vietnam, it did not take me long to decide right then and there that this sounded a whole lot better. I signed all of their papers seeking this WHCA assignment quickly, before they could change their minds!

It was amazing how much easier Basic Training got from that point on, knowing that no matter how bad my day was, I was going to the White House instead of Vietnam. Long, hot marches, gas chamber training, and being shot at in the infiltration courses were suddenly a lot easier to deal with.

I finished up Basic and began my eight-weeks of Switchboard Training. It was a breeze! I did graduate in the top 5% of my class and on the last day of school we were given our orders for our next duty stations.

When I got mine and started looking them over, I was shocked! My orders were for Germany! Well, the last time I had looked at a map, the White House was still in Washington, DC, not Germany! Wouldn't you know, if anything could go wrong, it would happen to a fellow from Altamonte Springs, Florida!

I had been given a number to call collect in case I had any problems; so I couldn't wait to get to a phone to make my call. When the Ft. Gordon base operator answered the phone, I said, "I want to make a collect call to the White House." When she stopped laughing, she said, "Yeah sure, soldier, everyone here wants to call the White House collect!" I finally convinced her I knew what I was doing and we got the call through.

I told the people in WHCA I had orders to go to Germany! They assured me the White House had not been moved and they would get the mistake straightened out very soon.

Well, I don't know whether you've ever had to deal with the government in trying to straighten out *anything*; but if you have, you know it doesn't happen very fast! So I had my serious doubts! I was pleasantly surprised the next day when I had new orders to report to Washington, D.C.

My Top Secret Clearance had not come through yet, and I wasn't going to be able to report directly to the White House without it. I spent a couple of days in a small Army post in Suitland, Maryland, U.S. A.S.E.S.C.S. Don't ask me what it stands for, but I do remember those were the initials for it! I also remember it had great food cooked by civilian chefs and the best, richest chocolate milk I ever drank!

Shortly thereafter, I moved into the barracks at Ft. Myer, Virginia, across the Potomac River from DC. I had my own private room and could see the Arlington National Cemetery, the Potomac River, the White House, Pentagon, Lincoln Memorial, and Washington Monument.

I was assigned to the headquarters office building of Defense Communications Agency (DCA). I worked there as a Xerox copy machine operator until I received my Top Secret Clearance. They sent me to a special Xerox Training Course to learn to clean and change the photographic drums and other maintenance duties. I was running approximately 5,000 copies a day on two Xerox 914 copiers. A lot of what I was copying was Top Secret material, even though I didn't yet have my Top Secret Clearance.

During the time I waited for my Top Secret Clearance to come through, I had two part-time jobs. I worked for a while in a bank sorting checks and I worked at McDonald's cooking hamburgers and fries. You'd be surprised how fast you can cook three dozen hamburgers! (I read somewhere recently that one out of every five adults in America had worked for McDonald's sometime in their lives.) It was a great work experience!

After six months of waiting for my Top Secret Clearance to come through, someone finally called me from WHCA. They were having trouble figuring out why there was a difference on my birth certificate between the date of my birth and the date it was actually recorded ten weeks later. I told them of my adoption and explained why the birth certificate had been re-issued. I said, "Why did it matter? What did you think I was doing at ten weeks of age? A little diaper espionage?" I got my Top Secret Clearance the next day.

I was told to report to the security people in the Executive Office Building (EOB) next door to the White House. They took my picture and issued me a photo ID pass to get in and out of the White House each day. *I had finally arrived!*

It was exciting to report to work each day and I was in and out of there as easily as you go in and out of your own home, office, or school. For a while, I had to show my ID, but after I had been there a couple of weeks, the guards got to know me and didn't even ask to see it.

I became good friends with one of the guards and he got me started selling Cutco knives. Ed and I went out demonstrating knives to single ladies and couples all over greater Washington and Virginia. I sold quite a few sets. They are great knives and I still have a set in my home I use every day.

It took the first few days on the White House switchboard to learn the names and code names of all the people for whom I would have to answer the phone. It didn't take long to learn it all and to learn how to operate the board. In addition to running the regular board to handle calls for military staff, etc., we also had to keep up with the police

Image in the Mirror

board. On that board, the policemen who guarded the White House grounds had to call in to us every fifteen minutes to let us know at which post they were stationed and to record their movements.

The communications center where I worked was located under the White House and behind foot-thick bomb-proof doors. These doors were guarded by surveillance cameras and cipher locks. One night, while I was on duty, there was a frantic call from the phone at one of the entrances to the Communications Center. The president was trying to get in to show someone around. The aide who was with him had forgotten the code for that day and could *not* get the door open. I ran up there to get the door opened quickly and came face-to-face with a very embarrassed President Johnson.

In case of an attack on the White House, the president and first family would be able to seek shelter and safety and have uninterrupted communications lines to the rest of the world. During the time I worked at the White House, I discovered the famous red phone to Moscow was *not* a phone at all, but a TWX (teletype) link.

I could call anywhere in the world free. I would call back to Florida and talk to my family and old girlfriends every day or so. I also had a friend in Weisbaden, Germany. She lived for a while at the Amelia Earhart Hotel; so when I worked midnights, I would call her at about midnight D.C. time, which would be about 7:00 a.m. German time, and give her a wake-up call. I spoke to her for several months. One night while I was on duty, one of the guards called me on the switchboard to say there was someone at the gate asking for me. I went outside and was pleasantly surprised to finally get to meet my friend from Germany. We sat and talked for an hour or so and then she had to catch a flight to somewhere.

Those were adventurous times working at the White House and getting to travel all over the country with the president and the first family. I was able to go to South America in 1967 when President Johnson went down there for a peace conference. I spent two weeks in Paramaribo, Surinam, which was the refueling stop for Air Force

One on its way to Punta del Este, Uruguay. It was a beautiful country and I met a lot of nice people while I was there.

Trips were always something to look forward to because we traveled in style with any of the first family. Wherever they went, we were there too. On at least one trip, I stayed at the Waldorf Astoria Hotel in New York City for only five dollars a night! That was the White House rate and I was being reimbursed TDY (Temporary Duty Assignment) pay for all my lodging and meals. I was able to visit parts of the world I wouldn't have otherwise been able to at the expense of the government.

Even if one of the president's daughters or Mrs. Johnson wanted to go on a shopping trip to New York City, some of us went with them in case they needed to call back to the White House.

I still have a baby blue Princess telephone one of the New York City telephone people gave me for a souvenir of a trip there with Lady Bird or one of the girls.

One trip I took was to the LBJ Ranch in Texas for two weeks of training on the ranch switchboard. I was disappointed in the size of the ranch house. I had expected the president to have some enormous house, but it really wasn't that big. If the Pedernales River in front of the ranch was up very high, you couldn't drive over the low-water bridge and would have to take a helicopter across.

I also took several trips to Chicago when President Johnson went there to visit his friend, Mayor Daley. It definitely was a cold, windy city!

I went on a trip to Billings, Montana, and after we were there for several days, we were told to pack it up and come on back to Washington. The president had changed his mind and cancelled the trip.

Here is a story I wrote while stationed at the White House.

Trip to Dulles
One evening, I took a drive out to the new Dulles International Airport outside of Washington, DC. At the time, this was

one of the world's most modern, technologically advanced airports and I was very impressed with what I saw.

Driving off the nice, big, smooth highway, we stopped beside a small entrance gate and took a ticket out of a machine that had automatically printed the date and time on it. It read 2349 hours, January 1, 1965. The gate swung open and we drove into the spacious parking lot. We had no trouble finding a parking place near the front of the huge terminal building.

There was a very light snow falling as my friends from church, Dave, Karyl, Clara, and I walked into the terminal building. We walked up a concrete ramp and then rode an escalator up to the main floor. After we stepped off the escalator, I looked up at a large board in front of me. Flight numbers, arrival and departure times were being posted automatically on the board. Every minute there was a "click-click" and the time was changing on a four-position, rectangular, modern clock.

On the runway side of the building there were approximately thirty gates for arrivals and departures of passengers. At each gate was a board overhead showing arrival and departure schedules and over the intercom system a voice was heard clearly stating the same information.

The building was truly ultra-modern in every respect! There were beautifully designed glass windows everywhere. If one became tired of standing, there were comfortable chairs throughout the building.

We walked into a large area that protruded from the building out to the control tower. We sat down in comfortable lounge chairs and looked out onto the runways with all their blue and white lights. There was a plane taxiing in on the long jet way to the ramp area about a half-mile from the control tower. We walked out to the observation deck to watch. There were coin-operated binoculars mounted along the wall ledge for those who were specific curiosity seekers.

As we stood watching the airplane taxi and stop in the distance, I was suddenly aware that this was only the second time in my whole life I had seen snow. As the four of us stood there under the enormous control tower, which towered 250 feet above us, I couldn't help but think of how marvelous everything looked. It was cold, but not too cold; there were thousands of sparkling blue lights all along the runways; everything was quiet and peaceful in the black of the night with soft white snow all around us. It was very refreshing! This was in so many ways different from the warm ocean breezes I had known so well in sunny Florida. We just stood there for a few moments admiring this part of God's beautiful world!

After about ten minutes, we returned to the inside. As the warm air hit us, we shook off all the remaining snow and turned our thoughts to Gate eight, where a mobile lounge car was just arriving from the plane that had landed a few minutes earlier. About fifty people walked out of the car into the terminal: men and women in Army, Air Force, Navy, and Marine uniforms; boys and girls. Businessmen officially visiting DC hurried through with their briefcases at their sides. They had all enjoyed a pleasant trip and their feet had not touched ground since they boarded the plane.

We decided to get a closer look at the mobile lounge (ML) after it had unloaded its passengers. As we stepped into the vehicle, our feet sank into a luxurious bright red carpet. The ML had black leather chairs and a seating capacity of seventy-two passengers with room for nineteen more to stand, if necessary.

As luck would have it, the driver, wearing his Dulles Airport uniform, asked if we would like to come aboard and look around. We were delighted to be given the opportunity and for the next forty minutes we were conducted on a "first class tour" of this magnificent vehicle. It was a mobile lounge (ML) used to take passengers from the terminal to their planes and vice-versa, no matter what the weather might be, in comfort and ease. The passengers needed only to walk about a hundred feet from the ticket counter to the ML and then be transported to their planes.

The agent-driver explained to us that Dulles is the only one of its kind in the world. They had twenty-two MLs like this one we were exploring and each one cost approximately

$225,000. They were powered by two eight-cylinder Chrysler engines... one at the front and one at the rear of the sixty foot vehicle. They travel between twenty and thirty miles per hour and with a control booth at each end of the car so they don't have to turn around on the runway. The car was even equipped with soft music coming out of the intercom system. The driver could talk to the passengers or to the control tower via two-way radio. There were even outside speakers. The ML was air conditioned by a large system that would keep it quite comfortable in the summer months.

There were two ramps at the rear of the ML that could be automatically maneuvered up, down, or from side to side to perfectly reach the passenger door of any aircraft. All a passenger had to do is step out of the ML directly into a waiting airplane or to step from the plane to the ML and relax as he/she was taken to the terminal. There was even a specially designed wheelchair for terminal-to-airplane-seat transportation for anyone needing that service. The ML was a fantastically ultra-modern convenience in all respects! As we left the ML, we thanked the driver for his time and interest.

We were quite wide-eyed and thrilled as we took the escalator down to the ground floor and walked to the front door. The cold night air roused us once more, and as we were heading for the car I noticed a snowball (that had obviously missed its mark) on the ground. Never having thrown a snowball, the temptation was too great and I hurled it at Dave. War was declared and I headed for the car. I arrived just as a cold, wet snowball found its mark on the back of my head. With much laughter, we managed to get into the car and headed for the exit gate.

Even though it seemed like such a short time, we had been in the airport for one hour and fifteen minutes. The man at the gate charged us fifty cents and away we went.

On the return trip home, our thoughts were still centered on the beautiful Dulles Airport and I couldn't help but say, "If I ever fly home or anywhere, I would surely like to begin the trip at Dulles International Airport."

When I first got to the White House, I started having trouble with my stomach. I went to the doctor's office there in the White House to see what was wrong. I remember sitting down in the reception area next to a very attractive young lady. I started flirting a little with her, and then in a few minutes she got up and went in to see the doctor. When I finally was called in, I asked the doctor why the young lady had been called in ahead of me since I had been waiting the longest. The doctor told me it was Luci Bird Johnson, the president's youngest daughter. I had been flirting with the president's daughter and didn't even recognize her! She was much prettier in person than on the TV. I never did get a date with her!

I was dating a lot of different girls I met either at church or through working at the White House. I was seeing a lady named Marty who worked at the FBI switchboard, and then met her younger sister, Sally.

We started dating in 1965, developed a serious relationship and set a wedding date for August of 1966. We got married in her hometown of New Castle, Pennsylvania.

In January of 1966, my grandfather, who I was named after, died at the age of eighty-four. He had been active in real estate in Altamonte Springs for almost forty years. He was well known for his bright red cars as he sped around town selling homes and lots. One of his favorite stories he used to tell all newcomers in the area was about the man who died and knocked at St. Peter's gate. When the gate opened, St. Peter asked him where he was from, and when the man answered "Altamonte Springs, Florida," St. Peter bid him enter, but said, "If you're from Altamonte Springs, Florida, you won't like it here."

In May of 1967, when my enlistment was up, I was told there would be no guarantees any of us would be able to stay at the White House. I decided not to re-enlist. I got out of the service and my wife of nine months and I moved to Altamonte Springs, Florida. We bought our first house there on Hermit's Trail.

Image in the Mirror

Florida Gas Company was saving a job for me and I returned to work in their accounting department in the Winter Park headquarters office. After a few months with them, I could see I wasn't going anywhere very fast so I started looking for something else.

JOBS, JOBS, JOBS

I was doing a lot of different things there in New Salem; storekeeping, postmaster, surveying, and blacksmithing... nothing very successfully.

In 1832, I decided to get into a little politicking in Illinois. I ran for state legislature. I lost! But I still didn't give up. I ran again in '34, '36, '38, and '40... four consecutive terms and I won. I was a good, "honest" politician. Something we need more *of in Washington these days!*

I've had a lot of different types of jobs during my lifetime, the longest time I spent at any one place was with Sears Roebuck & Company and with Big Canoe Resort, each for five and one-half years. I thought it might be interesting for you to see the wide and varied types of things I have been involved in. Most of it has been sales or sales management. Some of these have been successful and *many* of them have been failures. But how would I have known if they would work *if I never tried?* I never gave up!

Here they are in alphabetical order:

Jobs Listing for Fifty Years … From A to Z

Accounting, advertising sales, author

Babysitting, bagging groceries, bakery, board games designing, business card sales, bus sales

Calculator sales, camper sales, car sales, chocolate sales, clerical

Display panel sales/manufacturing

Encyclopedia sales

Fire extinguisher sales, freight company sales

Game room operation

Home sales, household products (MLM-x3), siding, windows, gutters, home health care technician, Home Depot, HVAC sales

Insurance sales (MLM, Multi-level marketing)

JSB portable phone sales

Knife sales (Cutco), Kathy's Kandy & Gifts Shop

Line server in S&S Cafeteria, log home sales

Magazine sales, McDonald's hamburgers, microfilm equipment sales, mini-emergency kit sales

Name tag sales/manufacturing

Owner/operator four-wheeler race track

Phone answering machine sales, pizza operation, portraying Abe, printing shop, pumping gas

Quartz clock sales/mfg.

Real estate office management and sales of land & homes

School desks sales, security systems sales, sewing machine sales, skating rink owner/operator, sorting checks at bank, storeroom manager, storm shutter sales, substitute teacher, systems manager, sheds sales manager, signs delivery each week

T-shirt design/sales, Terra Jet sales, theater operator/owner, time share sales, tour bus operator

Image in the Mirror

U.S. Army, White House Communications Agency
Vacuum cleaner sales
Water filter sales (MLM), Walmart Associate CSM
Xerox copier operations
Yard work, mowing and raking
Zwieback toast sales, Nabisco Company

If you believe in something strongly enough and think you might be able to make it work... then try it! Give it 110% to try to make it work. If after six months or so you can't make it work, then go on to something else with the satisfaction of knowing you at least tried your best! Always remember there are lots of people out there who would never have tried at all!

In September of 1967, I left Florida Gas Company and went to work in sales for Nabisco. I started my training in the Orlando area. I will never forget the man who helped train me in the Orlando area stores. His name was Pete Blanco. Pete had been with Nabisco for several years and he really knew his way around. We became good friends and I still run into him once and a while. We had some good times together stocking shelves in those Orlando grocery stores. After several months of training, I was given my own territory in Ft. Myers, Florida. I had over 100 stores to sell and stock with cookies and crackers. I had a company car and was making a whopping $12,000 a year. I was really rolling now!

My favorite stores to call on were on Sanibel Island at Bailey's General Store and the Bee Hive and the Little Store on Captiva Island. Every Wednesday the company paid the three dollar toll for me to take my little trip to "paradise." We sold a lot of cookies during the winter months, but during the summer months, business on the islands died. I enjoyed those trips to the shell gathering capital of the world. If you've never taken a vacation to Sanibel or Captiva Island, you should plan do so. You can fly into the airport at Ft. Myers.

On August 2, 1968, we had our first child, Homer S. Sewell IV. We called him "Chip" for chip off the old block or Chips Ahoy cookies I was selling. My father was still living, so there were three Homer Sewells running around.

I recently came across a letter dated September 4, 1968 from my Nabisco District Manager, Harvey Alexander. I won't bore you with the whole letter, but he ended it by saying, "Keep up the fine sales job you are doing. P.S. Hope the baby, Homer Sewell, IV, is doing fine. Or, I should say 'Chip.' We suggest you not let him start putting up stock until he is a little older. Some fathers start this training at about one year, but it is a little hard for them to reach the top shelf. So don't rush it. Ha! Ha!"

I would walk into a big Publix Market or other large grocery store and there would be my order waiting for me to price, rotate, and put on the shelves. You don't realize how many cookies there are in a store until you face a stack sixty feet long and six feet tall. When I first started, I was pigging-out on cookies. I could sample whatever I wanted to and did just that. Pete had told me there would come a time when I wouldn't be able to decide what I wanted to eat. He was right! Within a few weeks of sampling everything Nabisco baked, I couldn't eat any more. I had seen too many cookies.

After a year of being a glorified stock boy, I had enough of cookie selling and shelf-stocking to last a lifetime. I went looking for a job with Sears Roebuck and Company.

I started with Sears in the Edison Mall in Ft. Myers selling sewing machines and vacuum cleaners. Within six months, I was their number one salesman and became the Department Manager at about $18,000 a year. Our department was consistently in the top three or four in the nation of all the Sears stores of the same size.

I learned a lot about servicing sewing machines and vacuum cleaners, so customers with minor problems wouldn't have to leave their equipment in the service department to be repaired. I had a lot of happy customers, and my five salespeople and I got along beautifully together. We worked hard, but we had fun too.

One of my salesmen was a man by the name of Bob Lyons, and he always kept us in stitches...literally. Ha! Ha! Stitches! Sewing machines! Get it?

Have you ever seen someone do "Live Mannequin"? I would stand perfectly still on top of one of our canister vacuum cleaners. Bob and my other salespeople would come over and dust me off once in a while, as if I were a real mannequin. We were trying to get the attention of the customers who were passing by and we did!

One day someone took a picture of me standing on top of a vacuum and sent it to our Atlanta office to Bobby Sullivan, my Regional Manager. His reply was, "Just think what you could do if you moved!" Bobby definitely believed we should be grabbing the customers off the aisles to show them what we had to sell in our department! Bobby was *not* impressed!

One weekend, about fifteen young people stood in front of me for twenty minutes or so...just staring at me. I never moved! They all agreed, "Oh! It's just a dummy...a mannequin." As they all headed out into the mall about thirty feet away, one of the girls turned around for one last look. I couldn't stand it any longer so I gave her a big *wink*. She about died! "He's alive! He's real!" she screamed.

I want to share a lesson I learned with salespeople everywhere. My store manager, Mr. Richards, came by one time and asked me why we didn't have any customers in the department looking at our sewing machines and vacuum cleaners. I said, "There aren't any buyers in the store! They are all just looking!"

Boy, was that the wrong thing to say to a thirty-year Sears Manager! He marched me over to the mall entrance door and had a long talk with me. He said, "Homer, I am going to give you two boxes of buttons. One of these boxes contains buttons that say in big letters 'Looker' and the other box contains buttons that say in big letters 'Buyer.' I want you to stand here at this main entrance and stop everyone who comes into our store. I want you to *accurately* pin one of these buttons on them. Then all of the salespeople throughout the store will know which ones might need help and which ones to avoid!"

I got the point, and in all my years of selling, I have never forgotten it.

Lesson to be learned here is: There is no way to judge a book by its cover! We don't ever know whether someone is a buyer or just a looker. Lookers may be converted to buyers if we are friendly enough to them, knowledgeable about our products, and can show them how our product/service will benefit them. All people are potential buyers! Don't ever forget this valuable lesson if you want to be a successful salesperson.

More Jobs

One day, while I was storekeeping, a family stopped by my store. They said they were heading out west and their wagon was so loaded down with goods that there was barely enough room for the family. They told me this one barrel was really in their way and wanted to know if I would give them fifty cents for it and get it off their wagon. I finally agreed to do so.

I stuck the barrel over there in the back of the store because I didn't have time to worry about it right then. I later discovered a complete set of law books, "Blackstone's Commentaries on Law," in the bottom of the barrel. The more I read and studied those books, the more excited I got. This looked like something for me to give some serious thought to.

While I was in management with Sears in Ft. Myers, I decided to get into the all-terrain vehicle business. I had seen an ad in a magazine for an all-terrain vehicle that looked like something I could sell in South Florida. In 1972, I bought the franchise for Florida and Georgia for Terra Jet, a four-wheel drive vehicle that would go anywhere, including into the water. I flew up to Drummondville, Quebec, Canada, to the factory and really liked what I saw. I took out a loan at the bank, bought eighteen Terra Jets, and set up a sales office near the airport.

The Terra Jets were fun to drive. I had approximately $1,200 in them by the time I got them delivered from the Canadian factory and I sold them for $1,800 each.

One evening, I was demonstrating the vehicle to a young couple who were interested in buying one. I showed them how easily it climbed in and out of a big drainage ditch near my office. Then I got out to let the husband drive. That was my first mistake! He didn't know you had to be careful not to let water run over the back end and into the engine compartment. He tried to climb out of this steep water-filled ditch front-end first. When he did, the back-end was left in the water and the engine compartment quickly filled up.

I got the family out of the vehicle and stood there on the edge of the ditch watching my new Terra Jet sink. *My heart sank with it! I needed that sale!* I went back to the office, got my new Ford pickup truck, and a big rope. I hooked the rope to the Terra Jet and pulled it onto dry land. I drained the water, pulled the spark plugs, dried and replaced them, and it started right up. Needless to say, I didn't sell that couple a vehicle!

It took me a while to sell those eighteen units. I even delivered one with a special trailer I had made to fit it all the way to Hattiesburg, Mississippi. I finally decided this was not a good part-time business to be in.

Unfortunately, Sally and I were having problems, and in 1973 we were divorced.

I left Ft. Myers and moved back to Altamonte Springs. I was home again. I opened up a new Sears store in the Altamonte Mall, as the sewing machine and vacuum cleaner department manager.

My new store manager was Dan Holley, and you just don't find a finer man to work for anywhere. It was a pleasure and a privilege to work for and learn from a man of such character, integrity, and knowledge of the retail business. He was also a man who was very close to his wife, Bess, and their children, Debbie, Danny, and David. They are the "Ideal American Family." Some years ago, I heard that after Dan had left Sears, he and his sons were running a very successful residential contracting company in Columbus, Georgia. I have more recently heard from Dan and found out that Bess had passed away.

I stayed for another year in the retail business and then decided it was enough for me, so I left Sears in search of something different to do.

For a while, I tried a lot of different types of selling: phone answering machines, security systems, engraved plates for doors and desks, magazine advertising, T-shirts, and a mini-emergency kit I sold for a dollar. It had fifty items crammed into a thirty-five millimeter film can: things like a safety pin, a dime for a phone call, water purification tablets, hook and line, matches, aspirin, and other items you would need in an emergency.

In 1974, I was selling advertising for *Sunshine Artists Magazine* and as I went around to art shows I noticed the lack of good display systems. I decided there was a market for lightweight, portable, and easily assembled display panels. I made some inquiries with aluminum suppliers in the Orlando area and started a business I called A.I.M. Fixtures. The name stood for **A**luminum-**I**ntegrated-**M**odular and that was just what they were. I started manufacturing and selling them from my home in Forest City, Florida.

In September of 1974, I met a nurse named Kathy as I was going by bus from Orlando to Ft. Myers. Kathy was from New York and was living in Memphis, Tennessee, at the time. She was on the way to see her parents who lived in Punta Gorda, Florida. We visited on that bus trip for about three hours and I decided I wanted to get to know her better.

We called and wrote each other constantly. The phone bills were getting bigger and bigger. I even wrote love letters to her with my sewing machines at Sears, monogramming on long pieces of starched demo material. She invited me to spend the upcoming Thanksgiving holidays with her and her family in Memphis. I cooked Thanksgiving dinner for her twin sister, Paula, and Paula's husband, Dave, and her nieces: Susie and Jennifer. I even went to work with Kathy one midnight shift so we could see each other during the night. We had some great times together!

When she came down to Florida for Christmas, I gave her an engagement ring and we set a wedding date for Valentine's Day, February 14, 1975. We got married in a small, old chapel in Altamonte Springs and bought a house in Forest City, just a few miles from Altamonte Springs.

At the time, I was selling calculators for Singer-Friden all over the Orlando area. It was strictly on a commission basis. The home office was in Tampa. I was calling on stores all over Central Florida trying to sell my calculators. There was a lot of stiff competition and sales were not good. I ended up having to sue the owner to get all of my commissions. That was a bad experience!

In October of 1975, I was driving down I-4 in Orlando when I heard a public service announcement asking for volunteers to talk to school students about any subject of interest. I called to ask if they had anyone talking to students about the White House. I was told they did not, but would like me to do so. My intention was to talk to students about my personal experiences working the switchboard for the Johnson Administration. About that time, I started growing a beard and the students started calling me Abe. So began a thirty-five-year portrayal of our country's greatest president, as I took Abe part-time to school children all over Central Florida.

At the same time I was selling calculators and display equipment, I was getting into designing t-shirts. Since Kathy was a nurse, we designed one for nurses, "Love a Nurse, PRN." We sold over 12,000 of them from 1975 to 1977 through stores all over the country. For a long time we were buying the shirts and working day and night, with two presses we had bought, pressing transfers onto them. Then I found a company in Alabama that could sell us the shirts with the imprint already on them, and cheaper, too. That helped a lot!

One valuable lesson I learned was you should always shop around before you make decisions about buying anything. I've said for years that anytime you are thinking about spending over $100 for an item, shop the price at least three places. We really started saving a lot of time and money after we discovered that company in Alabama.

We were getting real creative with designs and I have copyrights on about a dozen designs for t-shirts and board games. I have made designs for dentists, pilots, pharmacists, a ruby mine in Franklin, North Carolina, and others. My most popular shirt has been the one we did for nurses.

I have always loved the mountains, so in 1976 we sold our home in Forest City and moved to Franklin, North Carolina. We bought a two and one-half acre home site on top of a 3,500 foot mountain just outside of town. I then proceeded to build our dream home.

Kathy was working in town at the Angel Community Hospital. In early 1977, when she was about six or seven months pregnant, I dropped her off at the doctor's office for her weekly visit and left to run some errands. When I came back to the office, the receptionist said the doctor needed to see me with Kathy. I sat down not knowing what he might have to say to us. They had done some X-rays and he wanted us to know we were going to have *twins*. Kathy asked the doctor if it was boys or girls. He said, "Mrs. Sewell, that bone doesn't show!" Back then it wasn't as easy to determine what sex your baby would be.

Well, I had always heard women were the ones to carry the twinning capability, but it usually skipped a generation. Kathy is a twin and it wasn't skipping anything with us! We were excited and couldn't wait to call our parents to tell them the *double* good news.

That same day, the doctor was seeing another patient and was holding one of those sound-amplifying devices so you can hear the babies' heart beat; a fetal heart monitor on the tummy of a very pregnant woman. All of a sudden, where everyone in the room could hear it, "Come on good buddy!" came out of the monitor. I guess somebody was outside on their CB radio and the monitor had picked up the signal. What a laugh we had!

On April 5, 1977 Kathy gave birth by C-section to our twins, Kimberly Irene and Jason Leon. They weighed six pounds and thirteen ounces and six pounds and three ounces. Mom and the babies were all doing fine, and in a couple of days, I took all three from the hospital to our new home on top of the mountain.

I kept building the display panels in the basement of our home for a while, but ultimately had to rent some warehouse space in town. We were selling them all over the country. I even shipped an order to an artist in Germany. Kathy and I were also still very much in the t-shirt business. The display business was not providing the steady income that we really needed to support our new twins, so I finally sold it to a young fellow who worked for me. His name was Mark Kresal, and the last I heard he was still in business. If you know of anyone who does art shows and wants a lightweight, all-aluminum display system, please have them call Mark Kresal with A.I.M. Fixtures in Franklin, North Carolina.

Kathy and I decided we would open up a candy store in Franklin. We found an empty shop next to the courthouse and opened "Kathy's Kandy & Gifts." We bought homemade candy from Mrs. Magnus's Candies in Orlando and had a pretty good operation going. I probably ate up a lot of the profits because I love any type of candy, particularly chocolate. We had great candies, but it was not making us enough money to live on, so after a few months of trying to make it work, we sold the equipment and closed the shop.

One day, when the twins were about three months old, I was playing with them and the phone rang. A fellow from up north somewhere had been given my name and number. He started talking to me about becoming a Shaklee Distributor. He wasn't about to hang up the phone until I said yes, so I finally did. All I wanted to do was get him off the phone and go back to playing with my babies. I never did buy or sell any of their products, although they do have great products for cleaning, etc.

Lesson to be learned here is: Don't ever let anyone talk you into something over the phone that you have absolutely no interest in doing. Don't ever give your credit card number over the phone to anyone you don't know. It is bad business to do that! There are those out there who could use your credit card numbers to charge all kinds of goods and services to your account! Make sure you know who you are dealing with before you ever give out your credit card number or Social Security number! In 2009, credit card and identity theft was our *number one crime in America!*

When the twins were about six months old, we sold our new house on top of the mountain to Hobbs and Edith Lanier from Savannah, who owned the twenty-five acres next to our house, and moved to Birmingham, Alabama. My brother-in-law, Dave, was the General Sales Manager for a big Toyota dealership and he offered me a job selling cars.

One day after having let several prospects leave the dealership ("walk") without buying anything, Dave called me into his office and asked me why I hadn't sold them a car. I told him they would "be back!"

Dave said, "Homer, do you see the big barrel over there in the corner? That is our 'Be-Back Barrel'! I want you to go over and stand in the barrel until they return!" The lesson I learned here was a "Be-Back" was a rare item in the auto business!

I sold new and used cars for Dave for about six months, but Alabama and selling cars were *not* for me.

In 1977, my dad was dying of cancer, so after six months of living in Birmingham, we moved back to Altamonte Springs, Florida. Dad died in January of 1978. I bought the house I had grown up in from Mother. I continued to sell cars at a Toyota dealership in Sanford for a few more months. I made some money, but I was not happy with what I was doing.

For a few months in 1978, I worked for a trucking company trying to convince businesses all over Central Florida they should use my company to handle their freight needs. It was a hard-sell, competitive business to be in, and I wasn't making much money at it. I was doing a lot of cold-calling all over Central Florida. For those of you *not* in sales, let me explain what *cold-calling* means: when you don't have a specific appointment to see someone, and you knock on doors hoping to present your wares, that's cold-calling. It is not fun! But it is a necessary part of being a successful salesman, regardless of what your product or service is.

One day, while I was helping out in the warehouse, I moved a large, heavy crate of some kind and pulled my first hernia. I was in a lot pain and ultimately had to have my first of five hernia surgeries to repair the damage.

In 1978, while I was recovering from the surgery, I designed and copyrighted a board game about building houses. You play it like Monopoly, except instead of buying up properties you are given a fixed amount of money for a mortgage. The idea of the game is to see who can get their house built first without running out of money. It is a fun game to play and teaches people who have never built a house all about the major steps involved: from buying the land, building foundations, walls, roof, interior, windows, etc. to the landscaping.

I've got a thick file from all the major game companies I sent it to for them to consider manufacturing and marketing. Most big companies will not even look at anything submitted to them unless it comes through a broker they are already working with or their in-house design people. One of these days, I will have enough money to have 1,000 of them printed, and I will market them myself. It is also a good educational aid. I showed it to a mortgage company in Winter Park, Florida, and they said if I ever did get it printed, they would buy them to give to people applying for a construction loan so they could see what building a house was all about.

Don't ever give up on something you believe strongly in. I haven't totally written off getting this game marketed. It has just been placed on the back burner for a few years while I go on to try other things.

I heard about Frank Messina, who had a shutter and window sales/manufacturing business in Longwood. He was looking for a salesman, so I talked him into giving me a try. I would drive as much as 100 miles to show people what we had in the line of storm shutters for their homes, mobile homes, patios, etc. I would demo the samples I carried, measure their openings, and give them prices. The prices ran from $1,000 to as much as $5,000 and I tried to get them to make a commitment to buy while I was there. I was closing a good percentage of them on the first call. Frank was happy with the job I was doing for him and the company. I liked meeting people in their own homes and showing them a good product at a good price. I worked for Frank off-and-on for several years. Frank, his family, and Polly the office manager were super nice people to work with, and I probably could walk back into Frank's office anytime and start working that same day.

A motto I learned early in sales and have encouraged others to follow is: "Nobody cares how much you know until they know how much you care!" This is an important thing to remember for anybody in sales or any type of business where you deal with the public. I have always tried to live by this motto and show people that I do care about them.

In the meantime, I kept selling t-shirts and got into making custom clocks. I made them in cypress slabs and could make them out of almost anything you could think of. I even took business cards, had them photographically enlarged to about 12" x 24" and mounted a quartz clock movement into them. I sold a few of these all around Central Florida and still make clocks for special people out of pictures, posters, or whatever. I made one for one of my nieces on the box of her favorite cereal: Fruit Loops.

I also began buying and selling items from the Orange and Seminole County School systems surplus warehouses. I would bid on and buy buses, desks, beds, computer consoles, and lots of other items. I have had as many as two or three big, yellow school buses in my backyard at one time. I would buy them for $200 to $600, drive them home, place an ad in the *Truck Trader Magazine*, and sell them for as much as $2,000. I didn't have to do anything except put enough gas in them to get to my house.

For those of you looking for a way to make some additional money, you might want to call your local school board and ask to be placed on their bid-mailing list for buses and other vehicles. Also ask them if they have a warehouse where you can buy surplus items. I probably sold over 500 school desks during one busy Christmas season. I bought them for fifty cents or less and sold them for five dollars. People would take them home, paint them, and have a wonderful place for their children to do their homework.

Remember, what is one person's trash might very well be *your* treasure! There are a lot of people out there making a nice living buying up other people's throw-aways (from garage sales, etc.) and reselling them at flea markets.

I wasn't making enough money at anything I was doing, and several friends suggested I might be good in the booming real estate market in Central Florida. I took the required forty-hours, six weeks course and then passed the state exam in 1978.

I placed my license and went to work with a large firm called Real Estate One in Altamonte Springs. Ann Pinnock was my office manager. About twenty years earlier I had dated one of her daughters. I did alright in real estate; but I could see it was not what I really wanted to do the rest of my life.

I kept hoping I could make it work and be able to earn some good money. I wanted to follow in my grandfather's footsteps. He had been successful in real estate in Altamonte Springs for many years. There are still "Homer" and "Sewell" streets named after him in Seminole County.

Buyers were not always loyal, and you could take a family around in your car all day looking and not finding just what they wanted. A few days later, you might find they had bought something with the help of another real estate salesperson. Again, this is strictly commission selling and you don't make a penny until you match up a buyer with a seller and go to a closing. A couple of my deals fell through just hours before closing. At one time, I had a $600,000 mobile home park listed but never could get it sold. That would have been a nice commission check! Don't ever spend your commission check before you have it in your hands! There can be a lot of disappointments in the real estate business!

In July of 1979, I was asked to ride on a float in a parade. It had a small log cabin as its central theme and with me there in front it made the perfect Republican entry. Here is a short note written in the *Orlando Sentinel* about that parade:

> "Joining the parade... Some Seminole County Republicans were slightly dismayed to find out the man portraying Abraham Lincoln on their recent parade float was—of all things—a Democrat. So they talked politics—and practicality—to him. And Homer Sewell agreed he would rather switch than fight. He registered as a Republican just before the parade. And the float won a first prize."

Over the years between 1978 and 1983, I worked for several real estate companies in Central Florida. In 1980, I went to school again and took the broker's exam. I received my broker's license and had my own operation for a while. I called my company Presidential Properties of America.

One of the things I tried was taking ninety-day options on mountain land in Tennessee and trying to sell the land to Central Florida buyers before the option expired. I knew a lot of people in Florida owned land in the mountains of either North Carolina or Tennessee. There was plenty of very cheap acreage if you knew where to look for it.

I placed ads in several East Tennessee newspapers and found some great parcels, tied them up with options, but never could get them sold in time to make money. I had bought a very expensive, heavy, VCR camera and shot footage of the properties. I then showed these to prospects in the Orlando area.

I came close to putting a couple of deals together, and one beautiful mountain-valley parcel I worked on would have netted me $20,000, but it fell through at the last minute. Nothing I did in real estate made me very much money.

I worked for a year for Barry Luckenbach and was his General Sales Manager for five Central Florida offices. I recruited, trained, motivated, and inspired over 100 people while working for Barry. He was probably one of the most knowledgeable real estate people in the Orlando area and I learned a lot from him. If you ever need any help in real estate anywhere in Central Florida, I highly recommend Barry Luckenbach and his office of trained salespeople.

I read somewhere about a new, cheap, aerosol-type fire extinguisher. Thinking I could make some money selling them, I bought the required fifty cases. I sold them through Boy Scouts and other fund raising groups. I would set up a meeting with a group looking for a way to raise money. I built a fire outside and then put it out with my handy little "Flame Out" extinguisher. I finally sold the last of them and made a few dollars in the process, but it was another bad experience. The man in Michigan who got me into the business went belly-up and ended up owing me about $250, which I never was able to collect.

The fire extinguishers worked great on most types of fires. But I found out they had not been approved for sale in Florida, so that didn't help matters any.

I was trying to keep up with my real estate prospects and saw an ad in a magazine for a new portable phone. Since I had a communications background from the White House, I saw this as an opportunity to make some money and help people keep in touch with each other. I had to buy a minimum of three units at $500 each.

Somehow, I rounded up the money and bought my initial stock. They were the size of a small hand-held walkie-talkie with a touch-pad on the front. It worked great and I could make phone calls from my car or anywhere. This was before we came out with the new cellular phones of today, which work better, are much, much smaller and lighter and are less expensive to own. I finally sold those three phones and moved on to sweeter things.

In 1982, I became the distributor-salesman covering five Central Florida counties for World's Finest Chocolate of Chicago. It was a really sweet job! I had all the sample chocolate I could give away or eat! They have been around for a long time and have one of the best fund-raising opportunities ever presented to any group. I called on churches, schools, Scouts, lodges, ball teams, bands, etc. all over Central Florida. I gave them free samples to see for themselves how good the chocolate really was and then wrote up orders. From the time I took an order to when the group had their chocolate delivered to them was less than a month.

I could have a custom-label printed up for their chocolate bars or boxes, along with a promo from a local fast food place. One promo I put together was with Wendy's hamburgers: buy one single and get one free. They were selling for $1.29 then, so the person buying the bar of chocolate not only helped the group doing the fund-raising, but also got back their money with the attached coupon. I had another promo with a local pizza store in Longwood: buy one large pizza and receive one free small cheese pizza valued at $3.50. What a deal! The group made about 50% profit from their sales and the company would buy any unsold products. I still believe it to be one of the easiest ways a group can make money!

I had some labels made up by a friend in Longwood who had a label-making company. It said to, "Eat the bar and save the wrapper. Call Homer for details about fundraising." I wrapped these around my little two-inch long sample bars of chocolate and they became my "calling cards."

If your group needs a good fundraising event, I still recommend World's Finest Chocolate in Chicago. Tell them Abe said to call.

For several months in 1982 I also sold World Book Encyclopedias. I sold enough sets to make some money and to earn a *free* set of encyclopedias and Book of Knowledge for my family. They are great books and are less expensive than some of the others on the market. We still use them and I recommend to all my students across the country that they read their entire set of encyclopedias ... a few pages at a time. It will help you with all subjects and your grades.

In May of 1983, I saw an ad in the *Orlando Sentinel* about a resort in the mountains of North Georgia looking for salesmen. I called and got an interview with the sales manager, Mike Connors, who was to be in Orlando recruiting. Mike told me he was looking for experienced timeshare salespeople. I had lots of sales experience and had sold general real estate but had not yet sold any timesharing. I finally convinced him to give me a try for thirty days starting June first.

On Memorial Day, I did a Lincoln program in DeLand, Florida, and then headed for the mountains. When I finally arrived at the Big Canoe Resort, an hour north of Atlanta, I was in love. I have always loved the mountains of North Carolina and didn't even realize Georgia had such beautiful settings. After being trained how to present the resort to perspective owners I was turned loose to do my own "tours."

I toured about thirty couples in those first two weeks and never made a sale! I was in serious trouble and getting a little discouraged. So was Mike. He called me outside one day and we had a long talk. He said, "Homer, I thought you told me you could sell." I told him I could, but just hadn't had any buyers yet. He was ready to send me back to Florida, but I persuaded him to let me finish my thirty-days-trial period. In those next two weeks, I sold enough to make over $5,000 in commissions. I was finally making some really decent money.

I bought a clean 1972 Mercedes 280SEL from my long-time friend, Ron Masten. It was a great car for touring with its big back seat and large windows for my prospects to look out at the mountains.

One of the couples I sold was from Marietta, and the following is a letter their daughter sent to me after I had visited her school where she was a teacher:

March 27, 1984
Dear Homer:

As you can tell from the enclosed letters, all of the students at Wood Acres thoroughly enjoyed your visit. I'm sure your visit and presentation will make any future studying of Abe Lincoln more interesting and much easier... after all, they "saw" and "heard" Abe himself!

On behalf of the staff, I would like to say "thank you" for a truly wonderful program. We were all "captivated" by Abe.

Personally, I was thrilled to meet you because of all the wonderful things my parents, S.L. and Alice Nixon, have said about you. I understand now why they think so highly of you.

There were several things that conveyed the presence of Abe... the clothes, the beard, and the stories. However, what really impressed me was your gentleness and calm manner. This is exactly how I've pictured Abraham Lincoln all of my life. I've always thought of him as a gentle person, calm and in complete control.

Mom and Dad have enclosed the newspaper article. I think it was a great "write up."

Hope to see you again.
Sincerely,

—Johnnie Preston

One of the salesmen at the Big Canoe Resort when I arrived was George Bessada from Egypt. They called us the "resident president" and the "resident camel driver." George was a good man. He and his wife, Nadia, had two sons, John-Mark and Daniel Isaac. Nadia was always up at the lake fishing when I took folks on tour. Over the years, George became a good friend and he is now (2009) teaching Marti the Arabic language.

I toured over 3,000 couples in the five and one-half years I worked for Big Canoe Resort. I certainly did not sell something to all of them, but I sold my share. I had a chance to visit with a lot of nice people during those years and many are still close friends. I loved working outdoors and showing the beautiful mountains of North Georgia.

The next time you take a vacation, you might want to consider buying and using timesharing. I found it to be a nice way to take a vacation. I used to own one week and enjoyed resorts around the country.

One of the people I sold a timeshare week to was a beautiful lady from Atlanta by the name of Jacque. At the time I sold her, she was working for Edwards Baking Company. Any time she would come to visit the resort, she would bring my friends and me lots of Edward's pies. Those were some of the best store-bought pies I have ever eaten! She also needle pointed me something that has become my motto to live by: "Be a Dreamer, a Stargazer, and a Rainbow Chaser." I have since added, "And Soar with the Eagles!" I use this on all of my brochures and stress it in all of my shows.

I toured airline pilots, business executives, doctors, lawyers, chicken farmers, and people from all walks of life while at Big Canoe Resort.

I was consistently in the top three or four of the twenty salespeople working there. In early 1984, I bought a nice lot for $3,000 in the resort next to Big Canoe called Bent Tree and made plans to build a home on it. Both resorts have great golf courses, and for those of you who have never played on a mountain course, you would be in for a real treat.

My family came up after school was out the summer of 1984, and we've been here ever since. We all love it here in the mountains.

I had always wanted to live in a log cabin, so we built a three-level, 3,000 square foot log cabin during the spring and summer of 1984. We rented a cute little A-frame cabin off Burnt Mountain Road outside Jasper while I built our log cabin. I rented it from Curtis Mabie, who was with the Dawson County Sheriff's Department at the time. Then he was, for a while, with security at the Atlanta airport and I would see him nearly every time I flew somewhere.

I heard about a company that makes great log cabin kits from white northern cedar. I got in touch with them and did some Lincoln work for them at a big home show in Atlanta. In lieu of paying me for the job, I took a discount from the price of the log cabin kit. I made my cabin available for folks to come see and was probably helpful in getting some log cabin kits sold.

We lived in our new log cabin for a couple of years until we got tired of the ten-mile winding road drive to town several times a day. We sold it and bought a house on the west side of Jasper, only one-half mile from the airport and one mile from the four-lane highway.

Perhaps my other motive for being so close to the airport is that some day I will realize my dream I've had since my first airplane ride in third grade. I've been working on it for twenty-two years and as of 1994, I had twenty of the forty hours needed to get my pilot's license, and I did solo. It seems when I've had the money to pay for it, I didn't have the time. And, when I've had the time, I didn't have the money. Isn't that true of so many things in life? When I took my first lesson in 1972, the cost was only nineteen dollars an hour for the plane, fuel, and an instructor. In 1993, the cost had risen to close to fifty dollars an hour!

Sometime in the near future I hope to be able to finish getting my pilot's license. Then I can walk to the airport, get into a rented plane (or my own plane), and fly off to visit with family, friends, or to be "Abe" somewhere.

I've gotten hundreds of letters from kids since 1975 and will put a collection of the best of them in my next book, *Dear President Lincoln*. Here is one I received in February of 1986 from a young student:

> Dear President Lincoln:
> Thank you for spending some of your time at Sardis Elementary School. We appreciate your concern on wanting

us to learn about Lincoln. I enjoyed your speech. I hope everybody else did too. I learned a lot from the slavery speech. I learned that everybody should be free. If you had not told me you were Mr. Homer Sewell, I would have thought you were Lincoln. Come back soon.

—Your friend, Lisa Nance

In September of 1986 I was invited by Dick Schreadley, editor of the Charleston, South Carolina, *News-Courier*, to come speak to the fortieth Annual Convention of Newspaper Editors from all over the country. Dick even wrote my speech for me! I had the opportunity to visit Ft. Sumpter, where the Civil War had begun on April 12, 1861. That was a wonderful experience for me.

In 1988, while I was still with Big Canoe, I noticed the skating rink in Jasper was for sale, so with some money Kathy inherited from her mother (and against her better judgment), we bought it. Now we were $150,000 in debt with a $1,800-a-month mortgage payment! And that was on top of the $800 monthly mortgage payment for our home!

I was determined we would make it work. We cleaned up the whole operation. No more drugs, alcohol, or smoking were allowed! We added a large game room at one end with thirty video games and five pool tables. We rebuilt the skate storage room and built a three foot high sixteen by twenty-four foot stage in the middle of the rink for those who wanted to dance. We added a large double pizza oven. We could bake twelve sixteen-inch pizzas at one time. I started making pizzas not only for the customers who came in, but started a delivery service for the Jasper area. Up until then, the only other pizza operation in town did not deliver.

There was now a clean, wholesome place for the young people of Pickens County to go on Friday and Saturday nights. We also had special group skating during the week. I got the whole family involved. Kimberly, Jason, and Chip helped out in the concession stand, made pizzas, gave out skates, took money at the door, did floor-guard duty, and whatever else needed to be done to run the operation. Kathy was there to help whenever she could.

I put the word out around town that I needed someone who could repair skates and help with other responsibilities. Rhoda Warren stopped by one day to see what needed to be done. I hired her and Rhoda became a real asset around the rink. She kept all those 300-plus pairs of skates in good working condition. She had a real knack for mechanical things and a lot of patience with young people.

During the winter months, when there wasn't much else to do outdoors, we were busy and able to pay the bills. But during the summer, our business died and after two years of struggling to make ends meet, we finally decided to shut down the skating rink. I had more dollars going out than coming in!

I should have known if the banker's daughter, who owned it before us, couldn't make it work, we probably couldn't either. We were in for a serious up-hill battle! But I had to try! We finally sold the building and it became a shirt manufacturing plant and more recently a strip mall for several stores.

A lot of small towns all over the country have nothing for their teenagers to do except cruise the main street, go parking, or looking for trouble. Students still come up to me in town wanting to know when I'm going to open "Flashers" back up so they can have a place to gather and have fun.

When it was obvious the young people were not going to come in sufficient numbers to pay the overhead, I asked them what they wanted that they would support. Some of them said, "Build us a race track for motorcycles and four-wheelers." So that's exactly what I did.

We have eight acres with woods and pasture, a stream down by the pasture, a waterfall, and a gorge across the street and lots of peace and quiet. I had never even visited a four-wheeler race track, but had an idea of what one should look like. I had several cases of 2,500-feet rolls of copy paper a church in Atlanta had given me. I took a couple of those rolls and walked off the course, trailing paper behind me to mark it.

I then hired a contractor with a bulldozer to build the track. It ended up being about one-half mile long with banked-turns, jumps, "table-tops," and lots of curves and switchbacks. I even put in an irrigation and sprinkler system to keep the track wet when there had been no rain. I bought trophies, printed flyers, fixed up a concession stand in the barn, and put the word out all over North Georgia that we were now open for business. Rhoda was there to help run the track. She helped with concessions, kept score, and took entrants' and spectators' money. I couldn't have done it without her.

At our peak, we had as many as fifty people coming to race and/or watch. Our only accidents were a broken wrist and a gashed leg. With as many as ten four-wheelers or motorcycles racing at one time, there could have been some serious accidents. We were lucky! It was exciting watching folks race around the track!

Although it was self-sustaining and something fun to do on Saturdays and Sundays, I didn't have the money to promote it properly and after a few months of operation, I decided to shut it down.

It was fun while it lasted. The track is all grown up now with tall grass and trees, but I still go down when I am in town and ride my twins' four-wheeler or motorcycle. I enjoy it and it's a way for me to relax.

In the fall of 1988, the timesharing business at Big Canoe was declining and the company decided to get out of it completely. They would concentrate on selling homes and lots. I was offered an opportunity to sell general real estate. I quickly decided it was not what I wanted and started looking for other opportunities.

In October, when I left Big Canoe, I had a job for a while doing part-time work for Georgia Temps. They placed people in temporary jobs in the fifty-one-story headquarters building of Georgia-Pacific Company in downtown Atlanta. For several weeks, I was the PBX operator on the seventeenth floor in the Wood Products Division. I was answering and routing as many as 800 calls a day to

Image in the Mirror

the fifty people on my floor. I did meet a lot of nice people there in Georgia Pacific and they featured Abe in their *Atlanta This Week* newsletter to employees. I drove the fifty-five miles each way for a few months until I realized it wasn't going to work out. They weren't giving me enough hours to support my family and I knew I needed to find something else.

Kathy worked as a nurse during all these years and it was her income that helped support the family when I wasn't working at all or not making very much money. Her favorite quote was, "When are you going to get a real job?" She has been a nurse for nearly thirty years and could get a good job in any state in the country. She always wanted me to go get a forty-hours-a-week punch-a-time-clock type job. It just wasn't me! The entrepreneurial spirit in me is too strong to punch someone's clock!

Even More Jobs

Some interesting things happened while I was a good, honest lawyer in Springfield...

All these years since 1975 I was continuing to portray Abe part-time, and studied more and more about his life. My ultimate dream had always been to find a way to support my family by being Abe full-time.

Mark, one of the guys who had sold real estate with me at Big Canoe Resort, called me from his home in south Florida one evening in 1989. Mark was into something big and wanted me to get into it too. He had discovered NSA water filters and its multi-level marketing (M.L.M.) plan. Mark had been one of our top salesmen at Big Canoe, so I figured he must know what he was doing and if it was good enough for him, it was good enough for me too.

So I bought into NSA and started selling water filters. They are good filters and probably priced competitively with other filters that do the same job.

The demonstration we were taught to do was a real eye-opener! I had some chemicals you would use to test the chlorine level in your pool. I would go into a prospect's home, which had chlorinated city water, and fill a clear plastic tumbler with tap water. Then I would hook up the portable filter and run another tumbler full of filtered tap water. I then placed six drops of the chemical into both glasses of water. The unfiltered water turned "pee-yellow" real quick! The water with the chlorine filtered out remained clear. Then I turned to the prospect and asked, "Mrs. Smith, which water would you like to drink? Shall I leave this filter hooked up for you?"

For people who were interested in having good, clear, clean non-chlorinated water, the filter did the job. I recommend to everyone who has city water to get some type of water filter that filters out the chlorine and other impurities that are poisoning our bodies.

For a while, I sold Electrolux vacuum cleaners around North Georgia. I also did some home shows for them as Abe. I sold a few and made some money in commissions. They are good vacuum cleaners and last a long time. I can remember Mom and me cleaning house in Altamonte Springs in the fifties with an Electrolux. I personally think some vacuum cleaners are over-priced. From my experience with Sears and Electrolux vacuums, I think the best buy on the market now is the Royal Dirt Devil Upright Deluxe. I bought one last year from Walmart (my favorite store) for about $129 with all the attachments. It works as well as vacuums selling for five times as much! You need to thoroughly evaluate what *your* needs are and what is the best buy for you to accomplish those needs.

Mike Harrison, who had worked for me at Sears, had tried unsuccessfully in 1980 or 1981 to get me into selling insurance for A.L. Williams. I told him then that I didn't like to sell non-tangible things like insurance. Again, in early 1989, someone contacted me about selling term life insurance for A.L. Williams. I finally, reluctantly, agreed to give it a try. I went to school to take the necessary hours for my Georgia insurance license and passed the exam. Now

I was a licensed insurance salesman. I still didn't like it! I sold a few policies and even talked Vi Montgomery, a friend from Altamonte Springs, into getting her license.

Both of us dropped out of it after a few months of cold-calling and not selling! They were a good company for term insurance, but selling insurance is just not my "cup-of-tea."

I was hired in February of 1989 to be Systems Manager at the Marietta District Office for the U.S. Census Bureau. My job would be to set up a computer system with fifteen terminals, two printers, etc., hire and train about twenty people, and be responsible for the day-to-day running of this system. We would be handling payroll for 800 to 1,000 people on a daily basis. I would be there for a one year contract and then for an additional six months to end in September of 1990. This was the time I had already planned to go full-time as Abe, so the timing would be great.

I did the job I was hired to do well enough that they had me helping train other managers for other offices in North Georgia. I was always at work on time and put in my eight hours, five days a week. I worked overtime, if necessary, without complaining.

On Monday, February 12, 1990 (Abe Lincoln's birthday), I was scheduled to do a program in the Atlanta area. The previous Friday, I told my manager I would be off the following Monday to do this program. He reminded me to be sure to take a day of either sick leave or annual leave. I assured him I would. I would not want the Census Bureau to think I was at work and on their payroll while I was at a school as Abe.

I had several days of both sick leave and annual leave accumulated. During the weekend, I was installing a hot water heater in my home and pulled something loose in my neck or back. I was in so much pain I couldn't lay down to sleep. I had to sit up in a chair to sleep.

It would be helpful for you to understand that when I make a commitment to appear at a school or other location as Abe, unless I am already dead, I will be there. Even though I was in extreme pain and was barely able to stand in front of all of those students, I was determined to be there. That Monday morning, I called in and told one of the ladies who worked for me to tell my manager I was out sick. I gave her the number at the school so I could be reached in case she needed me. I told her to put me down on the time sheet for a day of sick leave. In fact, during my program later in the day, I was called to the school office to take a call from my Census office. I handled a small payroll problem that had come up and then continued with my program for the students.

I already had an appointment to see a chiropractor that Monday afternoon just as soon as I finished at the school. I felt since there was a medical problem, I should call my absence "sick leave" instead of "annual leave." Now, don't forget, I had plenty of both types of leave available to me!

I want to put in my two cents worth right here about chiropractic care. I strongly believe in what they do. If it weren't for Doctor Steve Curry here in Jasper, and other chiropractors I've visited around the country, I would be in a lot of pain. I see him on a regular basis. Everyone should get adjustments by a good chiropractor frequently. One of these days our insurance companies will wake up and realize that if chiropractors were seen first (became the "gatekeepers" for the medical profession), there would be a lot less money spent for expensive MRIs, CAT scans, drugs, and unneeded surgeries. Drugs will only mask the problems if your spine is out of adjustment!

And speaking of chiropractors, I've got another friend who has been a pharmacist for several years and in 1993 graduated from Life College of Chiropractic in Marietta. Rick and his beautiful wife, Melissa, just had their first baby (a pretty little girl) in March of 1994. They've gone camping with us and we visit each other whenever we can. Rick is one of the most-fun-to-be-with friends I have. Regardless of how your day or night has been going, Rick will make you smile. Everyone needs a friend like him! May God continue to bless you, Rick.

If any of my readers have any doubts about what a good chiropractor can do to help you feel better all over, all the time, and without drugs; please give me a call. I will be happy to tell you how much I appreciate *my* chiropractor!

I did my program and went straight to the doctor. In fact, I went nearly every day for over a month. I was in so much pain I was not able to sleep except sitting up in a reclining chair. I still, to this day, have problems in the same area of my neck and back and have to have regular chiropractic care in order to be able to walk.

Even though I continued to be in extreme pain and made visits to the chiropractor almost every day, I was always at work and put in a full day of duties for the Census Bureau. I never missed a day of work!

Abe Lincoln Gets Fired from the Census…

On February twenty-first, one of the supervisors from the Atlanta office came into my office and in front of several of my employees, directed me to come with him. We sat down in the District Manager's office. He handed me a letter stating that I had violated sick leave policy. He asked for my ID badge and keys and fired me on the spot! No questions about anything, nor did he offer to change the type of leave I had taken to annual instead of sick. His statement to me was, "If I was sick enough not to be there at work; then I was too sick to be performing Abe in front of school students."

Needless to say, I was devastated! I had never been fired from a job and I wasn't going to take it lying down. I called an attorney friend and asked him what to do. I called the Equal Employment Opportunity Commission office and filed an E.E.O.C. complaint. After months of hearings and phone conversations back and forth between here, Washington, California, and Atlanta, I ended up with nothing! I figured they owed me my pay for the six months I was told I would still be working, plus something for all the pain and suffering my family and I had been through. We nearly lost our home!

I tried to get unemployment compensation while I fought to get my job back, but was turned down because they said I had violated company policy and therefore was not qualified.

If the man who fired me, because he saw an article in the newspaper about my being at the school, hadn't had it in for me for some reason, he could have said, "Well, Homer, let's change that to annual leave and everything will be alright." Everyone, including my own boss, Mr. Frances Brooke, said I was doing an excellent job and did not want to see me fired.

If it wasn't for a lot of help from my pastor, Max Caylor, at the Jasper United Methodist Church, my strong faith in God, and my banker, Mark Whitfield, at the Jasper Banking Company, we would have lost our home. I really appreciate all they both did to help during these most trying times.

I have always had a strong belief in God and know He will answer prayers and be there when we need him. I have tried to attend church as regularly as possible. These were some very hard times in my life, and prayer and God helped us through it. There were times when I wondered if tomorrow would be a better day, but I never gave up.

I am often asked about Abe's religious beliefs and I want to quote what he said when someone asked why he never officially joined a church.

"I have never joined any church, but when any church will inscribe over its altar, as its sole qualification for membership, the words of the Savior, 'Thou shalt love the Lord thy God with all thy heart, and with all thy soul, and thy neighbor as thyself,' that church will I join with all my heart and all my soul."

It was probably one of the worst times in my life. One of these days I hope to be able to find an attorney or someone who can help me fight the Census Bureau for their unfair labor practices. I was told if I had been an employee for *just one more week*, I would have had a lot more rights because of being a military veteran. I think they also knew that! For now, I must go on with my life.

Lesson to be learned here is: Even when you are being honest, fair, and above-board, someone might still try to discredit you. But, don't ever give up when you know you are right. Stand up and fight for what you believe in.

After the Census disaster in my life, I did whatever I could the summer of 1990 to make ends meet. I worked for a while for Digital Equipment Corporation in Alpharetta. I did word processing and answered phones for their Talent Tree Temp service. That was a part-time thing that did not give me very many hours.

During this same year, I developed stones in my gall bladder and it was decided my gall bladder needed to be removed. Knowing I was facing several days stay in a hospital, a lot of pain, and being cut open in the belly, I was not excited! About that same time, I saw an article in my favorite magazine, *Reader's Digest*, about a relatively new type of surgery called Laparoscopic Laser that made gall bladder removal and other types of surgery a lot easier on the patient.

I called Emory University in Atlanta and asked who in the area was performing this type of surgery. They said Dr. J. Barry McKernan in Marietta had pioneered this type of surgery and was teaching it all over the world. I called his office, made an appointment, and went to see this world famous doctor. I liked him right off the bat. He is a very warm, friendly, and extremely knowledgeable man, and it was easy to see he *knew* what he was talking about.

We scheduled the surgery for the following week and I had it done "out-patient." The doctor made five small incisions into my abdomen for instruments, TV camera, suction, etc. I got up and walked two miles the day after surgery! I've even got a video of the procedure.

Again in 1992, when I pulled another hernia, I called Doctor McKernan's office to see if he was doing hernia repairs with Laparoscopic surgery. There was so much scar tissue in my tummy from previous surgeries that I didn't relish the idea of going through it again the "old-fashioned way."

I was told he did perform hernia repairs using his new procedure, so I had it done again on an "out-patient" basis. I highly recommend this procedure whenever you or a loved one needs to have anything fixed or removed. Every day there are new advances in this type of medical treatment and *my* doctor is the leader in field.

Because of Doc McKernan, I was able to do my performances within a day or two of surgery instead of being out of work for a couple of weeks! Thanks Doc!

Early in 1994, I got a call from Doc McKernan's office asking if I would mind if they had their new PR person get in touch with me to do a human interest story about "Abe" and his surgeries. I told them I didn't have any objection and I got a call a few days later from Marilyn Pearlman of Atlanta. She came to see one of my school programs and then worked up some PR releases for Doc McKernan. She also arranged for me to appear on an Atlanta TV talk show that had featured my doctor the week before.

For a while, I placed my Georgia real estate license with two different companies in Jasper and tried general real estate again. I decided it still wasn't what I wanted to do.

I was trying to bring in enough money to live on until September, when I would go full-time as Abe.

In late 1989, I had been on a flight somewhere and sat next to a lady who told me if I ever wanted to go full-time as Abe, she had a friend in Kansas who booked talent into schools all over the country. I got in touch with him and signed a contract for the school year 1990–91 to begin in September.

Right after a Labor Day family camping trip to Shinning Rock Wilderness Area, our favorite place on the Blue Ridge Parkway in North Carolina, I hit the road as a full-time Abe. My nineteen-year dream had finally materialized! Would I be able to handle the stress of ten shows a week (at the time I was still doing half-day shows. I've since decided I can give schools and students more for their money by being there for an all-day program) and being away from my family for weeks at a time?

In that first nine months of being Abe full-time, I did 333 appearances in seventeen Midwest states! I was doing more appearances in more locations than most any other type of public speaker, singer, or other kinds of performer ever does!

My agent booked me all of those jobs and paid me in a timely fashion; but the man never bothered to come see my show or to meet me in person! I was within an hour of his office for two solid weeks and he never made an effort to come see my performances. I handed over $30,000 to him that school year 1990–1991. It was obvious he was more interested in what he could make off my performances and those of the other fifteen talents he handled than of taking time to meet me.

If I gave you $30,000, wouldn't you at least come take me to lunch or dinner and say, "Great show! And thanks for the money, Homer"?

At least it proved to me there was a need for my services and I could handle the schedule of being on the road all the time. My family didn't like my being gone, but the money was good. I was getting a check for $1,500 a week, sending $1,000 home and catching up on a lot of debts.

If you are in an area of the country I haven't worked in yet and you want to make some money as my agent, please call or write. I will tell you how to book some shows and make yourself some commissions. I would love to get to the remainder of the states that aren't yet on the list at the end of the book. They are Alaska, Hawaii, Louisiana, and Montana.

OFF TO WASHINGTON

I ran again in November of '60... for the big office... and guess what happened? I won that one! I became your sixteenth president!
   Right before that election, I received the nicest letter from a little eleven-year-old girl who lived up in Westfield, New York. Her name was Grace Bedell. Miss Grace said she thought I would make a good president; if I had any little girls, would I ask them to write to her, and I might look much more handsome if I grew some whiskers.

In all those miles of traveling, I've had a lot of interesting experiences and met quite a few people who encouraged me to write a book. I started gathering my notes.

I have wanted to write a book for years, and now that it is done, I am fulfilling one of the dreams I have had. I came across a quote the other day and I would like for those of you who didn't see it to have a chance now.

This quote is taken from the May, 1993 issue of my favorite magazine, *Reader's Digest*, and was quoted there from *Writer's Digest*, and was written by one of my favorite writers, Tom Clancy. He has written such wonderful adventures as *Hunt for Red October, Clear and Present Danger, Red Storm Rising, Patriot Games,* and *Without Remorse*, published by the Berkley Publishing group. If you are looking for some adventurous reading and haven't yet read these books and many more by Tom Clancy, you may want to do so.

"The foundations of successful writing are within anyone's grasp," says best-selling author Tom Clancy. "Writing is like golf or skeet shooting or any other human endeavor," he says. "The only way to do it is to *do* it." Clancy considers his accomplishments:

"My greatest good fortune was that I didn't know that I was doing everything wrong. If I'd done a single thing right, I probably would have failed. If I'd known how hard—statistically speaking—it is to get a first novel published, I might have given up and done what my wife told me to do: sold more insurance.

"What success really means is looking failure in the face and tossing the dice anyway. You may be the only person who ever knows how the dice come up, but in that knowledge you have something that millions of people will never have—because they were afraid to try."

Right-on, Tom! I love what he says and what he writes! And to think that I used to sell insurance, too! I could only *dream* of ever selling as many books as Tom Clancy has, but if we don't ever reach for our goals, we will *never achieve them*! I read somewhere that Tom now gets a $4,000,000 advance as soon as he is ready to start another book!

By the way, if you aren't already subscribing to *Reader's Digest* and reading it cover-to-cover each month, you need to. It is a great little magazine and I have my copies all the way back to the 1960s.

This is a good place for me to repeat my favorite little motto...

"Be a dreamer, a stargazer, a rainbow chaser, and soar with the eagles!" You will hear me say it over and over again!

I want you to write down, either on this page or another piece of paper, what ten things you most want to accomplish or achieve with your life in the next five years.

1. _____

2. _____

3. _____

4. _____

5. _____

6. _____

7. _____

8. _____

9. _____

10. _____

List them in order of their importance.

What do you need to accomplish these goals?

Break down your goals into small daily segments so you can achieve them daily. This will help build your personal self-esteem when you are able to accomplish goals each day.

Tell family or friends what you want to accomplish. This will force you to make them happen! You don't want to be a failure in front of friends. Post the list where you will see it every day... on your refrigerator or mirror.

Read all the self-help books and listen to all the tapes you can find.

Some Good Suggestions:
See You at the Top by Zig Ziglar
The Greatest Salesman by Og Mandino
How to Win Friends and Influence People by Dale Carnegie
The Greatest Thing in the World by Henry Drummond
Acres of Diamonds by Russell Conwell
And there are lots, lots more out there.

Go to your library and check out autobiographies of successful men like Victor Kiam, Dave Thomas, David Green, Sam Walton, and Conrad Hilton. Read and study about these people's successes and failures. Reading these books and others like them will motivate *you* to success!

Lesson to be learned here is: If you can dream it, you can achieve it!

Gettysburg

Some things happened in '63 that looked like they might cause the war to wind down a little... on January first, I issued the Emancipation Proclamation.

On July first, second, and third, outside the town of Gettysburg, Pennsylvania, there was a major battle. At that one battle, over 60,000 troops from the North and the South were either killed, wounded, or missing in action. It became a major turning point of the Civil War. As the townspeople of Gettysburg were burying those dead soldiers in a seventeen and a half acre portion of that battlefield, they decided since this had not been just any ordinary battle, this certainly could not be just any ordinary cemetery. It needed national dedication and national recognition. The date was set for November 19, 1863 and a lot of very important people were invited to attend.

My friend, Edward Everett, a great senator and former governor from Massachusetts, was asked to be the main speaker of the day. Finally, on November second, just two weeks ahead of time, I received a telegram at the White House asking me if I could come speak, "a few appropriate remarks, just a short talk," with the emphasis on short.

I wrote my little speech in the White House, revised it slightly on the train on the way to Gettysburg, and then revised it again for the third time in the home of Judge David Wills, the family I stayed with in Gettysburg.

The Gettysburg Address
Four score and seven years ago, our fathers brought forth on this continent a new nation, conceived in liberty and dedicated to proposition that all men are created equal.

Now we are engaged in a great Civil War, testing whether that nation, or any nation, so conceived and so dedicated, can long endure. We are met on a great battlefield of that war. We have come to dedicate a portion of that field as a final resting place for those who here gave their lives that that nation might live. It is altogether fitting and proper that we should do this.

But, in a larger sense, we can not dedicate—we cannot consecrate—we can not hallow—this ground. The brave men, living and dead, who struggled here, have consecrated it far and above our poor power to add or detract.

The world will little note nor long remember what we say here, but it can never forget what they did here. It is for us, the living, rather, to be dedicated here to the unfinished work which they who fought here have thus far so nobly advanced. It is rather for us to be here dedicated to the great task remaining before us—that from these honored dead we take increased devotion to that cause for which they gave the last full measure of devotion—that we here highly resolve that these dead shall not have died in vain—that this nation, under God, shall have a new birth of freedom—and that government of the people, by the people, for the people, shall not perish from the earth.

Mom, Look Who's Here!

Did I tell you about the nice family I stayed with in Gettysburg? Judge Wills fed me a couple of good meals and I enjoyed visiting with him and his family. I stayed with a lot of nice folks in my travels as an attorney.

When I travel around the country visiting schools and other locations, I prefer to stay with families. That way I am not staring at the four walls of a motel room and having to eat fast-food all alone. That gets old! I enjoy visiting with families and having a good home-cooked meal. I leave them a frameable certificate that says "Abe" stayed with them.

The times when I don't have a family to stay with, I look for one of my favorite places to eat: Cracker Barrel Restaurants. I can always count on a good "home cooked" meal with reasonable "down home" prices and great "presidential" friendly service. When you're traveling next time and want a great meal, stop by a Cracker Barrel and tell them Abe sent you.

As I have traveled, I've met some very special people all over America. It would take a complete book to tell you about all of them, but I do want to share a few of my experiences in this chapter.

I took the title of this chapter from a young student who lives in Grandview, Missouri. When I finished my program at her school on a Friday afternoon, she and her brother and sister asked, "Mr. Lincoln, why don't you walk us home and surprise Mom?" I didn't have anywhere I needed to be for the night or the weekend, so I agreed to walk with them two blocks to their house. When we arrived at the front door, Tonya, Melissa, and Timmy yelled inside, "Mom, look who's here! We brought Mr. Lincoln home to dinner." Terri and Mac invited me to supper and to spend the night. I accepted their invitation and we had a great time visiting.

When I arrived at the home of Principal Al, his wife, Pat, and son, Scott, in Sheridan, Indiana, he asked me, "Would you like to eat tonight?" I told him I would love to. He then told me that, "We were going to a Rotary Club supper meeting, and by the way, would you *speak* for your dinner?" I love food—and talking—I readily agreed and spoke for thirty minutes after dinner. I am always ready to eat a good meal or talk to folks … anywhere … any time.

While I was on a tour of the beautiful state of Colorado in 1990, I was having some trouble with my red, white, and blue sports car. I pulled into the little town of Swink late one afternoon with my radiator boiling over. As I was trying to figure out what to do, a very nice lady stopped by to see if she could help. Dorothy turned out to be the librarian at the school I would visit the next day. She was gracious enough to take me to a parts store where I bought a thermostat. She took me back to the car and found a high school student she knew who installed it for me. That weekend, I went with her to visit her friends, Jack and Lori, who were in the process of building a log cabin. I helped them put up some fencing for their animals. I then visited the fort where Jack works.

In Ripon, Wisconsin, I stayed with Leon, Barb, Jenny, and Paul. Leon drives a big tanker and picks up milk from a lot of dairy farms to make some of that great Wisconsin cheese. They showed me a little building where the first Republican Party meeting had been held just a few years before Abe became president. Ripon is also the home of Rippling Good Cookies.

When I was in South Texas, I heard about a man who lived in Ingram. I was going to be driving near his home. I called and was able to stop by for an hour or so to see Bill and Peggy. Bill is one of the few men still living who helped carve Mount Rushmore. He showed me around his home and shared some of the "small" pieces he had sculpted. I would imagine after working on Mount Rushmore, no other artistic endeavor could ever compare! He was a fascinating man and we had a nice visit. I am so happy that I had the opportunity to meet Bill.

Bea is a wonderful counselor at her school and I stayed with her and Phillip at their home in Amity, Arkansas. Phillip took me on a tour of his sawmill. It was interesting for me to see how they cut big logs down to small boards to make pallets. All that modern technology sure beats the way Abe used to split rails and sawed boards by hand! Bea cooked us a great southern meal.

I stayed in Westlake, Ohio, with Don, Maria, their twins, Amanda and Nicholas, and Mandy. Mandy may very well be our first lady president! She is studying hard and heading in that direction already. Don also showed me around one of his six temporary service offices and we talked about the possibility of me doing some TV commercials for his company.

Connie and Melba cooked me a great meal in their school cafeteria in Lyons, Kansas. I always enjoy eating a good meal in school and these two ladies *know* how to cook! Their cherry pie was excellent!

I went to Neal's ice hockey game and stayed with Biri, Catherine, Colin, and Neal in Olmstead, Ohio. I had never seen an ice hockey game and it was exciting watching all those youngsters flying around on the ice.

The award for living closest to the school I would visit goes to Anne in San Antonio, Texas. Her home was directly across the street. She took me on a boat ride at the River Walk in downtown San Antonio.

When I pulled into one little town in Wisconsin, I didn't know where I was going to stay. I don't like staying in motels, but I didn't have a family to stay with for the night. As I was reluctantly checking into a motel, I met Karen. She invited me to stay with her, Wanda, and their twenty-five cats. That evening, she took me to visit a family who had a dairy farm. While we were watching the cows being milked, one of them in a nearby stall decided it was time to "pee." She did and it splattered all over my black pants and frock-tailed coat. For the next two days, nobody would get anywhere near me at school! I smelled bad! I finally got my suit to a cleaner that weekend, and not a minute too soon!

I stayed in a big, beautiful log cabin in Montello, Wisconsin, with Rich, Monica, Ricky, and Christopher. Abe would have loved *this* cabin!

When I stayed with Wayne, Linda, Bryn, Jim, and Katie in Plover, Wisconsin, Wayne got a call to go out to a farm. Wayne is a vet and invited me to go along with him. So I changed clothes and helped him deliver a calf. That was an experience! There really are vets who still make house calls!

The award for largest family I've ever stayed with goes to Bobbie in Dallas, Texas. Her husband died a few years ago and Bobbie is raising Junior, Nicole, Jana, Joshua, Jennifer, Jamie, Jesse, John, Jeff, Julie, Joy, and Jordan all by herself! Yes, count them again, twelve kids. One dozen! She is quite a hard-working mother! And she also does a lot of volunteer work in the community. God bless you, Bobbie.

Image in the Mirror

One of the "sweetest" ladies I've ever stayed with was in Garland, Texas. Sweet (that's her real name!), Kenny, Kendall, and Ivy fed me great meals and Sweet later wrote me two of the nicest letters I've gotten from anyone. She is the PTA President and they should be proud to have such a hard working lady on their team. Kenny and Sweet, thank you for everything.

I stayed with teacher, Carol, and bank president, Randy, and sons, Scott and Nathan, in Troy, Ohio. Randy's bank paid me to ride on the bank's float in a big parade on Saturday. Then I ran into them again that summer while I was at Mount Rushmore. Great food! Great folks!

When I was on the way to Virginia in the summer of 1993, I stopped at a Wendy's to eat. I met a couple from Texas and they asked me to call them the next time I was in Irving, Texas. My next trip to that area, I stayed with Bob and Sheila for a weekend. Their children, Lindsey and Logan, are both very talented, beautiful models for TV and newspaper ads, and they took me for a walk/bike ride to a park a few blocks from their home.

In Round Rock, Texas, I stayed with Richard and Sara. She is a wonderful, talented, and caring principal at the school I visited and Richard designs computers for IBM. He is also a pilot with his own plane. One weekend, when I was in the Austin area, I helped him wash his plane and then we went flying for an hour or so. I love it! I relish every chance I get to *soar with the eagles!*

The award for biggest in-home fish collection goes to James in Flat Rock, Indiana. He is the school superintendent and his beautiful, old two-story home is full of fish tanks of various sizes and descriptions. He had fresh and salt water tanks and I don't even remember all the types of fish he had collected over the years. They were beautiful!

Oink! Oink! That's the noise I heard from a couple of hundred pigs I helped feed late one night when I stayed with Jim, Judy, and John in Rockbridge, Illinois. We ate some great pork chops for supper! I wonder where they came from? After we ate, I put on some big rubber boots and helped Jim feed and give shots to some of his pigs.

I stayed with Ray and Ronnie in Attica, Kansas, the same day that Ronnie had run over and broken off a valve to a natural gas line in their backyard. They were lucky there wasn't an explosion! Ray is the principal at the school.

I milked my first and *only* goat when I stayed with Tom, Sara, Kellen, David, and Paul in Three Lakes, Wisconsin. Milking a goat is different than milking a cow and it wasn't easy to get the hang of it. Tom is principal and raises bees in his spare time. He gives all of his teachers and friends fresh honey for the holidays. Sara has about a dozen goats and sells the goats' milk. Wisconsin is a cold place to visit in the winter, but I had a warm family to be with and ate great food!

Brad and Brenda are teachers in Westlake, Ohio, and Brad took me for a ride on his motorcycle along the shores of Lake Erie. We ate a big pancake breakfast at an old Veteran's Home.

Tom, Sharon, J.D., and Josh in Ironton, Ohio, had a big spread of food for me and a lot of friends who stopped by to meet "Abe." Tom took me to Masonic Lodge with him that night. I enjoy visiting other lodges whenever I can.

On a trip in Ohio, I was talking on my CB radio to a UPS driver. He invited me to come home and have a meal with his family that weekend. Steve, Delores, Steven, Sarah, Rachael, and Gracie fed me a good home-cooked meal in Broadview Heights, Ohio, and I had a nice visit. This was just one of the many, many cases of people taking me in and feeding me when I wasn't even going to their school. I must have an honest face or something that makes strangers feel comfortable around me!

I've had many interesting experiences with African-Americans while in my black frock-tailed coat and stove-pipe hat, but two stick in my mind. One time, I was at the Atlanta airport and prior to departure, I was having my boots shined. A security guard came over to me and politely asked me to come with her after I was finished. I followed her and she introduced me to her boss. She said, "Mr. Lincoln, I just wanted to thank you for what you did for the black

Image in the Mirror

people. Would you please autograph something for me?" I was more than happy to autograph one of my brochures for her.

When I took a group of students to Mount Vernon in March of 1994, I had another moving moment. As we were headed back to get on our bus, we were passing a long line of busses. A black driver was standing outside of his bus and when he saw me coming up the sidewalk, he got down on his knees in front of me, stuck out his hand and said, "Mr. Lincoln, I appreciate what you did for us and just wanted to shake your hand." I take portraying Abe very seriously, and these two simple gestures of sincerity meant a lot to me personally. I understood what they both meant and how the man I represent would have felt under the same circumstances.

I am sorry I can't mention *all* of the nice families who took me in and fed me good meals or I met and visited with along the way. There just isn't enough space to list all of you. Perhaps someday soon I will write another book just about my experiences with families across the country. I do appreciate your hospitality and I hope anytime you are anywhere near the mountains of North Georgia, you will give me a call so I can try to return the hospitality.

Lesson to be learned here is: "Do unto others as you would have them do unto you." Go out of your way to be friendly to a stranger *today*. Your smile, friendliness, caring, and compassion to others will reward you ten-fold in so many ways. Give someone a hug today.

The Importance of Letter Writing

I wrote a lot of letters while I was president. Some were happy, but a lot of them were very sad letters.

November 21, 1863
Dear Madam:
   I have been shown in the files of the War Department a statement of the Adjutant General of Massachusetts, that you are the mother of five sons who have died gloriously on the field of battle.
   I feel how weak and fruitless must be any words of mine which should attempt to beguile you from the grief of a loss so overwhelming. But I cannot refrain from tendering to you the consolation that may be found in the thanks of the Republic they died to save.

I pray that our Heavenly Father may assuage the anguish of your bereavement, and leave you only the cherished memory of the loved and lost, and the solemn pride that must be yours to have laid so costly a sacrifice upon the altar of freedom.
   Yours, Very Sincerely

—A. Lincoln

I included this letter because it has become a classic around the world and speaks so much of Lincoln's compassion, caring, and concern.

One of the projects I've been working on these past few years is to get the law changed that currently allows *anyone* to burn our flag. I have been encouraging my students around the country to write letters and I would like for you to do the same.

Please take time right *now* to write a letter and address copies of it to your senator, congressman, TV stations, newspapers, and the president. Tell them as a red-blooded patriotic American citizen, you want to see the law changed right now that allows anyone to burn our flag for any reason other than if it is torn, soiled, or damaged. And then it should be burned in a ceremony at your local American Legion Post.

I've been told by people I've met from other countries that if you burned the flag of their country, you would be *shot* or *hung* on the spot! If enough of my audiences and my readers will take time to write, perhaps someday soon we can get the law changed. Please, for the sake of our flag, write a letter *today*!

This might be a good place to quote something I recently read in a book I borrowed from Sally Smith. *In and Out of Rebel Prisons* was written in 1888 by Lieutenant Alonzo Cooper and published by R.J. Oliphant, Job Printer, Bookbinder and Stationer of Oswego, New York. Lieutenant Cooper was born in 1830, so he was thirty-two years old when he joined the Union Forces in 1862. His book is an excellent look at Rebel prisons and the way the officers were treated in those prisons. Enlisted men were kept in separate prisons from their officers. The section I quote comes from near the end of his book and describes a scene towards the end of the war when 2,000 prisoners were being exchanged.

> "When the head of the column came under the shadow of "Old Glory," both our cheers and our old dilapidated hats went heavenward with all the velocity that we were able to impart to them. Some were too feeble to more than faintly whisper their greeting to the dear old flag they loved so dearly, while tears of joy attested the genuineness of their affection for that beautiful emblem of liberty, the sight of which had so long been denied them.
>
> "I never before realized how much I loved the dear old stars and stripes, or how much protection there was beneath its shining folds. How I longed to press it to my heart and lips. And not me alone, but of the nearly two thousand skeletons who that day saw it proudly waving high over their heads for the first time in many months; there were few indeed who would not have fervently kissed and caressed it had it been within their reach. As a mother's love goes out to her first born that has come to her amid suffering and pain, so that old flag seemed a thousand fold more beautiful and precious to us, for the sufferings and privations we had passed through in its defense.
>
> "Cheer after cheer went up as the straggling column passed along, feeble hands were waived, and feeble voices joined in the huzzahs, with which we celebrated our return to 'God's country.'"

It is too bad some of our young people today have no idea what patriots of our country have gone through to keep our flag flying high. There needs to be more respect for our flag from young and old!

And a couple of more interesting quotes from an old book. These came from one of a dozen books I bought in a small used book store while visiting Gettysburg, Pennsylvania, in January of 1994.

This is a quote from a speech given in an address before the Union League of Philadelphia on February 12, 1938 by Joseph Fort Newton taken from his book, *We Here Highly Resolve*, published by Harper & Brothers in 1939.

> "No one is really masterful until he has first been mastered by a great idea, a great cause, a great passion, a great purpose. Something outside himself, greater than himself, worthy of the utmost devotion is needed to unify his life, organize his energies, and give power to his genius."

This is a strong message for all of us to think about! It certainly fits Lincoln and probably fits me too! My *cause* since 1975 has been to help our youth have a positive attitude about life, read more, stay off drugs, respect their parents and teachers, and *now* more recently, do whatever they can to help stop youth violence in America.

Here's another quote from this same book. This one is from the sermon delivered by Mr. Newton at the seventy-fifth anniversary of the Battle of Gettysburg, July 3, 1938. This is from the very end of his sermon and speaks strong words for us today:

> "That we here highly resolve, as one people, under one flag, that we join hearts in one faith, join hands in one purpose, uniting spiritual vision and political wisdom, and individual initiative with social obligation, for the safety and sanctity of our republic; for the rights of man and the majesty of law; for the moral trusteeship of private property, public office, and social welfare; for the education of the young in the laws of life, the freedom of the truth, and the service of humanity; for the lifting of poverty, through self-help, to security, comfort, and nobility; for the holiness of the home and the altar; for a life more abundant, a liberty more responsible, and a happiness more abiding.
>
> "May the God of our fathers, who has led us thus far down the ways of time, mercifully grant that our flag—symbol of blood-making not of blood-shedding—may never again float

over a field of war, but ever and forever over scenes of peace, honor, and progress; flag of unity and justice at home, of fraternity and good will among all nations; the ensign of a free people, uniting many races without rancor, many faiths without feud, many classes without friction; in a land where men not only live and let live, think and let think, but live and help live; that the high destiny of man and the holy will of God may be fulfilled in the history of our country. Amen."

It has now been seventy-two years since these words were uttered by a great speaker, but they are words very fitting for our society today. Please pay particular attention to what he said about our flag. What would Abe have said about someone burning our flag? I don't think he would have tolerated it! Do you? Please do as I have suggested and take time to write a letter about changing the law that allows anyone to burn our flag.

I can't emphasize enough to my young readers the importance of learning letter writing at an early age. The ability to communicate with the rest of the world is something we all need to be able to do.

I learned very early about how to get results with letter writing. If you want to find out what a good letter can do in a hurry, go into your cupboard and get a box of your favorite cereal, cookies, soup, or other product you really like to eat. Sit down and write a letter to the president of the company. Tell them how much you love their products and you and your family eat them all the time. Get Mom or Dad to show you how to address the envelope properly—if you don't already know—and send the letter to the address listed on the package.

Within two or three weeks, you will probably receive a nice letter from the company, along with some coupons good for *free* products. I've gotten lots of coupons good for free food and other items over the years by writing letters to companies. You can have fun doing it and writing the letters is a good experience for you.

I have taught my children to write letters when they liked a particular product or found something defective. My son, Jason, once bought a can of tennis balls with a defective lid. He wrote to the company and got two free cans of tennis balls. You need to take time to write, whether it is a compliment or a complaint. A company's customer service department wants to hear from its customers; good or bad!

The following pages contain some letters I have received over the years from schools. I wanted to share some of them with you.

Friendship North Ridge Elementary School, Lubbock, Texas

September 25, 1990
To whom it may concern:

If ever the word "pride," "honor," "motivation," and "patriotism" could be extended to describe an individual, it would be proper and fitting in Homer Sewell's abilities to portray President Abraham Lincoln. Sewell's entertaining stories of Lincoln's life is a rare personal exposure to the human side of the man called "Abe." Sewell's unique touch with youngsters makes this program a true hands-on learning experience.

Sincerely,

—Rod Davis, Principal

Denver City Intermediate School: "Kids under Construction" Denver City, Texas

February 3, 1991
Dear Homer:

Your portrayal of Abe Lincoln made a famous American come alive and history real and meaningful.

Our students were spellbound. When you are able to keep the attention of 4th, 5th, and 6th grade children for a full day you have accomplished a great deal.

I realized you had captured the audience from the quality of questions the children were asking.

I would say to any school person, if you book just one assembly program for the year... this is the one!

Thank you for making us proud to be Americans.
Gratefully,
—Gerald F. Judd, Principal

Greenfield Elementary School, Greenfield, Illinois

February 9, 1991
Dear "Abe,"
On behalf of the students and staff at Greenfield, I would like to express our appreciation and gratitude for your visit to our school. The presentations you made during the assembly for students in grades 3–8 as well as the classroom visits for students K-2 were educational, inspiring and enjoyable. Teachers as well as students have commented that your presentation was one of the best we have had.

We certainly will recommend your program to others and hope that we have the opportunity to visit with you again. Good luck as you inspire others to be dreamers and rainbow chasers who soar with the eagles as they "become."
Sincerely,
—Marilyn Schild, Principal

Smith Elementary School, Berea, Ohio

November 13, 1991
Dear Mr. Sewell:
On behalf of Smith School and the Smith School PTA, I would like to express our thanks to you for providing a most rewarding day for our children.

Your portrayal of Abraham Lincoln was marvelous! Your enthusiasm for the man and his life was transferred to each child. Both of my young sons came home from school and talked non-stop about what they had learned. Your advice to the children to be dreamers, stargazers, rainbow chasers, and to soar with the eagles was a very valuable gift indeed.

I am enclosing copies of several articles that appeared in local Cleveland and Berea papers.

Again, many thanks for a wonderful day!
Sincerely,
—Barbara M. Norris, President, Smith PTA

The Big Top Performers Lubbock Arts Festival, Lubbock, Texas

April 3, 1992

To whom it may concern:

I have had the fortunate opportunity to meet and participate in Mr. Homer Sewell's sharing of Abraham Lincoln. This man is truly "called" to characterize the sixteenth President of the United States. I was with Mr. Sewell in two very different situations: one at our area wide Arts Festival which drew approx. 90,000 people and in three of our elementary schools. He was a wonderful addition to our Festival. He took the time to give lectures, to hand out signed copies of the Gettysburg Addresses and meet people during the three-day event. At our elementary schools he was met with great enthusiasm. I would especially like to share one event which was an example of this man's character. We were walking down the primary wing of one elementary school when six deaf education children saw him coming. Their faces lit up and hands flew in excitement. Their teacher explained that they had been studying Lincoln since early November and they could not believe that he was in their school. Homer stopped and took time with each child. He allowed them to see his watch, try on his hat and tug at his beard and all the while shining a smile that was pure joy. This encounter was but one of many unscheduled and unplanned events which Mr. Sewell graciously handled. I would encourage every opportunity for children to experience what Mr. Sewell so wonderfully and knowledgeably calls his work.

Sincerely,

—Lynn Elms, Chairperson

Image in the Mirror

Yale Elementary School, Richardson, Texas

February 10, 1993

Dear Colleagues,

    I just spent the day with Abe Lincoln. Actually, President Lincoln spent the day here at Yale interacting with our kids, teachers, and parents in a very unique way. He put in a full day (8:00 AM to 9 PM) storytelling, visiting, conducting assemblies and grade-level questions and answers sessions... and even had a great time helping pull lunch recess. The sight of Abe Lincoln booming punts halfway across the Yale playground in his stove pipe hat is a sight to see. The kids loved him, and he obviously enjoyed working with them. He was outside to see them off at the end of the day as they left on buses and cars and he was back fresh and ready for the PTA meeting where he was just as good with the parents.

    The man portraying Lincoln is Homer Sewell, an actor from Georgia who does this full time. He has been to about 830 schools over the past few years and has talked to thousands of children. I believe he is very effective in delivering his message, which is a combination of patriotism, commitment to a drug-free life, and just good old American values. His fee can be funded by your PTA, your corporate sponsor, or it qualifies as an anti-drug program if you want to pursue that avenue.

    I highly recommend this program and am attaching information in case you want to contact him about a possible engagement for your school.

    Cordially,

—Dr. John Phillips, Principal

Big Springs Elementary School, Garland, Texas

November 14, 1993

Dear Homer:

    What a wonderful, educational, inspiring, and exciting day you provided for our school. I am still hearing praises from teachers, parents, and children about our visit from Abe

Lincoln. I cannot begin to thank you enough for the work which you do and the message that you present to a new generation of Americans.

Numerous parents have told me that their children have not stopped talking about your visit. We probably spent 30 minutes from an hour long PTA Board meeting praising you. After I elaborated about what a delightful individual you are, how wonderfully the children responded to you, and how relevant and important your message is the other officers piped up and said they had never seen their children so excited about a program. Just yesterday a friend from church told me that her fourth grader who never comments on anything talked for a full forty-five minutes about Abraham Lincoln and your program. It would be a gross understatement to say that the Big Springs Community was impressed.

I am enclosing a message which I intend to distribute to other schools and the few individuals whom I know that are involved in service organizations both here and in Alabama. You are welcome to use this letter for your own references in any way that you would like.

On a personal note Kenny, Kendall, Ivy, and I immensely enjoyed your stay in our home. We are the only family I know who now has a Lincoln bedroom and we were entertained and educated beyond our furthest expectations. You have led an incredibly interesting life. Homer, you will never know the lives that you have touched and the individuals that you have inspired. Your genuine love of people and your gift of demonstrating that sincerely is a trait to be treasured. I truly believe that you in your own right are a contemporary American hero and a wonderful person to exemplify the spirit and character of Abraham Lincoln.

If ever there is anything that we can do to advance your appearances please let us know. It is a noble and inspiring profession.

Your friend,

—Sweet Hopkins, PTA President

Here is probably a good place to say something about one of my pet peeves: answering correspondence. Attention: Corporate executives and anyone who receives mail: Please have the courtesy to answer your mail. Even if you aren't able to help or give the kind of results the writer might wish, at least acknowledge their letter. And do so as quickly as possible. I've sent letters to companies and executives who have taken a month or two to answer, or in some cases, never answered at all.

Lesson to be learned here is: Take time to send a *nice* letter or card to someone at least once a week. They will be glad to hear from you.

TAKING A TRIP

When the war was finally over, Mary started talking to me about going to a theater to relax and forget about the war. I said, "Mary, I don't have time to go to any theater. I've got a country to put back together again." She kept after me until I finally agreed to go on Good Friday evening; April fourteenth ... just five short days after the war had ended!

Early in 1991, I was asked by the National Park Service at Mount Rushmore National Memorial in the southwest corner of South Dakota to help them with their upcoming Fiftieth Anniversary Dedication Celebration to be held during the week of July 4, 1991. I was excited about the prospect of being there as history was being made with this celebration.

I have always enjoyed visiting our national parks and do so every chance I get. I hope that you and your family are able to spend time enjoying our great national parks located throughout America.

As a Mason, I was even more excited knowing one of our greatest Masons, President George Washington, was also on the mountain and there would be a look-alike for him as well as the other two presidents.

As time drew nearer, it was mentioned to me that President George Bush had been invited to participate along with a lot of famous people. All four of the presidents who are on the mountain would be represented during the upcoming celebration: George Washington, Thomas Jefferson, Teddy Roosevelt, and Abraham Lincoln. A look-alike for Gutzon Borglum, the sculptor, would also be there. The lady in charge of the program was having a difficult time finding look-alikes for all of the presidents and I was quick to be the first to say I would be there to help out however I could. She didn't know until just a couple of weeks ahead of time whether President Bush would be able to attend.

I decided even though it was a 1,550 mile drive to South Dakota, I would take my family. I wanted them to be a part of it, too. We packed the car and left Georgia on Thursday, June twenty-seventh.

We made one stop in Tennessee and then spent Friday night with our friends, the Grays, in Springfield, Missouri. We did a little boating with them on Saturday morning and I rode a jet-ski for the first time. It was a lot more fun than riding a horse. We then continued on our journey.

We tried to find a place to spend Saturday night, but after stopping at about two dozen motels all through Iowa, we finally gave up on getting a good night's sleep. I knew then how Joseph must've felt. There was no room in the inn! There must have been something big happening, because there just weren't any motels with rooms available anywhere!

Finally, at about 6 a.m. Sunday, after I had been driving all night, we stopped at a little restaurant, just across the border into South Dakota, to have some breakfast. I was telling the waitress we had been driving all night and really wanted a place to get a few hours sleep before going to Mount Rushmore. She and her husband invited us to go to their home. We were able to shower and get a few hours sleep. There really are still people out there who will take in total strangers. We appreciated their hospitality.

We arrived Sunday evening, June 30; about 7:00 p.m. Reservations had been made for us at the lovely First Lady Motel in Keystone, just three miles from the memorial. As soon as we were checked into the motel, I drove the family the final three miles so we could see the mountain. I don't know about the rest of the family, but I couldn't wait any longer. I just had to see the mountain right then! That night!

It was absolutely awesome! Beyond anything you could imagine! And all carved on the face of a mountain with air-driven-drills and dynamite, by a man with a dream! You talk about *never giving up!* Mr. Borglum certainly didn't! His son, Lincoln, took over after his death.

Monday morning, July first, I got dressed and went to the park to meet those in charge. I started walking around and being "mobbed" by visitors wanting to have their picture taken with me. *It was great!* I discovered that if I stood in just the right spot on the terrace at the visitor center, people could be in the picture with me and the memorial in the background behind and above us. I always pointed out they should be sure to get the handsome guy on the right in the picture; that was Abe!

I was there in character all day Monday and Tuesday. Wednesday, President Bush was there from 2:00–3:00 p.m. and the park was closed to the public. Only about 3,500 specially picked people were allowed to be there for the ceremonies that included President and Mrs. Bush, Tom Brokaw, Mary Hart, Mr. and Mrs. Jimmy Stewart, Barbara Eden, White Eagle, and others. The Secret Service said the four look-alikes could *not* come in character! What a disappointment! I had hoped all four of us could have gotten our picture in front of the memorial shaking hands with the president! So I was there in my jeans with my family to witness the official dedication.

Wednesday evening, all four of us "presidents" and Mr. Borglum were in a greeting line at a gala reception for about 500 VIPs in

Rapid City. We were able to meet and chat with Mr. and Mrs. Jimmy Stewart, Barbara Eden, Secretary of the Interior, and others. It was a great honor for me to have met and visited with Jimmy Stewart. He is one of the finest actors we have ever had.

Thursday, the five of us were in a 260-unit parade in downtown Rapid City and then it was back to the monument for more picture-taking and visiting with nice folks from all over the world. If I'd gotten a dollar for each time someone took my picture, I would be rich.

Friday, I was at the memorial for a full-day of picture taking and lots of just plain pride to be a part of it all! That evening my family and I stopped by Rapid City to speak to a group of about seventy-five people at a senior citizen village. This gave me another opportunity to visit with some of my favorite people: seniors. Then we headed out for the long drive back to Jasper, Georgia.

Oh! I've got t-shirts of the memorial, poster-pictures, and lots of photos we took, but the biggest souvenir I have was just being there. There are no words to describe my feelings upon seeing the image of Abe and the others carved on that big mountain!

Lesson to be learned here is: Nothing is impossible if you work at it hard enough! Don't ever give up on your dreams.

Search for Family

Mary and I had four sons: Robert, Eddie, Willie, and Tad. We loved our boys very much.

I've known all along I was adopted when I was only ten weeks old. As I have gotten older, I have wondered what my birth parents were like and did I have any brothers and sisters. Were my parents still living, and if so, where?

I love my adopted family very much and have always felt proud to be a part of the Sewell family and to have been adopted by a couple who gave me so much love; but I think all of us have a desire deep down inside to know about our roots and biological family background. As I have gotten older, the desire to find my roots has become stronger.

In 1981, I paid my dues and joined A.L.M.A. (Adoptees Liberty Movement Association) in hopes of finding a match between me and my birth parents, if they were looking for me. Nothing ever came of that.

When I made the decision in the summer of 1990 to go full-time as Abe and travel all over the country talking to students, I also started doing some serious looking in phone books for my birth name: Ferency.

One evening, during the summer of 1991, I got a call from Yvette Floyd in Orlando. I had recruited her into my real estate office when I was working for Barry Luckenbach in 1979. I had visited with her husband, Ron, and their children on a couple of occasions and we kept in touch with each other after I moved up to the mountains of North Georgia in 1983.

Yvette had called to try to recruit me to sell some MLM products. I told her I probably wasn't interested, but she sent me some samples to examine anyway. She also asked me if I had ever found my biological family. I told her I hadn't yet, but was still looking. She said Ron recently had an occasion to use a very good detective in Miami to help locate someone for him. His name was Joe Culligan, and she said I should give him a call. I called him just as soon as we hung up.

I said, "Joe, I'm Abe Lincoln and I am looking for my parents!" That got his attention! Joe told me he had recently finished a book, *You, Too, Can Find Anybody*, and he would have the *Maury Povich Show* send me a copy hot off the press. Joe has helped find long-lost family members for reunions on several talk shows including *Oprah* and the *Maury Povich Show*. He told me I should follow his suggestions listed in the book and if I didn't find my father within thirty days, he would find him for me *free*. That sounded like a great deal to me!

On Sunday afternoon, October 27, 1991, I got a call from Joe Culligan. He wanted to know how I was doing with my search for my family. I told him I had gotten a birth certificate for an Alex Ferency in Ohio. Joe asked me what his date of birth was and I told him it was 1927. He said it was the wrong Alex Ferency because my dad had been born in 1922. I knew then he knew something I didn't!

On October 28, 1991 at 5:05 p.m., just as I was leaving the house to go pick up Kimberly from cheerleading practice, the phone rang. There was a man on the phone whose voice I did not recognize. He said, "Is this Homer Sewell?" I said it was. He told me he was Alex Ferency. I said, "*The* Alex Ferency, the one who is my father?"

He said, "Well, that's what they tell me."

We chatted for about fifteen minutes. I found out he and my mother had gotten a divorce after giving birth to three more boys. So I had three brothers: Barry, born in 1944, lived in Long Beach, California; Stuart, born in 1947, lived in Hingham, Massachusetts; and Gershon, born in 1951, was in Israel, about thirty miles from Jerusalem. Dad was living in New London, Connecticut. Mom was remarried and living with her husband, Bill, in Dudley, Massachusetts, about two hours away from Stuart.

I found out I have international bloodlines: Mom's side of the family is Russian and Dad's side of the family is Hungarian.

After the divorce, Mom and Dad did not maintain a close relationship, so this made it more difficult to tell Mom I had found them and to put a reunion together. I asked when I would be able to see everyone, and Dad said he would let me know later when it could be arranged. He was trying to figure out how to tell Mom.

Dad and I corresponded back and forth for six months. He would send me audio tapes he made while driving his yellow taxi cab in the Hartford-New London area. I sent him a copy of a VCR tape of my Abe Lincoln program so he could see what I looked like.

Finally, on April 25, 1992, Dad called me again. We chatted for a few minutes and then he said, "Would you like to talk to one of your brothers?" I said I sure would, so he put Stuart on the phone. Dad had driven up to Stuart's house to break the news to him and his wife, Susan. We talked for a while. Stuart said he couldn't wait to call Barry in California and tell him *he* wasn't the oldest brother anymore! They still hadn't told Mother I had found them, and weren't sure how to go about doing it.

Five days later, on April 30, 1992, I happened to be home when the phone rang. An unfamiliar female voice said, "I'm not sure you want to talk to me, but..."

I interrupted her to say, "Sure I do, Mom!" I just knew it was her! We cried and talked for a while. I think she was glad I had finally found her and the long-kept secret was out!

Finally, I had located my long-lost family and now it was a matter of getting everyone together for a big reunion. We called back and forth every week or so. I even called to talk to my brother, Gershon, in Israel. Gershon is married to Rachel, an Israeli, and they have nine children. He has been a tour guide in the Holy Land for fifteen years. I also talked to Barry in California.

Perhaps this is a good place for me to say something about how my adoptive mother (the only mother I'd known for forty-nine years) took the news of me finding my birth family. I guess she was happy for me when I told her I had found my "other family."

I don't know the correct way to refer to these *two* moms. I don't want to hurt anyone's feelings. One *mom* gave birth to me on August 4, 1943, and I am sure, very reluctantly, gave me to the other *mom* to be raised, nourished, and provide for my needs from the time I was only ten weeks old. I know they *both* love me and I love both of them very much.

Finding my birth-mother does not take away any of the love I have felt for the *only* mother I'd ever known; neither does it lessen the way I feel in my heart for the mother who carried me inside her for nine months and then ten weeks later went through the difficult decision of giving me up, not knowing whether she would ever see me again. I feel sure it has been a hard burden to bear all these years not being able to share "the secret" with anyone. Unfortunately, in spite of my prayers, both mothers passed away before I could get them together.

After waiting all these forty-nine years, I didn't want to wait any longer and was anxious to meet everyone. I just didn't have the money to fly up to Boston, so I tried to get a talk show to pay for the reunion. We came close to doing it with the *Maury Povich* and the *Vicki Lawrence* shows, but just couldn't make it happen.

I was in Harrison, Arkansas, renovating the sixty-five-year-old Lyric Theater and have devoted the next chapter to what happened there from May to November of 1992. Dad told me he was going to be in St. Louis, Missouri, in early October for a church convention, so I told him I would drive up there to meet him.

When I arrived at the Holiday Inn and went into the lobby, there was a tall, handsome man I instantly recognized from the pictures he had sent me. It was my father! I walked up to him, gave him a big hug, and said, "Hello, Dad." At last, I was able to meet the man I'd sought for a long time. As we met for lunch, I discovered some of the similarities between us: we were each carrying identical brief cases, wearing the same black boots, had our beards trimmed the same, and both of us had identical noses and eyes.

We visited for a few hours between his meetings. I had a million questions, but there just wasn't time to get them all answered. I drove back two days later for another visit.

Finally, during the late summer, I made the decision that my family and I would drive up to Boston for a Thanksgiving reunion.

I drove from Harrison to Georgia before Thanksgiving and picked up my family. We drove straight through the 1,200 miles from our home, one hour north of Atlanta, to Hingham, Massachusetts, in the Boston area. I was tired, but would not have been able to sleep in a motel if we had stopped. I was too excited about finally getting to meet Mom, two of my brothers, and lots of other family members.

We finally arrived at Stuart's house about noon on Wednesday, the day before Thanksgiving. We met Stuart's wife, Susan, and their children, Fay and Alon, and lots of other family members. Barry and his new wife, Urda, had flown in the weekend before from California. We all had a great time visiting and eating! The next day, we drove about two hours up to Mom's house for the big reunion. There were thirty-one relatives there for the big dinner Mom had cooked.

I don't think I can put into words the feelings I had upon seeing my birth-mother for the first time in forty-nine years. The emotions were high and it was an exciting time for me, my family, and I am sure for Mom too. The pictures of Mom and me together for the first time say it all!

It was exciting finally getting to meet everyone. My *new* family instantly took us in as if we had never been separated. I met cousins, uncles, aunts, nieces, and nephews and they all accepted me like a shepherd finding a little lost lamb. We all got along great!

My cousin, Jennifer, is an actress in New York, so we had a lot in common. My step-dad, Bill, is a Mason, so we hit it off right away. One step-brother, Stephen, is a Rabbi in Yonkers, New York. I met other relatives who were attorneys, principals, teachers, and doctors.

The only one missing was my youngest brother, Jerry. His Hebrew name is Gershon. Israel was a long way off for him to join us for this big reunion! We did call him on the phone and were able to chat for a few minutes. I know he would like to have been able to be with the rest of the family. We talked about the four of us brothers getting together in Israel as soon as we could arrange it.

On Friday, Dad came up from Connecticut with his teacher-friend, Susan, to Stuart's house and we had another big feast.

The three days we were there we did a lot of visiting and eating lots of good food. It was fun trying to catch up on all the family news of the past forty-nine years! Time passed too quickly! The Jewish side of the family sure knows how to cook!

If you ever need to find anyone, you might want to go to your library or a book store and get the book, *You, Too, Can Find Anybody* by Joseph J. Culligan. It is an excellent source of how to find people.

Another exciting time as "Abe" was when I got invited by the Clinton Inaugural Committee to be part of the festivities in January 1993 for Bill Clinton's Inauguration. Even though our newest president was named after Jefferson, his favorite president was Abraham Lincoln. He was always quoting him and had a bust of Abe in his office.

I was at the Kennedy Center along with some other look-alikes to entertain children from around the country. I had hoped to be able to do my show for them, but someone had dropped the ball and didn't

Image in the Mirror

make plans for me to speak. I did get to visit Chelsea Clinton's old classroom via TV/phone link to Little Rock. Again, the Secret Service would not let any of us in costume get near the president when he visited the Kennedy Center. Bill missed a chance to meet Abe.

I was mobbed as I strolled along the mall area. I had the privilege of meeting some very interesting young students with VCR cameras, "US Kids TV." They interviewed me for their TV kids' news program.

I was able to see Stuart for a couple of days while I was in Washington. I also met my cousin, Sandy, and her husband, Chet, while I was there. They both work for *U.S.A. Today* newspapers, so they took me on a tour of their offices. Sandy is in charge of Sky Radio, a news and information service. It is broadcast directly to airplanes that have subscribed to the service. Chet is a political correspondent for several northern states and for Indian Affairs all over the country.

My family and I were able to spend some more time in late June of 1993 with Stuart, Susan, and daughter, Fay, in Virginia on a timeshare exchange. We had a great time hiking and just getting to know each other better. Stuart and I went on a hike by ourselves and *he* got us lost up on a mountain. We had a long hike bushwhacking our way back down to civilization, but we had fun just being together.

The kids got along great with their newly-found cousin. Fay, seventeen, is one of the top cello players for her age in all of Massachusetts. Her brother, Alon, was not able to join us in Virginia because he was in Israel for the summer. He is now attending Harvard University and in 2009 will become a Rabbi.

In October of 1993, Stuart, Barry, and I met in New York and flew to Israel to meet Gershon. Before we flew out of New York, Stuart and I took time to go for a nice boat ride on the Hudson River with our step-brother, Rabbi Stephen Franklin. He showed us all around New York City via boat. I took some great pictures of the Statue of Liberty, the Twin Towers, and other landmarks and then his wife, Karen, cooked us a great meal.

After a long twelve-hour flight to Tel Aviv, Gershon picked us up at the airport in a rental car for the start of our wonderful visit. We four brothers spent two weeks together for the first time in fifty years! We had a marvelous time touring Israel from North to South, East to West, and back again. I took over 400 pictures during the two weeks.

In one forty-eight-hour period, we swam in the Red Sea, the Dead Sea, and the Sea of Galilee. The country is a beautiful place to visit and gave me the opportunity to find out more about my Jewish heritage. Gershon carried his M-16 rifle and/or pistol almost everywhere we went. I hope and pray that by the time this book comes out, there will be some real peace in Israel.

Since Gershon has lived there for thirty years and is an official state licensed tour guide, he really knows his way around. We visited so many interesting places I can't even remember them all. We were able to stay a couple of nights inside the old walled city of Jerusalem. It was interesting seeing places over 2,000 years old!

We visited Masada, the historic Jewish fortress that rises 1,400 feet above the nearby Dead Sea. In A.D. 73, 960 Jewish patriots died there after fighting off the Romans for several years. We visited the ruins of several temples including the Temple Mount, where King Solomon's Temple had been. We saw remains of several battlefields and walked some of the same old cobblestone streets where Jesus had walked. It was exciting for me; being born Jewish, raised Protestant, and the four of us brothers together for the very first time. We also visited with some of our distant relatives.

One day, we visited the temple outside of Jerusalem where Samuel the Prophet is supposed to be buried. We were up on the roof admiring the view of the city when a storm started blowing toward us. We stood up there in the rain, and after the rain stopped, a beautiful rainbow moved directly over the top of where we were standing. It was an eerie feeling.

Lesson to be learned here is: Tell someone you love how much they mean to you every day!

A Bad Experience at the Theater

There was an actor by the name of John Wilkes Booth. He wasn't as famous as his brother, his father, or uncle. In conspiracy with several others, John Wilkes Booth decided to do something to make a name for himself. Oh! I'm sure they had other reasons also. At first, they were going to kidnap me and hold me ransom to get us to release some of the rebel troops. When they failed at their kidnap attempt, John Booth decided to do something much more drastic.

"I am not afraid to die, and in fact, would be more than willing, but I have an irresistible desire to live until I can be assured that the world is a little better for my having lived in it."

"I had a rather bad experience the last time I was in a theater…"

That was the opening line for my performance from the stage of the sixty-five-year-old Lyric Theater in Harrison, Arkansas.

On May 18, 1992, I was in the Houston, Texas, area for a school program. When I finished, I decided to drive to Branson, Missouri, and see what all the fuss was about in that town. My friends, Dana and Beverly Gray, live in Springfield, about an hour north of Branson, so I thought I would go visit them and check out Branson.

The Grays had been telling me about all the activity going on in Branson and I had heard the segment on CBS's *60 Minutes* show where the comment was, "Would the last person leaving Nashville on the way to Branson please turn out the lights!" It had gotten my attention along with millions of others. Now, admittedly, I am not into country music, but I did see the possibilities of being able to get off the road, settle down in one location, and let folks come to me. I had already done over 500 shows all over the country in the two years since going full-time and liked the idea of settling down in one place.

When I arrived in Branson, I stopped by six theaters trying to see if they might like to have something in addition to country music. Finally, at the Cristy Lane Theater, my seventh stop during a bad rain, I went in to talk to them. The man at the counter just happened to be Cristy's husband/manager, and I said, "I had a rather bad experience the last time I was in a theater, but expected to have a much better experience soon" and I was looking for a place to do it.

The manager asked me, "What are you? A comedian?"

I said, "I wasn't a comedian, but a serious actor and was looking for a place with an open time-slot." He thought about it for a few minutes and then asked me how soon I wanted to start? I said, "ASAP."

He said, "How about this Sunday at 4:00 p.m.?" I told him that was fine with me.

I shopped around in antique shops and rounded up an old table, chair, hat rack, books, and a few other props I needed for a stage production of my one-man show.

Unfortunately the producers were not wholehearted in their support of the show, and after a week we decided to part company. But it was fun while it lasted!

Image in the Mirror

I had been staying about forty miles south in Harrison, Arkansas, and noticed the old Lyric Theater sitting empty on the courthouse square. I should have stayed away from it and from the town of Harrison!

I did some checking around and found out who owned the old theater. I made arrangements for the owners, Kent and Glenna Regan, to show me the inside of the theater. I found out it had been closed for eighteen years. I looked around and fell in love with it in spite of the fact that it was dirty, musky, full of pigeons and other varmints, and needed a lot of TLC.

I made some arrangements with the owners and signed a lease/option-to-buy contract good for one year. I figured if I couldn't make it work in one year, then I didn't need to be there.

I started organizing a major renovation project for the "Old Gal" and worked day and night for weeks. I had to bring it up to 1992 codes for wheelchair access and many, many other requirements before I could open the doors to the public. I had a lot of volunteers come by to help haul out the trash and clean it all up.

Tom Lockett and his wife, Julie, and their daughter, Wendy, came by early-on and were there helping every chance they had. Tom and Julie both worked for the newspaper, *The Harrison Times*, which was right next door to us. I could not have accomplished all of what needed to be done without their help and the help of others like Ruth Taylor, Darlene and Susan Farmer, and many others.

I was determined to have the doors opened in time for the big July Fourth celebration being planned at the courthouse square across the street. Everyone kept telling me it couldn't be done! That motivated me to work that much harder. I put in a lot of long hours and was able to get opened—in a fashion—for that weekend.

I had borrowed $25,000 from the owners to do all of the construction of new bathrooms and other things that needed to be done, like painting and re-plastering the walls. I also borrowed another $25,000 from a friend.

From the very beginning, the town seemed to be supportive of what I was trying to do to get their old theater re-opened. They were all excited and dropped by every day to see the progress I was making. Fay Hodge brought us donuts every morning. Avo McBee made some delicious pies and cakes, and Ruth Taylor cooked some great meals. John Hudson helped me with my accounting records and he and his family were very supportive. I appreciated all of the people who were interested in what was happening to the Lyric.

When we did get open, we found out just how much Harrison *did not support outsiders!* I did everything I could think of from a marketing standpoint to get the community to come see the show. I even offered *free* tickets, but the townspeople just would not take an hour-and-a-half out of their schedules to come get motivated and inspired by "Abe."

The ticket was only five dollars. I billed it as, "An Abe for an Abe"! I tried to get the local motels to offer special prices to their guests who had nothing else to do in the evenings. I had a total of about twenty people over a two month period that were sent from local motels. Before Christmas of 1992, I started realizing I was not going to get enough support to survive there in Harrison.

In contrast to today's theaters, this old theater had a lot of character you can't find anymore. It had three big, beautiful, hand-painted murals approximately twelve by twelve feet along each wall, a big stage, and a big balcony area. It was a perfect place for me to do my shows.

I had built a box up over one end of the stage to represent box seven and eight of the Ford's Theatre, and each night I climbed up into that box and had someone step in and shoot me. We really had a dramatic presentation. All of those who saw the show loved it! I had them laughing one minute and crying the next and we received great reviews from everyone who came to the theater. I finally decided to give it back to the owners.

One day while I was working in the theater, J.D. Ramsey, a principal from a school I had visited in Missouri, stopped by to see me. He wanted to know about the possibility of using the theater for sales meetings on Monday nights. I wasn't doing any shows on Mondays, so I told him he could. He and some friends started conducting MLM meetings on a regular basis. The more I listened to them, the more interested I got. I finally signed up as a Melaleuca distributor/marketing executive. The company has great household products and a good marketing system. I've made a little money signing up some of my friends, but I haven't taken the time to really work the business. I bought the products each month for a while and my family used and enjoyed them.

Another venture into the job market began in late July of 1993. I was talking to my newly-found brother, Barry, in California. I told him I was going to have to get some type of job to get some dollars coming in to pay the bills. I couldn't sit around all summer waiting for school to start and hoping to get some bookings for Abe. He said I should call a long-time friend of his in Atlanta. His name was Larry Human and he owned a bottled water business. I called Larry, arranged for an interview, and he hired me on the spot.

Larry had been running his water business for three years by himself. He really needed someone who could help and give him some time off. I started on August second and spent the week of my fiftieth birthday loading and unloading forty-two-pound five-gallon bottles of spring water in and out of vans. With my back prone to get out of shape easily and the fact that I've had five hernia-repair surgeries, I didn't need to be lifting anything heavy. But, in the water business, it is hard to be in the warehouse and *not* get involved in lifting or moving one-ton pallets of fifty-four bottles of water around with a manual pallet-jack! Not fun!

There was a fellow by the name of Tommy who had been working with Larry off and on for several years. He was one hard-working guy and I tried to help him however I could. All companies need more dedicated, conscientious employees like Tommy, who never complain about anything and do what they are asked to do without questioning.

I was kept busy doing payroll, posting payments, balancing checkbooks, checking drivers and their load sheets in and out, and fielding customer service complaints. I'd go in about 7 a.m. and didn't get out of there until 5 p.m. Those ten-hour days were hard on this old man!

I finally left Larry and the water business in October of 1993. I had had enough of this type of work to last a lifetime!

In January of 1994 I had an opportunity to visit some schools in Ledford and Hartford, Connecticut area. This gave me another chance to spend some time with my dad. It was nice to be able to visit and catch up on some of the things I had missed growing up. Dad showed me some pictures, some listings of family ancestors, and other information he had about our family. Perhaps someday soon I will be able to sit down with him or Mom and take a close look at family albums I wasn't there to be a part of.

Dad and Susan took me on a tour of New York City, including the Twin Towers. After eating some good Italian food at a restaurant near the hotel where we were staying, we were getting on an elevator to head up to our rooms. A man and woman came up to the elevator just as the doors were starting to close. She said, "Is there room for two more?"

I said, "Sure, come on in." The woman said to us, "Hi, I'm Hattie Jackson and I sell Hattie's Sauce." Pretty quickly, the doors were opening to let us off at our floor and as I was getting off the elevator, I turned to her, handed her one of my business cards, and said, "Hattie, I'm Abe Lincoln and I'm here to help you!"

She was one of the most bubbly, vivacious ladies I'd met in a long time. She invited us to come up to her room a little later to tell us all about her sauce. I was impressed with her and the sauce she's cooked up to bring new life to hot dogs, hamburgers, salads, and other foods. I told her I would do whatever I could to help her get her company up and running. Here was a lady who had never given up on trying to get this sauce marketed, seventeen years since the idea was first conceived. I was inspired by her faith in herself and in American Free Enterprise. She will go places and I hope to be able to help her get there! She is going to give away some college scholarships from profits of her new company.

I also took time to run up to Dudley, Massachusetts, to have lunch and dinner with Mom and my step-dad, Bill. We had a chance to visit for a few hours and catch up a little more on all those long-lost years. Mom sure knows how to cook some good meals. In fact, both of my moms were great cooks!

As you can see from reading this book, I take what I do as Abe pretty seriously. I feel there is a real need for our young people to hear the messages I have for them. I started doing Abe back in 1975 just a few months after Kathy and I were married. She knew I always dreamed of being Abe full-time and was not happy about the prospect.

A lot of times since going full-time in 1990, students have asked me if I had a wife and family back home. I usually joked with them and said, "Yes, I am married. Or, at least I was the last time I was home!" Kathy didn't like the idea of me being away so much and leaving her to raise the twins by herself. I know it was hard on them, but I tried to get home as often as I could and make something special of those times we had together.

During the Christmas holidays of 1993, our family was in Utah skiing at our favorite place and Kathy told me she had gotten tired of me being on the road all the time and wanted a divorce! What a Christmas present that was! So, as of March 10, 1994, we were both single again.

The kids and I must go on with our lives and Kathy will go on with hers without me in it. Jason has decided he wants to go to a different high school, so he is now living with Kathy thirty-five miles away and closer to her office. Kimberly is still with me in our home in Jasper.

For any of you who have recently gone through a divorce, or are contemplating one soon; it will be hard on you, but you *will* survive. Life is too short to remain in a relationship if you are not happy. My pastor, Hoyt Jenkins, has been an inspirational help to me during these trying times of being single again after nineteen years.

I did one of my programs in January for the Fairglen Elementary School in Cocoa, Florida. They mentioned they would be taking a sixth grade class trip to Washington the last week of March and invited me to go with them. I've always wanted to escort students on just such a trip, so I agreed to go with them.

One of the teachers, Ms. Donna Welton, has been taking students on these trips to Washington for eight years and she has it all very well organized. I flew from Atlanta to Orlando on the new Valujet Airlines and met the twenty-nine students and their nine chaperones at 2:30 p.m. on Sunday, March 27, at the old Sears parking lot on US One in Cocoa. We loaded all of our luggage into the bus and left promptly at 3 p.m. Our two bus drivers, Elvin and Rick, with Destiny Tours, were a lot of fun to be with.

Our first stop was just north of Jacksonville for supper at Long John Silvers and McDonald's restaurants at about 6 p.m. About 10 p.m. we stopped at a truck stop in South Carolina so everyone could wash faces, brush teeth, and get ready for a long night's ride on the bus.

Two hours out of Washington on Monday morning, we stopped for the breakfast bar at Shoney's. Everyone was excited we were almost to our destination.

At 10 a.m. we arrived at the Doubletree Hotel in Arlington, Virginia. We got all the students and their luggage settled into their rooms—four students to the room—with two adults in the adjacent rooms. The first thing everyone wanted to do was take a shower and change clothes.

We then met our Washington tour guide, Mrs. June Humphrey. She had been touring folks around Washington for twenty-four years and really knew where everything was. I met her husband, Captain Bill Humphrey, who had worked for Admiral Rickover. I would love to spend some time with Captain Humphrey. I'll bet he has some interesting stories to tell about his times spent working for one of our country's greatest admirals.

Our first stop was at the Vietnam, Nurses, Soldiers, Jefferson, and Lincoln Memorials. Everyone wanted their pictures taken with "Abe" at the Lincoln Memorial. From there we had lunch at the Old Post Office building. Some of us took a trip to the clock and bell tower at the top of this beautiful old landmark.

We then went to the Ford's Theatre and the Petersen Boarding House across the street. This was a very interesting but sad time for me. There were lots of visitors who wanted to have their pictures taken with "Abe," so I obliged them. The students also had a chance to buy some souvenirs from the street vendors.

From there we went to the Smithsonian Museum of Natural History and the group I was with got a special "presidential" tour from one of the employees in charge of that building.

We drove past the White House, Old Executive Office Building, several embassies, and other government buildings. We ate at the Crystal Station and then rode the Metro train to the Rosslyn Station, which contains a 437 foot escalator to street level and is the third longest continuous span escalator in the world. The students enjoyed their train and escalator rides. We then took a night driving tour and a quick trip through the Kennedy Center.

On Tuesday, after a breakfast at Roy Rogers Restaurant or McDonald's, the students took a tour of the National Cathedral. While they did that and the zoo, I went back to Ford's Theatre and met with the "US Kids TV" film crew for about three hours.

The National Park Service personnel are responsible for the day-to-day operation of the Ford's Theatre, and they saw the reaction from visitors on Monday and Tuesday mornings. They asked me if I would like to perform some of my show. It was a pleasant surprise for me to be invited to speak from the same stage Abe had witnessed the play, *Our American Cousin*, on that fateful Good Friday night, April 14, 1865. It brought tears to my eyes when I thought about what had happened to Abe that night.

I did perform about thirty minutes of my show for approximately 500 people and then posed with several groups of visitors for picture-taking with Abe. I ran into a family from Florida who had been my next door neighbors when I lived in Altamonte Springs thirteen years previously.

When I finished at the Ford's Theatre, I boarded the Metro train to try to catch up with my tour group. I went to the zoo, Union Station, and the Smithsonian, but kept missing them. I finally decided to go back to the hotel and wait for them there. They all came back about 4:30 and got dressed to go to a dinner theater to see "Annie Get Your Gun." All the students were looking mighty handsome and pretty in their fancy clothes. One young student told me she "would much rather be in her jeans!"

On Wednesday, we packed up all of our belongings and checked out of the hotel at 8 a.m. After breakfast, we went to the Arlington National Cemetery. We saw the changing of the guard at the Tomb of the Unknown Soldier and visited the JFK grave site. I took four students with me and visited the tomb of Robert Lincoln, the only member of the family not buried in the Oak Ridge Cemetery in Springfield, Illinois.

We went to the House of Representatives and the Capitol and the students enjoyed seeing where our nation's laws are being made. Our Senators and Congressmen were out on spring break.

Some students asked me why the flags were flying at half-mast all over Washington, and we found out it was because Representative William Natcher of Kentucky had died of a heart attack at the age of eighty-four.

I would like to quote some lines from an article about him by Leslie Phillips in the *USA Today* newspaper:

> "He will be remembered for his extraordinary voting record during his forty-two years in the House. His last recorded vote, the 18,401st consecutive one, occurred on March second. An austere gentleman, Natcher eschewed the ways of Washington from the moment he was elected in 1953. He never hired a press secretary, never paid consultants, nor so-

licited campaign contributions, and he routinely returned 70% of the allowance members are given to run their offices. He sent out one press release a year to tout his voting record."

I quote this article because it sounds to me that Representative Natcher was one of a rare breed of *honest* representatives in Washington! We need more people like him who are doing what they were sent to do … government of, by, and for the people. More about this later!

We took a trip south to Mt. Vernon, George Washington's home, and then back to D.C. to the Smithsonian National Air and Space Museum. There just wasn't enough time to see it all.

We dropped June off about 5:30 p.m. and headed back to Florida. We drove straight through and arrived in Cocoa at noon on Thursday. It was a very rushed but educational trip for everyone.

I am now giving some serious thoughts to taking some school groups to Washington myself. If your school would like to have "Abe" escort you to Washington and show you around for either a three-day or five-day trip, please get in touch with me for all the particulars.

Lesson to be learned here is: Even when today is *not* going your way, remember to make the most of it and "The sun will come out tomorrow."

Life Happenings and Travels Log

I have continued to try to support myself doing what I enjoy most—portraying Abe—anywhere, anytime. There have been times when even with all my optimism, I have felt very discouraged. All it takes to "recharge my batteries" is the reaction I get from another school where teachers, students, and parents tell me that I'm doing a great job and I get the encouragement to continue. I still need to find a corporate sponsor so I don't have to worry about how to pay the bills when I've not been doing the number of school visits I need.

March 3, 1996, I had purchased a motorcycle from one of my tenants and was driving it down to Atlanta to visit one of my girlfriends. About halfway there, I ran off the highway at fifty miles per hour. I broke my neck in five places and my right wrist in two places. The doctors said I was lucky to be alive and not paralyzed! I sold that motorcycle as soon as I was able to and will never again ride one. If any of you, young or old, ever think you need to ride on two wheels (other than a bicycle); please be careful. Motorcycles give you *no* protection in a collision with cars or trucks, and you can very easily die or become seriously hurt.

As you can see from the list of places I've visited, I spent the summer of 1995 doing shows at campgrounds and other locations at or near Mount Rushmore. I spent a couple of weeks in the area in 1996 and returned for all of July and August of 1997 at one of my favorite campgrounds, Rafter J. Bar Ranch Campground; owned and run by Tom George and his family near Hill City. The KOA campground is located a little closer to Mount Rushmore and is also a very nice place to stay. The Black Hills of South Dakota are a beautiful place to spend some time, whether you look like Abe Lincoln or not!

I have had students ask me for years why I didn't drive a Lincoln. My comment has always been that I would love to, but could not afford to buy one. August of 1997, while I was working in South Dakota, I saw an ad for a used Lincoln. I went to look at it, loved it, sold my Toyota Cressida, and drove the Lincoln back here to Georgia. It rides nice, but sure uses a lot of gas!

In late 1995, I started renting rooms in my home here in the mountains of North Georgia. I now have six tenants who rent from me on a regular basis. It helps pay for the mortgage and utilities for my home and gives me someone to keep an eye on things and feed my animals while I am on the road. I now have three dogs, two cats, two birds, and a lot of goldfish inside and out.

In May of 1997, I decided to get creative in my front yard and constructed a small goldfish pond approximately ten by fifteen feet and about three feet deep. It has a fountain in it and then I pump the water up a hill approximately fifteen feet to another fountain and have it come cascading downhill into the pond. It looks nice and is relaxing to sit on the bench nearby and listen to the water running. As of December 1997, I have begun construction of a twelve foot by twelve foot deck with a gazebo on it overlooking the pond and waterfall.

Since my divorce in March of 1994, I'd been dating a lot of different women and had a couple of them want to settle me down and have a serious relationship. I am not ready for that yet and don't know if I ever will be again.

I've also gotten involved in several businesses that have not made me any money: including, but not limited to, real estate, air purifiers, some home-use products, home remodeling sales, etc. There just isn't anything out there I really want to do other than speaking to groups of people of all ages all over the country as Abe.

So if your company (or anyone you know) is looking for someone to tie-in with, that will help project an image of honesty, integrity, fairness, and American free enterprise, please get in touch with me, because I've got something to offer them that will *double* their sales volume in one year! Honestly!

In school years 1998–1999 and 2000–2001, I went back to my agent in Kansas and he booked me into about 400 schools in thirty-five states. I was only back in Jasper, Georgia, for less than two months for those two years. I was in three different towns almost every day of school, and it was a hectic schedule for sure.

For a while, I dated a lady named Barbara, who had started out renting a room from me. We spent the summer working at Mount Rushmore in the beautiful Black Hills of South Dakota. She dipped ice cream and fudge while I was next door in the gift shop getting my picture taken about a thousand times a day and autographing my book and others about Abe Lincoln. It was a wonderful experience and I met a lot of nice people; employees and visitors alike.

As the summer drew to a close, Barbara and I discussed the fact that I had signed back up with the same agent I had in 1991 and would have me on the road for nine months. Barbara really wanted to go with me on his tour, but knew we would need a bus or motor home to do so. We started looking around for something we could afford. We finally found a good deal on a twenty-eight foot Southwind. It had everything we needed to live on the road: bathroom, kitchen, beds, and guzzled gas at the rate of five to seven miles per gallon. It had an ugly twelve-inch brown stripe all the way around it, and we decided that needed to be replaced by red, white, and blue. We bought several dozen cans of spray paint at the Walmart in Rapid City, South Dakota and proceeded to get the job done. We named it the *"AbeMobile,"* because my twins, Kimberly and Jason, had always called any vehicle I drove the *"AbeMobile."*

Perhaps it will be interesting for you to see what my diary for the next two years looked like as we traveled all over this great country of ours. We also sent in articles that were published in the *Pickens Progress* newspaper.

At the end of August, we packed it for the trip back to beautiful Pickens County, Georgia. After some mechanical problems en route, we finally arrived home at 3 a.m. Friday, September fourth. We had one week to get organized, repacked, and leave for our trip. We left Georgia on Friday, September eleventh and headed north to Dudley, Massachusetts, to visit with my mother and stepfather. We slept a few hours at a rest area in Maryland on Friday night and then headed on north. We arrived in Dudley at about 7 p.m. Saturday evening just in time to have a big meal with my mother and Stepfather Bill. We visited with them until Sunday afternoon. We then headed south to New Jersey for my first school. After spending the day with students in New Providence, New Jersey, we then headed to Hicksville on Long Island, New York. If you ever thought traffic was bad in Atlanta, you should see the mess in downtown New York! I hope we don't have to endure that kind of traffic ever again.

After that, we headed for some beautiful scenery in Vermont. We spent two days doing schools in Arlington, Vermont, about ten miles from Hildene: Robert Lincoln's home. We then headed south to Wilkes Barre, Pennsylvania, and spoke to students at Wyoming Seminary. They invited me to eat with them and the principal presented me with two pens from the school. The building was over one hundred years old and the students and faculty were very friendly. Then on to Penndel, Pennsylvania. On Wednesday, September 23, we visited with students at a 100-year-old Quaker school in Lahaska, Pennsylvania. In trying to decide where to park the *"AbeMobile"* for the night, I was looking around and discovered an old cemetery adjacent to the school. People were buried in that cemetery all the way back to Lincoln's time. After school, we took time to visit and ride one of the few remaining carousels in America. It was an exciting experience for me riding a carousel. I was like a kid again!

We then drove to Landsdale, Pennsylvania; and then on to Maryland. We broke down again and Barbara spent a week keeping the *"AbeMobile"* company at a repair shop near Aberdeen Proving Grounds, Maryland. We were within a few miles of John Wilkes Booth's home. Tim and Lisa picked us up and took us to dinner at the Golden Corral restaurant. We had a nice visit with them and their four children. I rented a car and drove each day to schools in Arcola, Virginia, Huntingdon, New Paris, Houtzdale, and Russelton, Pennsylvania. After eight days, we had a new radiator and other repairs taken care of and headed out to Chardon, Ohio. We spent the weekend at Jellystone Park campground near Mantua, Ohio.

On October sixth, we did schools in Rocky River and Lindhurst, Ohio, and then on to Poland and Richmond, Ohio. We were in Poland because of having met Linda and Bob at Mount Rushmore. They invited us to a nice dinner at their home. Friday, October ninth found us in Wheeling, West Virginia. We spent the weekend camping at White Water State Park in Indiana. Monday found us in Liberty, and the rest of the week we visited schools in Hope, Jamestown, Daleville, and Ft. Wayne, Indiana, and Tipp City and Ohio City, Ohio. On Friday, October sixteenth, we moved north to Lansing, Michigan. After school Friday afternoon, we drove about 100 miles to Port Huron, Michigan, and spent the weekend with Guy and Joyce Bailey. We had worked all summer with them at

Mount Rushmore and they had invited us to come spend the weekend with them when we got into Michigan. We had a nice relaxing visit with them, their children, and grandchildren. We even took a trip across the bridge into Canada.

The week of October nineteenth, we visited schools in Hartland, Rochester Hills, Napoleon, Ypsilanti, Dearborn Heights, Clio, and Hazel Park, Michigan. We finished up in Michigan on Monday at Grand Rapids and headed west for the traffic congestion of Chicago, Illinois. It was not fun driving the *"AbeMobile"* in Downtown Chicago. On Wednesday, we drove back into Indiana to visit in Kingsford Heights. During World War II, it was called Victory City and the town boasted a large factory that made munitions for the war. Then back to Chicago and more fights with traffic and rude people. We have found that the people in the north are not nearly as friendly and polite when it comes to letting you merge into traffic. We slept in the parking lot of the school and within a mile of the Sears Tower. We got "egged" that night, and the next day I did assemblies for a group of "not very well behaved students." The principal and the teachers had left me in charge and they obviously did not know what good assembly behavior was all about. Then I drove south to Benson and back north of Chicago to Wheeling, Illinois.

We spent the weekend camping at a beautiful, quiet campground called Potato Creek in Indiana. I changed the valve cover gaskets on the *"AbeMobile"* in hopes of stopping some oil leaks. We went for a walk in the woods and around the campground. The leaves were changing and the colors were beautiful. It had been cloudy and drizzling off and on all day.

It had been sad seeing crosses placed along the highways in our travels indicating those who had died in accidents. Please drive carefully so you don't end up being a statistic somewhere along the highway.

I hope all of you there in Pickens County are doing well and looking forward to the holiday season. I don't know what your weather has been doing there, but we are now in Wisconsin and have been having some bad weather since we last reported to you.

Two weeks ago, I spoke to students in Hobart, Indiana, on Monday morning and we then drove over to Momence, Illinois. After visiting with the students there, we drove to a Cracker Barrel restaurant and had a nice dinner with Max and Donna Daniels from Wheaton, Illinois. We had seen them when we were in Charleston, Illinois for a convention earlier this year. Max is another Abe and Donna plays the part of Mary Todd in their visits to schools and other locations. I have known them for several years and Max is known for his humor. We had a nice evening visiting with them.

We had a day off on Tuesday, so we spent Monday evening at Starved Rock State Park campground in Central Illinois. We just about had the whole place to ourselves. Wednesday found us in Cuba, Illinois, in the morning and the evening in Gridley; then on to two schools in Chillicothe, Illinois. We were excited about spending Friday in Galena, Illinois, because we knew that General US Grant had lived there. After school, we stopped by for a quick visit and tour of his beautiful home.

We spent Friday night in Cuba City, Wisconsin, at a garage and had a new starter and fan clutch put on Saturday morning. In southern Wisconsin, we kept seeing signs about a House on the Rock. We decided to stop for a visit to see what it was all about. Words can't very easily describe what we saw in our three hour visit there. Disney World and other attractions have *nothing* on this place. The two men who put it all together had an imagination that reached all the way to the moon and back!

We then drove further north into Wisconsin and stayed at a beautiful glacial lake campground; Devil's Lake State Park. On Sunday afternoon before we left, we took a three-mile walk around the lake. I have not seen water so clear in a long time. It was a very beautiful place to spend a weekend.

On Sunday evening, we headed on over to North Freedom for Monday morning and to Waupun for the afternoon. Our trip that afternoon to Mauston caught us in the worst snow, ice, sleet, and wind storm of the century. We heard on the news later that the winds were fifty to over 125 miles per hour. Semi-trailers were flipped over all along the highways. It took us over six hours to drive the 200 miles to Two Rivers. We were only able to drive thirty-five to forty-five miles per hour as we feared being blown off the highway in the *"AbeMobile."* I don't think I've ever been so scared in my entire life! Not a fun time to be on the road.

After speaking to the students at beautiful Two Rivers, we headed south along the shore of Lake Michigan to Kenosha and visited two schools there on Wednesday afternoon and Thursday. Then it was off to Lake Mills and Steven's Point for Friday. The *"AbeMobile"* started heating up again and it looked like we had major engine problems; either a blown head gasket or a cracked block. We wouldn't know until another mechanic looked at it.

It turned out that we needed a new engine. We found out that the overheating problems had caused major engine problems; so we decided to go ahead and spend the money to have a new engine put in. I had to pay over $5,200 to pay for the new engine and new carburetor, radiator repairs, etc. So hopefully we will not have any more problems. We may look around and find something to trade in the current *"AbeMobile"* for a newer model.

Back on Monday, November sixteenth, I took off in a rental car to make the rounds for a week all over Wisconsin. I visited Pittsville, Prairie Farm, Rice Lake, Eau Claire, and Chippewa Falls, Wisconsin, and Wyoming, and Edina, Minnesota, while Barbara stayed with the *"AbeMobile"* in the parking lot of a repair shop again.

I then went back and picked her up and we lived out of a rental car and motels for two weeks. We missed the roominess in the *"AbeMobile."* We headed out on Sunday for Dubuque, Iowa Falls, Waterloo, and Lake Mills, Iowa. We also took a trip across the line

Image in the Mirror

into Adams, Minnesota, to speak to a church school there. The night before Thanksgiving, I spoke at a church pastored by some friends of ours in Albion, Iowa.

We were invited to spend the Thanksgiving weekend with a nice family I had met while in Iowa last year. Don is a Methodist pastor in Albion and Beaman. He preaches at both churches (which are about eighteen miles apart) each Sunday morning. They have two daughters, Faith, seven, and Hope, eleven, that they adopted several years ago. Two very smart little girls who were constantly reading to us and Faith was drawing us lots of very nice pictures. We took time on Thanksgiving to take a nice long walk on what had been railroad tracks. More towns across America are converting their old railroad tracks and right-of-ways into bike and walking paths, and there was a nice one near Don and Trish's home in Beaman. We enjoyed our little walk and saw a couple of deer in the woods.

You may already be aware of the fact that Abe Lincoln (the other one) signed into law our National Holiday of Thanksgiving. I like to point this little-known fact out to my students in my travels and remind them to give thanks to God for all the blessings He bestowed on them each year including, but not limited to, a wonderful country to live in, a school with a principal and teachers who love them and want nothing more than to see them grow up to be something special and successful, and to thank Abe for the holiday. It was the best Thanksgiving I've had in a long time.

We left Sunday after Thanksgiving to head south to visit three schools in Boone, Iowa, on Monday and then on to Adair, Chariton, and Burlington, Iowa. We also made stops in Alexandria, Palmyra, and Salem, Missouri, before being able to head back to Wisconsin Friday evening to pick up the "*AbeMobile.*" We then headed south to Highland, Illinois, for Monday's school.

We miss ya'll back there in Jasper and are anxious to get home in two more weeks. We will be home for two weeks and then are off for five months all the way out to California and Washington before schools get out in May. Hope all of you had a nice Thanksgiving holiday and are getting ready for the Christmas season.

What's the weather doing back there? We have had unseasonably warm weather these last couple of weeks and hope the snow and cold hold off until we can get back to beautiful North Georgia.

Since last we visited with you, we have finally arrived home in Jasper for a couple of weeks. We got in Friday night and now have less than one week until Christmas. We hope all of you are having as much fun shopping and getting ready as we are.

The *"AbeMobile"* is doing just fine since we got the new engine in it. We have put about 2,000 miles on it since we left the repair shop in Wisconsin two weeks ago.

It was good to get back into the *"AbeMobile"* after spending two weeks in motels and the little rental car. We left Watertown, Wisconsin, on Sunday December sixth and drove down to Highland, Illinois, where I spoke to a school there on Monday. We then drove on over to St. Clair, Missouri, and then on to Edinburgh, Elnora, and Tell City, Indiana, before heading for Mr. Lincoln's birth state of Kentucky for schools there on Friday in Henderson and Oakland. We spent Thursday at two schools in Tell City right near the southern border of Indiana and Kentucky. The counselor there was Sally and she was one of the most organized ladies we have met on this trip so far. She was a big help in setting up and assisting me in running the Abe's Store in both schools. We sold a lot of Abe souvenirs to the students! We give the school library 10% of whatever we sell so they can buy more books.

We spent the weekend in a nice state park in Kentucky. We didn't get to do much hiking because it rained all weekend. It was nice to be able to relax back in the *"AbeMobile"* and get caught up on some reading and correspondence.

Sunday afternoon, we drove on over to Prestonsburg; then on to Emmalena, Hindman, Inez, Barbourville, and Helton, Kentucky. A word about winding roads in Kentucky coal country: If you ever think the roads at home are bad, you should drive a twenty-eight-foot motor home around the mountains in Kentucky. Wow! I was scared! I was somehow able to keep the dirty side down and the shinny side up on some very narrow, winding roads with no guard rails and steep drop offs to streams or gorges as coal-loaded *big* trucks went speeding by us.

We were glad to get out of those hills and onto some wider, straighter interstate roads in South Carolina and North Carolina. We visited a school in Wellford, South Carolina, and then headed for Mount Olive, North Carolina, before heading home on Friday. Mount Olive's big claim-to-fame is their pickle factory. They ship out so many pickles now that they have to import cucumbers from Florida to meet their demands. They also grow a lot of cotton and raise pigs.

I had to repair a broken water line down by the barn, so I was up early Saturday morning to get that done. I will be seeing my children, Chip, Kimberly, and Jason in the next few days and we will be cooking Christmas dinner for a lot of family and friends.

We wish all of you the very best of holiday seasons and hope to be able to visit some of you while we are in town for a couple of weeks. Please give us a call at 706–692–3682. We would love to hear from you and tell you all about our experiences.

Here it is, the end of January, and we have been so busy we haven't had time to get you folks updated on what's happening with us in our travels.

We arrived home the week before Christmas and rushed around trying to get some last minute shopping done. We cooked Christmas dinner for a total of eighteen family and friends. We had a nice dinner and some time to visit.

Sunday, January third, I headed south to Venice, Florida, and spent the day visiting with the students there. I also stopped by to see my mother, sister, and brother in Central Florida. Then I drove up to speak to a school in Spartanburg, South Carolina. I was supposed to visit a school in Joelton, Tennessee (north of Nashville), but the school was closed due to an ice storm.

Even though the original *"AbeMobile"* was running just fine after I spent so much money getting the new engine installed and other repairs done; I was worried about what would go wrong next. So I started looking around for something newer to trade. I found a thirty-seven foot, 1990 model Pace Arrow and was able to make a trade. It is so much nicer than the twenty-year-old, twenty-eight footer we had started out in. This one even had a washer and dryer so we didn't have to find a Laundromat anymore. Barbara spent the week while I was in Florida and South Carolina getting the new RV all packed up and ready to go for the five months we would be gone on this trip.

We left Jasper on Sunday, January tenth to head for Lewisburg, Mt. Pleasant, Michie, and Medina, Tennessee. I drove the little red Passat (The little red *"AbeMobile"*) up to Hopkinsville, Kentucky, and left Barbara at the school in Clarksville, Tennessee. The new *"AbeMobile"* started giving us trouble about this time. I called the mechanic several times at Carl Black GMC dealer in Marietta where Chip works. He had completely gone through the new RV for us before we traded to give us some assurance that we wouldn't be having problems. I thought it sounded like a case of bad gas or a bad fuel filter. I crawled around under it during a freezing rain storm trying to find the fuel filter so I could change it. When I finally located the filter, I then drove around Clarksville for several hours that night trying to find a parts house with the right filter. When I finally realized no one had it by 9 p.m. that night, I bypassed it with a short piece of hose and off we went.

We didn't get more than about thirty miles and then it wouldn't go over twenty miles per hour on the interstate. That is scary! All those big rigs flying by us at sixty-five miles per hour and we were hardly able to move. We finally decided to pull off for the night. We found a church parking lot to spend the night. I left Barbara at 3 a.m. the next morning to drive about 350 miles to a school in Black

Rock and then on to Little Rock, Arkansas. I called our trusty Good Sam Club at 8 a.m. and had them come tow the "AbeMobile" and Barbara to a mechanic. He replaced both filters and it ran fine; now the problem was getting Barbara and the "AbeMobile" to Memphis so I could meet them and drive on to a school for first thing on Friday morning in Checotah, Oklahoma. I told the mechanic I would pay him an extra $100 to drive the RV to Memphis so I could meet them. There just wasn't enough time for me to backtrack all the way to Clarksville, pick Barbara up, and then drive all the way into Oklahoma in time for school at 8 a.m.

I arrived from Little Rock about 5 p.m. Barbara left Clarksville at 3 p.m. and finally arrived there about 8 p.m. We were supposed to meet across the river from Memphis on the Arkansas side. The guy who drove Barbara to Memphis decided he didn't want to go through town, so he just left her in a parking lot to wait for me. I was getting frantic by 9 p.m. and so was Barbara. My cell phone was not working properly and I didn't know how to reach her. Finally, at about 10 p.m., I called 911 and so did she, and our friendly police in Memphis helped get us together so we could head back across Arkansas to Oklahoma. Barbara was in tears by the time we finally got reunited. We got to our school around 3 a.m. tired and more than a little concerned that we weren't going to ever find each other that previous evening.

From Checotah, we drove to a school in Hartshorne. We camped for the weekend at Crawford State Park in Southeastern Kansas. I then spoke in schools that week in Girard, Emporia, Topeka, Wellsville, Shawnee, and Overland Park, Kansas, and one school back south in Miami, Oklahoma. We camped that next weekend in Waynesville, Missouri, and went over to Springfield to visit with some friends I have known since 1974. Beverly was still in the hospital since having a brain aneurysm last October eleventh. She is doing much better and is supposed to be able to get out of the hospital around February eleventh. Dana and Beverly also have twins,

Christie and Richie, who are a couple of years younger than my twins, and an older son, Willie.

We then drove to schools in Dixon, Hartville, Rich Hill, Roscoe, Hardin, Camden Point, and Edgerton, Missouri. The little town of Roscoe only had dirt roads and about seventy-five students in grades kindergarten through seventh. We drove right by without knowing, had to turn around in a cemetery, and go back to find the school. We also visited Wakarusa and Leavenworth, Kansas. Leavenworth has a fort, a federal prison, a state prison, and a military prison.

We stayed this last weekend of the month of January in Cottonwood RV Park, north of Columbia, Missouri. It was cold and raining all weekend. I did manage to get the rest of the lettering on the side of the new *"AbeMobile."*

The weekend we spent near Columbia, Missouri, we took time to take in a movie, "Patch Adams" with Robin Williams. It was a great movie and will probably win an Oscar. If you haven't seen it yet you should go.

That week found us visiting schools in Moberly, Guilford, and Burlington Junction, Missouri; Nebraska City, and Omaha, Nebraska, and a trip to Vinton, Iowa. When I finished my schools in Nebraska City, we visited a thrift store and I found a bicycle in good condition for only fifteen dollars.

The night before I was to go over to a school in Vinton, we stopped to visit with our friends Don and Trish in Beaman. We parked the *"AbeMobile"* in the parking lot of the church where Don is pastor. This was the same family we spent last Thanksgiving with. It was a bad snow and ice storm that night and the temperature got down to thirteen. Our water froze up until the next day.

The next weekend we spent at the Grand Island RV Park, Nebraska. We found a couple of flea markets and thrift stores to visit. We also found an RV dealer who carried a special rack to attach to the ladder on the back of the *"AbeMobile"* to hold our bicycles. Now all we needed to do was to find a good deal on a bike for me.

This week found us visiting schools in Polk, Sutton, Bellwood, Palmer, and Grand Island, Nebraska, before heading south back into Kansas to visit Alma, Longford, and Clay Center.

Grand Island is where millions of sand hill cranes stop in their Southern migration route.

When we were leaving Nebraska Wednesday afternoon, we were hearing radio reports of a bad storm that had already dumped eight feet of snow in four days on I-80 in Nevada and was heading east. We were hoping it wasn't going to find us. The winds were bad on Wednesday and Thursday and it was difficult keeping the "*AbeMobile*" on the road in some places. On Thursday, as we were heading north to Longford, it was snowing and blowing badly. I tried to call the school several times to be sure they hadn't dismissed. Finally, the principal answered and said they were still in school and were anxiously waiting for Abe to arrive for his visit.

We slipped and slid on the ice a couple of times and were wondering if we might have to have them come get us out of a ditch for my visit. We did get there in one piece and it was a nice group of students I visited; all forty-two of them in a school for kindergarten through sixth grades. It is now one of the smallest I have visited in the past twenty-four years! The old brick building had been built in 1918.

I spent Friday observing Abe's 190th birthday at two different schools in Clay Center.

After leaving there on Friday afternoon, we decided to go a little out of our way before heading south to the little town of Delphos, Kansas. This is the town where Grace Bedell Billings lived after leaving Westfield, New York. Grace is the little eleven-year-old girl who, in October of 1860, wrote to Mr. Lincoln to suggest he might look more handsome if he grew some whiskers. So at her suggestion, he let his beard grow. It was a very small town with a monument on the square about Grace, and we stopped at the cemetery outside of town so I could take a picture of her gravesite. While we were in town, we spotted a junk shop with a bicycle outside for ten dollars. So I have a bike, too.

On Saturday, while camping at Falls River State Park in Kansas, we decided we would take a bike ride, but my bike needed a new rear tire and tube. We took a trip over to the nearest Walmart in Chanute and spent six dollars for a new tire and tube. After I got it all put back together, we took a ride around this beautiful park on a big lake.

What did you do for Valentine's Day? I hope you did something special for your sweetheart.

What have you been doing since last we visited two weeks ago? We have moved further west and are spending a few days at the end of the month of February here in beautiful Colorado Springs, Colorado, within sight of Pikes Peak.

Sunday evening, two weeks ago, while we were still in Kansas, we went to see the new movie, "Message in a Bottle." It was a good love story for Valentine's Day, but had a sad ending. Have you seen it yet?

We started off the week in Independence and then on to Andale, Augusta, Russell, Kinsley, Lakin, Garden City, Johnson, Grainfield, and Brewster, Kansas. Russell is where Senator Bob Dole was born. We had hoped to be able to meet him, but he only stops by once and while for a short visit and was not there while we were. We spent the weekend in a small campground in Oakley, Kansas. On Monday, we headed for Colorado.

On the way, we had our first of three tires blow out on us. Even though the "*AbeMobile*" only had 7,000 miles on it when we bought it, and now has 12,500, I guess the ten-year age on them is catching up with us. While waiting for the Good Sam Club to come from Wichita to change the tire, we went into a restaurant to get some supper. While there, we met and spent some time visiting with a man by the name of Jim, who, at sixty-six and retired from the Post Office, spends several months a year bicycling all over America. He was a very interesting man and has seen a lot of our beautiful country by bike.

We made our first stop in Colorado in Brush and then on to Haxtun, Greeley, and Karval. I left Barbara Tuesday night while I drove the Volkswagen (the little red "*AbeMobile*" Junior) 200 miles up to Douglas,

Wyoming, to speak to a school there. I ran into high winds and blowing snow while on that trip, but the scenery was awesome. Karval will give Roscoe, Missouri, a run for the smallest town we've visited. It was all of six square blocks in size and the school I spoke to was kindergarten through twelfth grade with only ninety students.

On Thursday, while I was at school in Greeley, Barbara spent the day in two different repair shops getting eight new tires put on and an oil change to the tune of $1,200. On Friday, we drove on over to Colorado Springs, where we spent a beautiful, sunny weekend. The temperatures are in the mid seventies for the first time in a long time. We went for a walk around old Colorado Springs and stumbled into a store where they make thousands of custom character dolls that sell for $37.50 to hundreds of dollars each. They have had several Abe dolls in the past and are working on a new, young Lincoln reclined against a pile of logs and reading a book. They were quite unique and I may be able to help promote them in his travels.

This weekend we drove up almost to the top of 14,100 feet Pike's Peak. At about fourteen miles up of the total of twenty miles, the gravel road started to get very narrow and icy as we neared the top and we decided to turn around before we reached the top. It was a scary but spectacular drive. I've never seen such distant views of lakes, valleys, and snow-covered mountains. On Sunday, we went for a drive through Garden of the Gods Park in the Colorado Springs area. It has some very unusual rock formations, something like some of the ones we saw in the Badlands of South Dakota. It was beautiful.

I made some stuffed peppers and we invited our next door neighbors, Walter and Sabrina, to eat with us. They are from California and are spending time here in Colorado selling computer software. They are also full-time RVers and live out of their fifth-wheel camper. I saw on the national news that you had some snow, so I hope you had an opportunity to enjoy it. Hope everyone there in Georgia is doing well. If any of you want to e-mail us, you can reach us at AbeUSA16@AOL.com.

We have done a lot of traveling since last we visited three weeks ago. We have been driving so much I've not had time to update you until now.

While we were in Colorado Springs, Colorado, we were fortunate enough to find a good RV repair man who was able to get our refrigerator and generator repaired. Our new extended warranty insurance covered the repairs except for the $200 deductible. Thank goodness for insurance plans. Those repairs would have cost us about $1,500. It is good to have a refrigerator that works like it should and the generator comes in handy when we are not parked at an RV park with electric hookups.

I visited schools in Bennett and Pueblo, Colorado, while Barbara took care of the repairs. We then headed north to Elizabeth, Colorado, before crossing over the mountains in Loveland Pass. We were at 12,000 feet and then down to and through a beautiful gorge with a river running alongside of the highway. What scenery!

We then drove 125 miles through the Sevier and Great Salt Lake Deserts on a one lane gravel road to speak to thirty kindergarten through sixth grade students on an Indian Reservation in Ibapah, Utah. There were times when we wondered if we would make it through the deserts on that gravel road. The only life we saw during that trip was a lone llama out in a field, some horses and lots of ducks and other birds in a wildlife preserve we drove through. It was desolate, but beautiful in its own way.

We then drove on north and west to Spring Creek, Nevada. By that Saturday afternoon, we were in Spokane, Washington. We had come over 1,700 miles since leaving the Denver, Colorado, area on Wednesday. We crossed the six states of Colorado, Utah, Nevada, Idaho, Oregon, and Washington. What a long drive through some beautiful mountains!

On Sunday, we drove about thirty-five miles across the line from Spokane into Couer d'Alene, Idaho, to look around this beautiful resort town on a mountain lake. We walked the 3,300 feet world's

Image in the Mirror

longest floating boardwalk and I joined the Fraternity of Eagles while we were there.

On Monday, I spoke to two schools in Spokane and then we drove on to Granger and Sunnyside. On the way south, we stopped by on Tuesday afternoon in Goldendale, Washington, and visited and had dinner with my cousin, Michael Levitz. He is the Deputy Prosecuting Attorney in Goldendale.

We drove on to Tualatin, Oregon, and stopped for a look at a beautiful waterfall outside of Oregon City. While trying to get turned around to speak at the school in Hillsboro, we got stuck behind the Grange Building. The backend of the *"AbeMobile"* got hung up on a downhill slope in the driveway. We thought we were going to have to call our Good Sam Club to get a wrecker, but a nice man in a big truck stopped by, hooked up a chain to the front of the RV, and pulled us off the slope we were stuck on. We then drove on down to Salem and had dinner with my cousin, Curt, and his wife, Barbara. Curt and Barbara raise llamas and have forty-five of them. We spent Friday night in their huge arena where they show their llamas. We had a nice visit with them before heading out Saturday to drive down the Oregon Pacific coast.

We stopped at Coos Bay and spent the night Saturday at the Lucky Loggers RV Park. The drive along Highway 101 runs right alongside the Pacific Ocean, with lots of cliffs, up and down mountains, and lots of curves that were a challenge for the *"AbeMobile."*

The 200 mile drive through the mountains to Hayfork, California, was one of the worst and slowest we've had yet. We ran into fog, snow, ice, a lot of steep roads, and were such slow-going that it took us almost six hours to make the 200 miles to school. Then after school, we had no choice but to go right back through the same mountains again. It wasn't quite as bad in the daytime as it had been the night before.

We backtracked to Crescent City and Fort Dick for schools there. On the way south, we saw a large herd of elk on the side of the road. I was able to get some video footage of them as we passed by. We drove through the Redwoods National Park and later through another redwoods area where we saw giant redwood trees big enough to drive a car through. We also saw giant sequoia trees towering a long way into the blue sky.

We drove south to San Jose and Livermore. We spent the weekend at the Solano County Fairgrounds RV Park. On Saturday, we took a trip over the Golden Gate Bridge into San Francisco and wanted to take a boat ride out to Alcatraz Prison. When we got to Pier 41 to the ticket office, they told us they were sold out until Monday for trips out to the old prison. We were disappointed. We did get to ride the famous San Francisco trolley cars from one end of the line to the other end and back. We had to wait in a long line at each end for about an hour, but it was worth it. The hills in San Francisco are bigger than anything I've ever seen anywhere. While walking around on the piers at Fisherman's Wharf, we saw a lot of neat shops, lots of people crowding around, several musical groups entertaining us, and a juggler. There were also about 150 sea lions enjoying a sunny Saturday afternoon by sunning themselves on some floating piers.

If any of you ever think your gas prices are high where you are, you should check out what we've been having to pay to fill up the "*AbeMobile*" here in California: from $1.35 to $1.59! Ridiculous! They sure try to rip-off the tourists. When I spoke to Jason the other day back there in Alpharetta, he said gas prices there were running about seventy-two cents; one-half of what we are paying out here. The "*AbeMobile*" takes about seventy-five gallons to fill it up and gets only five to six miles to the gallon. How would you like to pay the $300 a week we have to pay for gas?

We will be here in California until April seventeenth and then we go to Arizona. The last weekend before we leave California I will receive the "Lincoln of the Year Award" in Burbank.

We are still in sunny California in the San Francisco Bay area this weekend. We will be in this expensive state for two more weeks.

Image in the Mirror

I have never seen grocery or gas prices so high! We stopped to fill up the "*AbeMobile*" the other day, and when I went back to turn off the pump, it had stopped at $127.50 for seventy-six gallons of gas at $1.68 a gallon! There is *no excuse* in ripping off the public at those prices. The oil companies are making a killing off not only the locals, but those of us who are visiting. There is talk all over the state of a boycott on April thirtieth to protest the high prices.

The scenery here is beautiful with all the rolling hills, mountains, ocean views, etc., but the people are not as friendly as we've encountered in other states, and their high prices are not fun. We are spending close to $500 a week for gas. We can't wait to head to Arizona in two weeks and hopefully lower prices.

Two weeks ago, while we were in the Ukiah area, I drove over to the Pacific coast to Mendocino and had dinner with a long-lost cousin, Dalen, and her husband, Paul, and children, Moshe and Zoe. I had not seen them since Dalen was about four years old and I was about fourteen. They had come east to Blackshear, Georgia, to visit our grandparents. I came back telling Barbara about what a beautiful area it was and we decided to go spend the following weekend there. We did and walked on the beach, saw some beautiful sunsets, did some shopping in some really neat shops, and just relaxed. On Saturday evening, we went to a cancer fundraising concert and heard a really good trio who played Charleston-era swing music. It was different, but enjoyable. We spent the weekend at the Pomo RV Park in Fort Bragg. It was one of the most beautiful campgrounds we've ever stayed at. Each site had its own privacy screen of trees and bushes. We also took a walk through a forty-seven-acre botanical garden right on the Pacific Ocean. There were dozens of hummingbirds buzzing around and all the flowers were in full bloom. What a treat that was!

We left Ukiah and drove south to Petaluma and then on to Newark. I got a haircut in Newark and got scalped! The lady from Hong Kong who cut it took off too much. I hadn't had hair that short since leaving the army in 1967. While in Newark, one of my cousins, Susan, came from across the bay to see my show and to meet me for the first time. We then drove over to Linden, Fairfield, and back north to olive country, Corning. It is the olive capital of the world. The school I spoke to there was twenty-two miles out of town out in the middle of nowhere. One of those places where "You can't get there from here."

On Friday, we drove across the Golden Gate Bridge again and took a boat ride with Susan. We were out on the San Francisco Bay for about an hour. We drove under the bridge and around the island where Alcatraz Prison is located. We had wanted to take the tour of the old prison, but that tour was sold out for several days ahead. We enjoyed the ride and the scenery and I didn't even get seasick!

This week was a slow week for me, since most of the schools were out for Easter vacation. We hope you and your family have had a nice holiday. I spoke in Newark again and a few miles away in Fremont. We spent the weekend again back at the Solano County Fairgrounds RV Park because it was the cheapest place to spend some time, only fifteen dollars a night there for full hookups when most other parks in the area would be thirty to fifty dollars a night. We had the whole place to ourselves. I did visit a computer show on Saturday and bought some software to try to get my web pages up and running.

After leaving the San Francisco Bay area two weeks ago, we headed south to Oakhurst up in the mountains, and then on to Lamont just outside of Bakersfield. We continue to be amazed at the high prices of everything out here; from gas to groceries. We spent that weekend at the Kern County Fairgrounds in Bakersfield. Their price was only ten dollars a night with full hook-ups. What a deal!

On Saturday, we drove 150 miles south to Huntington Beach to spend some time with my cousin, Terry, and his wife, Mary, sons, Kurt and Kevin, and other family members. We took a walk on the pier at the beach and went out to eat at the Island Restaurant. We enjoyed some wonderful, very large salads. After spending Monday and Tuesday without a school to visit, we then drove back down to park in front of Terry's house for Tuesday and Wednesday evenings. Mary cooked some great meals for us and a lot of visiting relatives and friends of theirs. I did a presentation for them after dinner. The meal and Abe were enjoyed by all attending. We missed an earthquake that hit very near right before we arrived. That was one California attraction I was happy to miss!

On Wednesday of that week, I drove about 100 miles south to speak to a Catholic school in San Diego. We had a great time seeing Huntington Beach. On Thursday, on the way up to Hermosa Beach, we stopped by Long Beach to meet my brother, Barry. We had lunch with him and his girlfriend, Rosalind. The house where they live in Laguna Beach was right in the midst of all the mudslides they had a few months ago. A lot of houses were destroyed.

We parked the "*AbeMobile*" Friday afternoon up on beautiful Lake Castaic near Santa Monica and drove down thirty-one miles to the big Hilton Hotel across from the Burbank airport for the Association of Lincoln Presenters Fifth Annual Convention. I was given the "Lincoln of the Year" award for 1998. There were approximately twenty-five Abes at the convention, and over 100 members of ALP. On Saturday afternoon, we drove out to Forest Lawn Memorial Gardens and saw several presentations. What a beautiful memorial park it was!

On Sunday morning, we left early for the nearly 450 miles drive to the Phoenix area in Arizona. As we came past Palm Springs and through the desert, we realized that summer must be here. It has been in the nineties since we arrived in Arizona and is still quite hot, even though the sun has gone down as I write this piece.

Two weeks ago, it was good to finally get out of California and those expensive gas prices. At $1.60 to $1.85 a gallon, we were spending about $125 to fill up the "*AbeMobile*" two to three times a week in California and we found gas prices down closer to $1.09 to $1.29 in Arizona, New Mexico, and Texas. What a difference!

On Monday, I spoke to students near Phoenix, Arizona, at Chandler and then on to six different Indian Reservations and schools at Bapchule, Laveen, Many Farms, Chambers, Lukachukai, and Ganado. They were nice students, but do not know what good assembly behavior is all about. Their principals did not expect them to sit still and listen, and I had to stop several times during my presentations to ask them to be quiet and listen. More about this and my feelings about the subject at the end of this article.

While driving from the southern end of the state to the northeastern corner, we stopped by the Grand Canyon. It was awesome! What a beautiful piece of God's creation it was. If you haven't had the opportunity to visit it you should.

We then drove about 300 miles and I spoke to students at four schools in Belen, New Mexico. We stayed that weekend at the LaMirada RV Park in Belen. On Wednesday of last week, we drove about 700 miles to the Dallas, Texas, area. I spoke at Frisco, Texas, and then drove up to do a program in Waurika, Oklahoma. While in the Dallas area, we visited and ate supper with some friends of mine from my previous visits to Texas. Bobbie Kerr has adopted fifteen children over the years and is doing a great job of being a mother to Jennie twenty-two; Jesse, eighteen; John, seventeen; Jeff, sixteen; Julie, fourteen; Joy, twelve; TJ, twelve; Myesha, eleven; Megan, ten; Tara, seven; and Joel, four, who are still at home. Bobbie just graduated from college and is now going to seminary. We wondered how she could possibly do it all and keep her sanity. God must have a special place for mothers like her.

Friday, after leaving the Dallas area of north Texas, we drove through some really bad traffic approximately 400 miles to the Corpus Christi area and are staying for the next several days at the Mathis Motor Inn RV Park. The weather is a little cooler and the drive in and around Corpus Christi is beautiful. It is right on the Gulf of Mexico, so now we have been from the Atlantic Ocean on the East Coast all the way to the Pacific Ocean in Washington,

Oregon, and California and to the Gulf of Mexico. We are seeing a lot of this beautiful country of ours.

In light of what happened recently in Littleton, Colorado (I had spoken there to several schools a few years ago), I wrote a letter and e-mailed it to a lot of schools and friends around the country. I am putting forth my suggestions about how to prevent these bad things from happening in our schools. I would encourage you to help do something about discipline and respect with your children and those you might come in contact with.

Two weeks ago, we were still in Texas in the Corpus Christi area. It was hot, but the gas was a lot cheaper at ninety-nine cents per gallon. I spoke in Portland at two schools there, and then on Thursday afternoon we drove southwest of San Antonio to Uvalde. I spoke at four schools there on Friday. We stayed at the Quail Hollow RV Park. It had lots of big shade trees and was a very nice campground.

On Sunday, we drove about eighty miles from Uvalde to Eagle Pass, Texas, parked, and walked across the bridge to Piedras Negras, Mexico. We shopped around for a couple of hours. I bought an eagle wind chime and another eagle about twenty inches tall for my collection. We had a double-dipped ice cream cone for forty-five cents each. We were not bombarded by little children begging for coins as we had been told we would. I can now say I've been from the Atlantic Ocean to the Pacific Ocean and the Gulf of Mexico and from Canada to Mexico and lots of states in between. We have seen a lot of this country these past few months.

We returned from our trip across the border and went to a local movie theater to see "Entrapment." It was a good action movie.

This past Monday and Tuesday, I spoke at two more Uvalde schools, and then on Tuesday afternoon, we headed back to Georgia. We drove 400 miles on Tuesday and 700 miles on Wednesday and arrived home late Wednesday evening.

I started my two-day visit to Jasper early Thursday morning digging in the mud at the barn to repair another broken water line. It was good to be back for a while and catch up on all the new things happening in Jasper.

My son, Jason, has now gone into the U.S. Army and is at Fort Jackson, South Carolina, for basic training and advanced training. My son, Chip, and Kimberly came up on Friday and along with my long-time friend, Ron Masten, from Florida; we had a nice dinner together.

On Saturday morning, I left Barbara and the *"AbeMobile"* in Jasper and took off in the Lincoln to drive up to do schools in Delaware, Maryland, and Virginia. I didn't even get to Dawsonville before the alternator went out on the Lincoln. So two hours and $200 later, I was on the road again. Hope all of you are well. Hug someone today and tell them how much you love them.

After I finished my nine-month, 300-plus schools, in thirty-five states tour in Virginia on May twenty-first; I then headed further north to the Boston, Massachusetts, area to spend some time with my mother and brother, Stuart, and family. I helped Stuart get ready for a big weekend. Stuart's nephew, Dan, was going to have a Bar Mitzvah on Memorial Day. So there were a lot of parties and lots of good food to eat for that celebration of Dan's coming to manhood.

I then drove back the 1,250 miles to Jasper on Monday and Tuesday. I arrived home on the first of June. We have since been busy trying to get caught up on things around the house. Since we are never home to enjoy it, I am thinking of selling the house and the beautiful eight acres and will continue to live in the *"AbeMobile"* until I decide to get off the road and slow down a bit.

I helped out with the dedication of a new medical facility on Highway 515 just south of the 108 intersection. On Flag Day, Monday the fourteenth of June, I had a visit with the students at the Community Christian School in Canton. Those students enjoyed visiting with our sixteenth president, and they learned some valuable lessons about respect for themselves, parents, and teachers.

We will be leaving in the next few days to go back out to Mount Rushmore, South Dakota. If your summer plans call for a trip to the

Black Hills, be sure to look us up in Hill City, about nine miles from Mount Rushmore at the Rafter J. Bar Ranch Campground. You may want to stay in a cabin at the resort. It is a wonderful place to spend some time if you are camping or traveling through the area.

Well, it is the end of summer, schools have started, and we haven't slowed down to give you an update. We left Jasper on Sunday, June twenty-seventh to drive the *"AbeMobile"* out to South Dakota. We arrived in the Black Hills at Rafter J Bar Ranch Campground on Tuesday afternoon, June 29. The trip was just over 1,500 miles. No problems with the RV except that it loves gas too much.

I did my first show at the campground on Thursday evening and continued to do three shows a week at one of the most beautiful campgrounds we have ever stayed at. We heard that there were approximately 400,000 people who attended the Sturgis bike rally. Next year, it is the sixtieth year for the rally, and year 2000, so they expect to have more than 500,000 attend.

I continued to work on my new Web site (www.AbeUSA16.com), and finished my second book, *The Life and Times of Abe Lincoln*, for young children ages four through twelve. I have someone in Alabama illustrating it for me, and she has already done a beautiful job on all of the pictures for the book. I am anxious to get it off to some publishers to look at. All students in Pickens County and all over the country are invited to join my *free* club, Abe's Ambassadors Club, on the Web site. If every student in the country would join and sign the ten-point pledge, we would have fewer problems in our schools and students would have more respect for parents and teachers.

On August nineteenth, I was invited to speak to a group of 250 National Guard Recruiters from six northwest states who were gathered in Lead, South Dakota, for a convention. They gave me a standing ovation after my fifty-five minute talk. Before I began my talk, I reminded those gathered that Abe didn't have any interns in his White House. They all appreciated the humor.

We left South Dakota on Monday about noon and arrived back home at 5 a.m., Wednesday, August twenty-fifth. Our only problem on the trip was that we blew out a tire in Paducah, Kentucky, and spent two hours waiting for our Good Sam Club to send someone to change it.

We drove the next weekend to New York, north of the Big Apple. I spoke on Monday on Long Island at Interstate 77 in Ridgewood. I then drove the car into downtown New York City through a lot of bad traffic. Those yellow taxi drivers are *wild*. They will run over you in a heartbeat! I couldn't wait to get out of that traffic and get back to the country. On Tuesday, I spoke to the students in Leptondale, New York. We drove on down to Sterling, Virginia, and I spoke there at Sully Elementary School on Thursday. Wednesday was a day off, so we drove into Washington, DC. I got to see the Lincoln Memorial, the White House, the Capitol, and the Washington Monument again. There was scaffolding all around the Washington Monument, because they are working on cracks and resurfacing some of the exterior. It was still open to the public, so we got to go to the top for a great view of Washington. It was nice to visit, but I wouldn't want to live there and fight the traffic every day. On Friday, I spoke to the students at East High Elementary School in Elizabethtown, Pennsylvania.

We spent the weekend of October ninth and tenth at the Country Haven Campground near White Horse, Pennsylvania. It is owned by an Amish family. We spent the day on Saturday shopping in Intercourse, Bird in Hand, and Lancaster, Pennsylvania. I found a lot of really neat handmade items and we had a wonderful lunch at a small Amish-run diner.

We have covered a lot of territory since last reporting to you four weeks ago. On Columbus Day, I drove to St. Anselm Catholic School in Philadelphia. They were a well-behaved group of students. Then on to Ashkar Elementary in Hughesville, Pennsylvania, Woodhome Elementary/Middle in Baltimore, Maryland, Norrisville Elementary in Maryland and on Friday of that week, spoke at the Broad Street

Elementary School in Gibbstown, New Jersey. We then drove until about midnight to park in front of a closed state park near Mineral, Virginia. We camped Saturday evening at the Christopher Run Campground. It was overlooking a big, beautiful lake. On Monday, I spoke at the Jouett Elementary School in Mineral. I had Tuesday off to get some well needed rest and get caught up on correspondence. We then drove over to Grandin Court Elementary in Roanoke and on to Sontag Elementary in Rocky Mount, Virginia. On Thursday, I spoke to Limestone Central and Northwest Elementary in Gaffney, South Carolina, and we drove to Homer, Georgia, where I spent the day at Banks County Middle School. We are not sure whether I was named after the town or the town was named after me.

We then made a quick pass through Jasper. We slowed down long enough to pick up our mail, check on the house, and the new roof being installed, and had dinner at the Cracker Barrel in Canton with my twins, Kimberly and Jason. We spent less than an hour visiting with my kids because we had a four hour drive to get to the other side of Nashville, Tennessee, to Mousetail Landing State Park. I had to speak there at a craft show on Saturday. We finally got parked after midnight.

On Sunday morning, I flew out of the Nashville airport to Green Bay, Wisconsin, rented a car and drove 510 miles to Bemidji, Minnesota. I was there to speak to their students and help dedicate a new Lincoln School on Monday. I spent Sunday night with the Heath family, a local pastor. I then drove back on Monday afternoon to the Green Bay airport, turned in the rental car, and slept in the airport for four hours before catching a 6:00 a.m. flight back to Nashville and the *"AbeMobile."*

Tuesday was an off-day, so we spent it driving over to Williamsburg, Kentucky, where we parked at the Williamsburg Motel/RV Park. I drove out each morning to schools there in Kentucky: Hall Elementary in Gray's Knob, Beaver Creek in Topmost, Rockcastle County Middle, and Mt. Vernon Elementary in Mt. Vernon. Barbara spent Thursday parked in the Ford dealership in Williamsburg getting $622 worth of brakes and a new tire taken care of on the *"AbeMobile."*

We spent that weekend near Lawrenceburg, Kentucky, at the home of Jim and Mary Sayre. Jim and Mary are also members of the Association of Lincoln Presenters. Jim got the "Lincoln of the Year Award" for 1995 and I got it earlier this year for 1998. Mary also portrays Abe's wife, Mary Todd, at some of the engagements they do. They have a thirty-acre farm with a pond on it. On Sunday, we went to church with Jim and Mary and then had a picnic and did some fishing.

I walked out on a rickety, old dock and sat on a rickety, old chair. Mary and Barbara were hoping I would fall in, but I surprised both of them and stayed dry. Neither of us had been fishing in years, and it was fun even though we didn't get any fresh fish to eat. Mary did fix a lot of good southern meals for all of us. Jim's dog, Buffy, who is really a dachshund, but is so fat that I kept calling her a miniature hippopotamus, kept us entertained running around chasing anything that moved near the pond. She got all muddy in the process. Jim spoils her rotten! He kept saying she was undernourished, but every time we ate, he was sneaking her food under the table. She was *not* undernourished, Jim. On Monday, Jim visited the afternoon school with me. He didn't have his suit on, but students who came through the cafeteria and saw both of us eating did a double take. I told them I was 190 years old and that Jim was my son.

On Monday evening, we all went to hear Jim speak at an annual Lions Club meeting. I was the one not dressed in my suit then and folks were doing a double take again. They had door prizes and Barbara and I both won a fifty dollar savings bond from one of the local banks. We had a nice, relaxing weekend visiting with these wonderful friends. I had met them at three previous conventions in Gettysburg, Charleston, Illinois, and Burbank, California. Jim is always teasing me about turnips. He knows I won't eat them, but has shipped me turnips on a couple of occasions.

This past week, the first one in November, we have seen the temperatures drop to the twenties in a couple of places, but have had good weather most of the time. On Monday, I spoke at Edna Tolliver and Jennie Rogers Elementary Schools in Danville, Kentucky. We had Tuesday off because of Election Day. I spoke at Hopkins Elementary in Somerset, North Metcalfe, in Edmonton, Stevenson Elementary in Russellville, North Junior High and Niagara Elementary in Henderson, Kentucky.

We drove from just south of Evansville, Indiana, on Friday afternoon to the Add More Campground just north of Louisville, Kentucky. I got up at 4:00 a.m. on Saturday and drove 200 miles to speak at a Catholic Men's Conference in Columbus, Ohio. Thom Lisk had asked me to come up there and will probably be one of my new agents. There were about 800 men attending and I received a standing ovation for my delivery of the Gettysburg Address. Saturday afternoon we went to see the movie, "The Bone Collector" and did some shopping.

We are looking forward to having nearly a month off in December. We want to spend some time doing some things around the house in our favorite place to be: Pickens County. I am hoping to be able to finish the gazebo I am building and get a spa installed. Hopefully, starting after this tour ends in May, we will be able to spend more time at home. I am getting burned-out with all of this traveling. I am right now the same age Mr. Lincoln was when he went to the Ford's Theatre on that fateful evening of Good Friday, April 14, 1865. I would love to make it until at least next August when I will turn fifty-seven and be one year older than the other Abe was. Let's hope so!

On Monday, November eighth, I drove to Louisville, Kentucky and spoke to students at Brandeis Elementary School and St. Agnes School, and then on to Bethany School in Glendale, Ohio. The school was located on beautiful grounds with lots of big, old trees. It was at one time an all-girls school run by Episcopal sisters. We then drove over to Lapel, Indiana, and spoke to the students at the Lapel Elementary, then came back to Anna, Ohio, and spoke to the students at Anna Middle School. We parked at the Lake Cody Campground near Lima, Ohio. I did some fishing, but didn't get any bites. It was too cold and windy, I guess. On Friday afternoon, I drove to Middletown, Ohio, and spoke to Central Academy Elementary School.

On Saturday, we drove over to Lima and had some brake work done on the Volkswagen. We had to leave it overnight and got a ride back to the campground with a teacher who was there getting his car worked on. We were able to go back on Sunday afternoon and pick up the car.

On Monday, I spoke to Parkwood Elementary and Lowell Elementary Schools in Sidney, Ohio, and to Westwood Elementary in Lima. Then I drove down to Columbus and spoke to an Avon sales meeting, which happened to be meeting in the same hotel I was speaking on Tuesday morning at a Speakers' Showcase. Then I drove up to Clyde and spoke to South Main School there. I then drove the Volkswagen over to speak to Bronson Junior High School and Chicago Street Elementary Schools in Bronson, Michigan; then on to the Lynn-Kirk Elementary School in Austintown, Ohio, and Apple Creek Elementary School. We then moved to the Amish Country Campsite near Winesburg, Ohio. We had a chance to eat at the Amish Back Door Restaurant. It was a really good, home-cooked meal. We did some shopping at a really big indoor flea market and bought some more tins for our collection, an eagle clock, an entrance mat that says, "One old goat and one cute chick live here," some more angel-making craft material, and some locally-made candy. We also fired my new signal cannon to check it out. It looks like a miniature Civil War cannon, fires a ten-gauge black powder shell, puts out a lot of smoke, and sounds like a real cannon.

On Monday morning, I fought through Pittsburgh rush hour traffic to get to the Norwin Middle School West in Irwin, Pennsylvania.

It was worse than Atlanta's traffic. Then it was on to Brookpark Memorial Elementary and Waterloo Primary in Atwater, Ohio. We then drove 350 miles across Ohio and Indiana, got in about midnight, and parked at the Blackhawk Campground near Cloverdale, Indiana, to spend ten days.

For Thanksgiving, we cooked a thirteen pound turkey, dressing, string beans, sweet potatoes, corn, spinach soufflé, pumpkin pie, and all the fixings in the RV, and enjoyed a big meal with just the two of us. We gave thanks for this wonderful country of ours and all that God has given us this year.

We heard a shop keeper, when we were looking around in town, mention that she had placed an ad in the local paper to advertise her birds for sale. We inquired about what she had and were informed that she had a male and female cockatiel about six weeks old and another pair only three weeks old. They had all been hand-fed. We decided to get the male, Peatie, who was six weeks old. He has been a good companion to keep us company while on the road. Barbara made a cover for his cage with eagles and flags all over it. I am going to try to teach him the Gettysburg Address. We shall see about that!

We spent some time over the weekend fishing and getting a few bites, but no fish on the hook. We found out there are more covered bridges here in this area (forty-two) than anywhere else in the country, so we set out to find three of them. We also visited Cataract Falls at one of the bridges. On the last Monday of this month, I made a short trip from the campground to Rosedale Elementary and Meridian Elementary in Brazil, Indiana.

It has been a few very cold and snow-covered weeks since we last reported in to you. We have heard from friends back there in Pickens County that you have also had some bad weather. Any time you feel you are having it cold there, think about what we have endured up here in Minnesota and Wisconsin for the last three weeks. We have seen actual temperatures range from fifteen below to highs of fifteen above and wind-chill factors to thirty below. Everywhere we travel, there is nothing but snow; some as much as a foot or more in depth, and drifts up to six feet or more. Our water pipes in the "*AbeMobile*" have been frozen for days at a time. It is *not* fun to take baths from a pot of hot water on the stove! We are ready to get out of the cold and find warmer climates further west and south.

On Tuesday, January eighteenth, we were in the Twin Cities area of Minnesota. I spoke at the Beaver Lake Elementary School in Maplewood. We took a trip over to the Mall of America and looked around in the second largest mall in the world. We rode the roller coaster. There was also a merry-go-round, a Ferris wheel, and lots of rides inside this big, beautiful mall.

While we were parked at the Beaver Lake school, a big snow and ice storm came through and dumped about five or six inches of snow all over us. The state and county road folks up here know how to deal with it a lot better than we do in Georgia. They start scraping, salting, and sanding as soon as it starts coming down, so the roads stay passable most of the time.

I then drove the car 160 miles over to Wisconsin to speak at the Holy Rosary School in Medford, Wisconsin; came back, and spoke to the Middleton Elementary School, and a father-son banquet at the Woodbury Lutheran Church in Woodbury, Minnesota. We stayed with the Doyle family in Woodbury. It was nice to be warm and be able to take a hot shower for the first time in several days. Our pipes had been frozen again. I had met them at Mount Rushmore last summer.

The week of the twenty-fourth of January took me to G.D. Jones Elementary School in Wausau, the Merton Primary and Intermediate Schools in Merton, Randall School in Bassett, First German Lutheran School in Manitowoc, the St. Paul Lutheran School in Appleton, and the Valley View Elementary School and the Red Smith Elementary School in Green Bay. We stayed with the Weidner family in Green Bay for a couple of nights while we got the heater fixed in the RV. The fan motor and burner had both gone out on the heater. We spent $300 for the fix, but it was nice to get more heat going finally.

The final week of January was spent traveling to St. John's Lutheran School in Watertown, Nature Ridge Elementary School in Bartlett, Illinois, Dickinson Elementary School in DePere, Prospect Elementary School in Lake Mills, and Southside Elementary School in Sparta; all in Wisconsin except for the trip back down to the Chicago area for the Bartlett school. The principal at the St. John's Lutheran School was nice enough to allow us to park in their parking lot for a few days and hooked us up to electricity. There are no campgrounds open up here this time of year, so it is nice to be able to park somewhere we can get electricity hooked up to the "*AbeMobile.*"

We are spending this weekend parked in the driveway of the Rothberger family here in Fort Atkinson, Wisconsin. Lance is a doctor and Linda teaches at school, runs a travel agency, and keeps all the books for Lance. Their children, Tim and Sara, will be at the school tomorrow that I will speak to; St. Joseph's Catholic School in Fort Atkinson.

The other Mr. Lincoln spent a couple of weeks here in the area back in 1832 during the Black Hawk Indian War. He was captain of a small group of army soldiers who were chasing the Indians from Illinois to here in Wisconsin. There are also some Indian mounds located nearby on the shores of Lake Koshkonong, so we visited them yesterday. Linda took us to the Hoard Historical Museum in town. They have a lot of really wonderful old things there, including an entire room devoted to Mr. Lincoln and a rather large collection of books donated to the museum. That was interesting to see all of the things there.

After spending the weekend of February fifth and sixth in Fort Atkinson, Wisconsin, with Dr. Lance and Linda Rothberger, I spoke at their children's (Sara and Tim) school, St. Joseph Catholic School. I was reminded several times by teachers and students alike that the other Mr. Lincoln had been in the area 168 years earlier during the Black Hawk uprising. We then drove over closer to the edge of Lake Michigan and spoke at Somers Elementary in Kenosha,

Salem Grade School in Salem, both Concordia Lutheran Schools in Racine, and then back to the other side of the state to speak to the students at Elroy Primary in Elroy. This was twenty miles away from where we had been the previous Friday at Sparta, home of the giant bicycle. We then drove to Carbon Cliff, Illinois, to speak at Apollo Elementary. While driving that afternoon toward the Kickapoo State Park to spend the weekend, we had another tire blow out just fifty miles from our destination. We spent four hours on the side of the highway waiting for Good Sam to send us a repairman to change out the tire. Instead of getting parked and settled in at 6 p.m., we finally got in about 10 p.m.

On Valentine's Day, I spoke at the Northview School in Rantoul, Illinois. We went out to eat and to see the movie, "The Beach." I hope all of you had a wonderful day with your favorite Valentine. Then we finished up our visit in Illinois at the Moweaqua Elementary in Moweaqua and the Bond Elementary in Assumption. We then drove over to the west side of St. Louis and spoke to Clearview Elementary in Union. We drove back to St. Louis and parked at the Rossman School. This very rich, private school was founded in 1917; I think.

We unhooked the car and drove about fifteen miles downtown to the arch. I had my heart set on being able to take the tram car up to the top, but we didn't get there until 5:45 p.m. and the last tram to the top had been at 5:15. That was a big disappointment since we had passed close enough to see the arch in the distance several times in the past two years, but had never been able to stop and see it up close. We did get to visit the museum under the arch for a few minutes before they closed. We planned to come back on Thursday after finishing up at Rossman and Conway Elementary; but, as luck would have it, a rain and ice storm came through town and we were not able to go back downtown to the arch before leaving town.

We then drove to Jefferson City, the capitol of Missouri. We drove for about an hour to spend the weekend at Lake of the Ozarks State Park. We finally got into some warmer weather and have it in the fifties these last few days for the first time since leaving Jasper. We took a nice walk on Sunday afternoon and gathered some pieces of driftwood. There were lots of deer in the park and more peace and quiet than we have had in a while.

I had President's Day off today, so we spent the day shopping and taking care of some errands. We moved over closer to town to the Ozark Trails Campground and the owner helped me weld a small crack in one of our wheels on the *"AbeMobile."* We found a small bust of Abe. I did a live radio interview with a station in the Twin Cities, Minnesota, via cell phone. When I was asked about what "Abe" would have to say to our current politicians, I told the radio audience that "he would tell Bill Clinton to tell the truth."

We have seen a lot more of this wonderful country of ours since we lasted reported in three weeks ago. On Washington's Birthday, I spoke to the students at Alton Elementary School in Alton, Missouri, and then on to Campbell Elementary School in Campbell, Missouri. By the time I got home late that night, I had driven 515 miles that day and spoken for six hours. Then it was on to Dixon Elementary and Dixon Middle Schools in Dixon, and Camdenton Upper Elementary School in Camdenton before heading to Brookridge Day School in Overland Park, Kansas. We then drove on south and spent the last weekend of February at Fall River State Park in southeastern Kansas. There is a big lake there and we walked along the shore and gathered some pieces of driftwood to make some craft items with.

The next week took us to West Bourbon Elementary School in Uniontown, St. Elizabeth Ann Seton Catholic School in Wichita, Bennington Elementary School in Bennington, and Ray Marsh Elementary School in Shawnee; all in Kansas. I drove the car south one day to speak to students at Dale Elementary School in Dale and then drove over to Gatewood Elementary School in Oklahoma City, Oklahoma. I also took a trip across the river to Mill Creek Elementary School in Independence, Missouri.

We drove over to Maxwell, Iowa, on Friday evening after leaving the Kansas City area and spent the weekend parked in front of the home of our Methodist Pastor friends, Don and Trish Burket, and their two girls, Hope and Faith. We went to a fundraiser dinner with them on Saturday evening and to church on Sunday. We had a nice visit with them again. Trish and Barbara spent some time on Saturday shopping while Don and I rounded up parts for a tune-up for the "*AbeMobile.*" We had a mechanic Don knew from his church put in new plugs, a distributor cap and rotor, and a new starter. The starter had been dragging more and more lately, so we figured while we had someone who knew what he was doing, we would head off any future problems and have that replaced. I dropped about $300 to get that all done. The RV starts and runs a lot better now.

This past week took us to Corinth Elementary School in Prairie Village in Kansas, and then on to Leonard Lawrence Elementary in Bellevue, Tara Heights Elementary in Papillion, both in the Omaha, Nebraska, area. I also spoke at Garfield Elementary in Clarinda, Iowa, and Hiawatha Elementary School in Hiawatha, Kansas. We then headed west Friday afternoon to Grand Island, Nebraska. This is where over 500,000 Sandhill Cranes stop between February and April during their migration from the south to the Arctic. What a beautiful sight they are! Bird watchers come from all over the country to witness this migration every year.

On Saturday, we spent the day shopping. We found some more books to add to our collection, more tins, and more music boxes. We went to see the new movie, "Reindeer Games" and ate dinner at Golden Corral. We also bought and installed a new antenna on top of the RV.

On March fourteenth, I spoke to the students at Engleman Elementary School in Grand Island, Nebraska, and we left the Sandhill Cranes and headed back to Kansas to Decatur Community High School and Oberlin Elementary School in Oberlin. We then drove to the southwest corner of Nebraska to speak at Benkelman

Elementary/Middle in Benkelman. On St. Patrick's Day, we were at Platte Valley Elementary in Sedgwick, Colorado. We were out in the middle of nowhere, so the principal asked me to fire off the cannon. The students, staff, and visiting parents enjoyed hearing this authentic sounding miniature cannon. I also found a beauty shop open that evening we arrived, so I got my ears lowered. I know I need a haircut when my stovepipe hat doesn't fit properly.

Some teachers at the school told us how good the food was at Lucy's Café, so that evening we drove over to find out for ourselves. I had the house special, "Buffalo steak burger." There was so much food, we took part of it with us and enjoyed it the next night. We also bought a whole pecan pie that Lucy's eighty-three-year-old mother made. She comes in each day to bake pies and we can tell you she knows how to make pecan pies as good as any we have had in Georgia or anywhere else. We enjoyed it for several days.

After leaving the friendly folks there in Sedgwick, we drove down to Colorado Springs and stayed at the Fountain Creek RV Park we had stayed at last year while in the area. We drove through a blowing snow storm and a lot of slow traffic between Denver and Colorado Springs. The *"AbeMobile"* was not driving very well; so on Monday, we found someone to work on it. We spent $300 getting new plugs and wires put in. One of the plug wires was broken, so that was a major part of our problems. We wished we had put in new wires when we had plugs put in back in Iowa two weeks earlier. It would have saved us some money.

We slept in that Saturday morning and then went shopping in some thrift stores we had discovered last year. On Sunday, we got up and had a big breakfast at Waffle House. I had two helpings of "Georgia ice cream" (grits). We then drove about sixty miles to Canon City to the Royal Gorge. We walked across the World's highest suspension bridge, rode the tram to the bottom of the gorge, and then took the aerial tram across the gorge. It was all beautiful and we took some wonderful pictures.

On Tuesday, I got a call from Victoria at *Georgia Magazine* back there in Woodstock. She was writing an article about re-enactors and included me in the article. She needed some pictures and the ones on my Web site weren't of good enough quality to use. I promised her I would email her some new pictures taken with the digital camera set on a finer resolution. We drove about five miles to the Garden of the Gods Park. I took about thirty pictures and we picked out several to send to her for the article. Keep an eye for your new *EMC* magazine when it comes out. "Our Abe" will be in it.

My only school for the week was ninety miles away in the Denver area at Belleview Christian School in Westminster. They were great students and one of the principals took me on a tour of the old "castle" building that housed a radio station and some of the classrooms. It sits on 500 acres that the church bought seventy or eighty years ago. What a view from the top level! They have two schools in California, so we are hoping to be able to visit them while we are there in April.

On Friday morning, we left Colorado Springs and drove about 300 miles over two mountain passes and alongside some beautiful frozen rivers to Durango, Colorado, and then on to Arizona, Nevada, California, and Texas before returning to Jasper.

A lot has happened since we visited two weeks ago while still in beautiful Colorado. Gas prices are running from $1.69 to $1.99 and grocery prices are a lot higher here than back in Georgia. Hope all of you are doing well. We will be heading that way soon. When we left Colorado on Sunday, we stopped at the Four Corners monument where the four states of Colorado, Utah, New Mexico, and Arizona come together. On Monday, March twenty-seventh, I visited the students on the Navajo Indian Reservation at Kayenta Community School, Kayenta, Arizona. We then drove over to the Hopi Reservation and spoke to the students at the Hotevilla-Bacavi Community School.

While visiting these two schools, we were on the eastern side of the Grand Canyon, and by the time we got to Las Vegas, we had gone around the "big hole in the ground" to the western side. But it was *not* an easy trip. We had left Hotevilla about noon to head west to Las Vegas and stopped in Flagstaff to get the oil changed in the "*AbeMobile*" and in the car. We finally located a Jiffy Lube where the manager told us he could do the service for us including changing out the two fuel filters that I felt might be causing our lack of power going up hills. It is not easy trying to get maneuvered into and out of tight places with the thirty-seven feet of the motor home, plus the tow dolly and the car. After spending a couple of hours there, we were ready to get back onto I-40 heading west. Knowing that I-40 also goes east to Nashville and Knoxville, it was tempting not to make a turn in that direction. As we were pulling out of the Jiffy Lube, the manager noticed one of the tires on the tow dolly looked worn enough to be of some concern. So instead of getting on I-40, we drove around looking for a tire place still open at 5 p.m. We found a Firestone Store and as I tried to pull into their driveway, I got the hitch buried into the pavement. Their driveway was too much of an angle for us and we couldn't move backward or forward. We were stuck! I got out and unhooked the car and the tow dolly and worked for an hour with crowbars and jacks trying to get the hitch unstuck. A local policeman directed traffic around us as we blocked the road. While I got us out of this predicament, the store changed out both of the tires on the tow dolly. We finally left Flagstaff, tired and $225 poorer about 7 p.m.

The "*AbeMobile*" did run much better after getting those filters changed, and we finally got to the Western RV Park in Downtown Las Vegas close to midnight. We were jammed in with other RVs, but full hookups for only ten dollars a night is a great deal. On Thursday, we drove out to the Hoover Dam and took a tour. That is one awesome dam! You have to see it to believe it. We took a lot of pictures. We also visited a few of the casinos and spent some quarters in the slot machines. Las Vegas has to be one of the most lit-up cities anywhere in the world and certainly is on the top of the list of places I have visited on this tour these past two years. We went to a night show at the Mirage Hotel and Casino and saw a beautiful volcano erupt with light and fire. We also went to the Treasure Island Resort and saw a realistic pirate fight between two ships. One of them actually sank in front of our eyes. It was quite a sight to see!

On Friday, I spoke to the students at the Clyde Cox Elementary School in Las Vegas and we then drove on to the Los Angeles area of California. We stayed the weekend on the beach at McGrath State Park. We took Peatie for a walk on the beach and took some beautiful Pacific Ocean sunset pictures. He loves the outdoors and we keep his wings clipped so he won't fly off. I am still trying to teach him the Gettysburg Address, but all he is saying so far is "Hi Baby" and doing a lot of whistling.

On Monday, I drove eighty miles through Los Angeles traffic to Alhambra to speak to the students at Northrup Elementary School. We neither one like all this traffic and are anxious to get back to Jasper's traffic. On Monday evening, we ate dinner with Linda Buchanan. She used to rent a room from me and is now back with the post office in Ventura. It was nice seeing her again. On Tuesday, we located a beautiful campground near Santa Paula on a river with mountains all around and only ninety dollars a week for the two weeks we will be here. We have taken some nice walks and picked up some long tail feathers from some local peacocks. We also took some pictures of them.

On Saturday evening, the eighth of April, we drove about 115 miles south to Huntington Beach, California. We took a walk on the long pier into the Pacific Ocean as we had done last year when we were there. We then had dinner with my cousin, Terry, his wife, Mary, and her mother and other family and friends. I was asked to do another show for them, since some of the family had not seen me last year. We had a nice visit with them and drove back to the "*AbeMobile*" in Far West Resorts RV Park near Santa Paula.

On Sunday, I left Barbara in Ventura with Linda and she spent two nights visiting with her while I drove nearly 850 miles to speak at the Oak Creek Intermediate School in Oakhurst, then over to the

Kennedy Elementary School in San Jose, and then back to pick her up on Tuesday evening. I had spoken at Oak Creek last year on our trip out to California and they were so impressed they wanted me back again this year.

On Friday morning, we got up at 3 a.m. to drive about ninety miles to the Los Angeles airport and Barbara got on her first airplane to fly four hours to Cincinnati, Ohio. We rented a car in Cincinnati and drove two hours down to Elizabethtown, Kentucky, for the Sixth Annual Association of Lincoln Presenters Convention. I am one of the few Abes who has attended all six conventions. We had a nice time visiting with friends, Jim and Mary Sayre, Max and Donna Daniels, B.F. and Dorothy McCleran, the Conines, and many others from all over the country. We visited Abe's birthplace, his boyhood home, museums, and took a train ride. We ate at an old hotel on Saturday evening and had a wonderful prime rib dinner. We packed up and left the motel about 8:30 a.m. on Sunday morning. We had an interesting passenger who we dropped off at the Louisville airport, Teddy Zalewski from Cambridge, Massachusetts. He portrays Teddy Roosevelt all over the country and he and I have known each other since we were at Mount Rushmore in 1991 for the Fiftieth Anniversary Dedication with President Bush. It was nice visiting with him during our ride to the airport.

On Monday, after the trip to Kentucky, I drove eighty-five miles to speak to the students at Emperor Elementary School in San Gabriel. We left beautiful Far West Resort on Wednesday and drove about 125 miles to the Loma Vista Intermediate School in Riverside and then another 100 miles to the Grapevine Elementary School in Vista. We took a nice long walk on the beach. While in Riverside, I drove over to Laguna Beach to see my brother, Barry, and his girlfriend, Rosalind. We went out to eat and had some wonderful lobster tacos.

We left Vista about 11 a.m. and drove 400 miles southeast and spent the night at a Flying J near Tucson, Arizona. On the drive through the desert, we stopped to take some pictures of the giant saguaro cactus.

Each one is as different as a fingerprint. On Saturday, we drove another 600 miles and are now parked at the Monahans Sandhills State Park near Monahans, Texas. Over 10,000 years ago, when the glaciers came through here, created rivers and then dried up or moved further away, all these big, ever-changing sand dunes were created. It is a different kind of beauty watching them blow and move as we sit here.

On April twenty-fourth, we left the beautiful Monahans Sandhills State Park in Texas and headed for Dallas. We stayed at Dallas West RV Park and I spoke to the students at the Parkhill Junior High School in the Richardson area of Dallas on Friday. Two of the children that my friend Bobbie Kerr has adopted go to school there. We went out for pizza with nine of her children. After school, we started on the long trip back to Jasper. We arrived home Saturday afternoon.

We have been busy trying to visit our families and get chores done around the house. Of all the places we have visited these past two years, Jasper sure looks good to us. As the old saying goes, "There's no place like home."

On Monday, May first, I drove the thirty-eight miles to Alpharetta to speak to the students at the Manning Oaks Elementary School. Then I left Barbara and the "*AbeMobile*" parked in Jasper and drove the Lincoln up to Tipp City, Ohio, and spoke to the students at Broadway Elementary School. I had been at that school nine years ago, so it was past time for a re-visit. I then drove further north to the Youngstown area and spoke to students at South Range Elementary School in Canfield and Beloit Elementary School in Beloit. I left there Friday after school and drove to the Chicago area. I walked with Ms. B's fourth grade class from J. B. Nelson Elementary School in Batavia in the big VFW Loyalty Day Parade on Sunday. The entire class entered a poster contest and one of Ms. B's students won the poster contest and a pizza party for the class.

So now you, the reader, have an idea of what it is like to be on the road constantly for two years. It was indeed fun, interesting, and educational; but was also very tiring.

When I got off the road in May of 2000, I needed to find a job. I went to work for the Canton Walmart store for about three months as a cashier and then CSM (Customer Service Manager). I took care of about thirty registers scattered all over the store.

After pestering the local Home Depot there in Canton for a few weeks, I finally talked them into giving me a job. I started out there making three dollars an hour more than Walmart was paying. I started out in the Flooring and Wall Department and then transferred to the Hardware Department, Electrical Department, and ultimately during the three years I was with them, I was the official greeter and lead generator for installed sales.

After getting off the road in 2000 I fixed up the barn for Barbara and I to move into. I didn't want to kick out any of my tenants from the big house. Shortly after we moved in she also moved in three of her grandchildren. It got to be too much for me to work five jobs to support the four of them, and finally after a year or so Barbara and I broke up.

I then dated a lady named Vickey for about three years. We could only see each other on weekends because she provided round-the-clock care for an elderly man in Canton and was only off on weekends. I knew that relationship was not going anywhere.

In 2003, I noticed on the AOL site as I was logging in that they had a contest going on. So I filled out and emailed in a little blurb about, "Abe Lincoln being alive and well in Jasper, Georgia." A couple of months later, I got a call from a lady at AOL Headquarters in Virginia saying that I was one of four winners of their "Fifteen Hours of Fame" Contest. I received about $1,200 worth of electronic stuff and for fifteen hours in October of that year, every time anyone logged on, they got to see a three-minute video of Abe. They had flown in a special film crew and for three days had followed me around and shot a lot of film. It was a nice piece and you can still see it if you visit my Web site.

In 2005, I worked with Jason and his crew supervising the painting project for a big apartment complex in Woodstock, Georgia.

This was also the year I went looking for a new church. My friend, Ed Almond, had told me about a wonderful little church and a great pastor at the Tate Methodist Church. So I visited a few times and then moved my membership there from the big Methodist Church in Jasper. I joined the choir and have enjoyed being there since.

In 2006, I joined the T.A.P., Taxpayer Advocacy Panel, as a volunteer to help see what I could do to help make changes to the IRS. It was interesting and I did get to take some nice trips to Washington, D.C. for annual meetings and Denver and Orlando for meetings. They picked up the tab for all the expenses, but it was time consuming, so I finally after two years had to drop out in early 2008.

Also in 2006, I was hired by Darryl and Eileen Payne, the owners of Hometown Home Health Company in Jasper, only two miles from my home. I quickly learned how to service and set up wheelchairs, hospital beds, motorized chairs for disabled folks to get around in, oxygen concentrators, and lots of things that people might need in their homes. It was hard work, but I enjoyed working for the Paynes. I met a lot of really nice patients as I helped take care of their needs.

In the summer of 2006, I got a call from the President of the River Explorer in New Orleans. He was interested in having Abe entertain his passengers for two weeks in August and September. They paid for my airfare to get to St. Louis to catch the boat, gave me lots of great food to eat, and a nice cabin that would have cost me over $2,500 for the week. I saw a lot of beautiful country as we traveled up and down the Mississippi River. We stopped by to take side trips to sites of historic interest. I was asked to entertain the passengers twice each week for about an hour and for that got paid $1,200 for the week. What a way to make a living!

I was able to get the time off for the trips in 2006 and 2007, but when I asked for the time off to the Time Line Event in September of 2007, Eileen refused to allow me to have the time off, so I quit. Had I not quit, I would not have been able to attend the Reinhardt College event where I met Marti. More about her in another chapter.

In the spring of 2008, Marti and I spent a couple of months down in the Savannah area helping Jason with a big contract he had to convert 200 apartments to dorms for nearby Savannah State College. We stayed out on Tybee Island and were able to take nice long walks on the beach each evening when we finished work. Marti and I love taking walks on the beach and hope to be able to make some more trips to the beaches of Savannah and places in Florida.

During the decade of the 2000s, I have had some personal losses. I have now lost my adoptive mother, Dorothy, my adoptive brother, Mike, my birth mother, Millie, and my birth father, Alex. I have also had some wonderful additions to my family. One of my twins, Jason and his wife, Tiffany, have now made me a grandfather twice with the birth of my five-year-old grandson, Rylan, and his two-year-old sister, Addie. They are a great addition to the family and it is always fun spending time with them.

Lesson to be learned here is: Life is all about choices and priorities. What is most important to do today? Don't put off until tomorrow what you can and should do today.

Romance and Marriage

Did I tell you what happened to me in 1839 in Springfield, Illinois? Things had been going along pretty good in my life since I had become an attorney in '36 and was back and forth between lawyering and politicking. Well, in '39 I had gotten invited to a dance and that is where I met Miss Mary Todd from a rich banking family in Lexington, Kentucky. I didn't really want to be there. I was bashful and shy around women, didn't know how to dance, and was afraid I might step on someone's toes. I did reluctantly agree to dance with her and stepped all over her toes with these size twelve boots. The dance was finally over with, thank goodness for both of us. In spite of the fact that I had stepped all over her toes, we did start going out and finally set a wedding date. But, guess who didn't show up for the wedding? I chickened out! After fifteen months, I was looking in the mirror one day and said, "There is probably not another woman in the whole state of Illinois who would even have anyone as ugly as me. Perhaps I bet-

ter get over there and see if Miss Mary Todd will give me another chance. I went visiting and apologized for not showing up for the previous wedding. I talked her into giving me another chance and we eventually set another wedding date for November fourth of '42. That time, both of us and the preacher showed up. In the next ten years we had four boys: Robert, Eddie, Willie, and Tad.

In September of 2007 I was invited to be part of a four-day timeline event at Reinhardt College in Waleska, Georgia, about eighteen miles from my home in Jasper. There were several actors/actresses there to entertain and educate approximately 3,500 students from all over North Georgia.

Shortly after arriving there on Tuesday morning, I saw *her* for the first time. She was heading off with a long-time friend, John Carruth, from Rome, to speak at a local school. Finding out more about her had to wait until the next day when she would be there on campus with me.

I approached John and asked him who she was and if she was single? He informed me that indeed her name was Martha Ann Smith and she was single. She was dressed in a long dress with hoop skirt, corset, hat, etc. She was playing the part of a Confederate widow and there I was as President Lincoln. When I approached her, she let me know very quickly that she didn't even like Abraham Lincoln. I certainly didn't take "*no*" for an answer and proceeded to follow her everywhere.

She happened to mention that she needed some help getting into and out of her corset, so I was quick to volunteer for that assignment. She later wrote a poem about our meeting and I will share that with you.

To Homer S. Sewell III, giving assistance, accompanied

by charm (and not always becoming a president) needed by a small, southern woman that indeed, could not dress herself.

Image in the Mirror

From the lessons in corset-lacing to garters and cotton hose,
this aloof female gives deepest thanks and fondest memories.

This and the accompanying poem were written by her and given to me on November 30, 2007.

Corset Lessons for a President
It started with lacings, as we both know.
To be helpful you said, but I knew this not so.

As we walked side-by-side to designated places,
I breathed too easily in all of those laces.

You claimed no knowledge of this tedious task.
I had my doubts, until many questions were asked.

My pleas, "They must be tighter," you would not hear.
Not even, "Mr. President, this you must do, my dear."

The man thought he was in absolute total control.
After all, what did a small Southern widow know?

The point being, I could not get dressed
Without steady hands, for they could cause a mess.

What a scandal we were, behind the unlocked door
That would hold no one back, if they wished to see more.

On the second day, his plan was revealed.
A soft kiss on the shoulder and my fate was sealed.

I played my cards, of the crotchless kind,
Surprised he was, but with a "trifle never mind."

Who was this man steadfast in my way?
Each day that passed, not a harsh word could I say.

The garters came next, a slight hand to the thigh.
This president was lucky not to get a black eye.

His eyes caught mine, with a hesitation so small,
He removed them quickly or not be there at all.

The touch done so gentle, with manners that passed
To a Southern Belle many had called a sweet lass.

He knew what he wanted, certain things on a platter.
The way it was served, really did not matter.

I think this is the way that some women fall
Even now to presidents, that will issue a call.

Mr. Lincoln will read these words that have been spoken
And know in his heart the ones that were broken.

It began as a lie, for the truth was not told
And one played a game that became old and cold.

It is said that eyes are mirrors to the soul.
Will we ignore and forget all we played in this role?

The politician prevailed, for they are free of sin.
While their real hearts are probably made of tin.

Bitter-sweet through eternity, it shall always be.
For what became of Lincoln and the Southern widow in me?
—Martha Ann Smith

Before the end of the week, I was in love and knew that I wanted to marry her. I asked her for her phone number, which she reluctantly gave me. Her birthday was coming up and I wanted to take her to dinner for that occasion.

Image in the Mirror

About this time in January of 2008, I was driving to church one Sunday morning and about one mile from the house I got hit head-on in my Toyota pick-up from a car running a stop sign and causing another heavier Ford pick-up to run into me at about thirty-five miles per hour. It totaled my truck and my neck. I went for several months to extensive physical therapy to try to regain some use of my neck and back and to help cut down on the pain.

We started seeing each other, but I needed to break off the relationship that I had had with Vickey for three years. I was finally able to do that when Marti and I left town in April of 2008 to attend a convention in Indiana.

Our relationship grew, but we did have our problems as do a lot of romances. She mentioned to me that she had always wanted to take a trip to Egypt and Israel, since she had studied ancient civilizations in college. We started looking into it and found an upcoming two-week trip in September/October 2008.

We rounded up the bucks to pay for the trip and left Atlanta on September twenty-sixth to fly to New York City and then on to Cairo, Egypt. As we were landing, we could see the big pyramids from the plane and the next morning Marti was finally able to "hug a pyramid" and make a life-long dream come true.

The rest of that week we were all over Egypt in buses, trains, boats on the Nile River, and a camel ride. We were inside some of the tombs, including that of King Tut. The temperatures were as high as 118 degrees on some days, but it was not unbearable. We saw things that most folks can only dream of.

After a week in Egypt, we then crossed the border into Israel and spent a week there. Marti was in tears because she wasn't ready to leave Egypt. We swam in the Dead Sea and got mudded up while there with famous Dead Sea mud. It is supposed to be great for the skin. We spent time in the old walled city of Jerusalem and saw many sites that were as old or older than Jesus. We also got re-baptized in the Jordan River. And we were able to spend a little time visiting with my brother, Gershon, and his wife, Rachel, who live just outside of Jerusalem.

When I realized, in spite of lots of setbacks, that I wanted to marry Marti, I decided to ask permission of her Uncle Paul to marry her. Marti's dad had died many years ago, so Uncle Paul was taking the place of her dad and she was very close to him. I then made plans to take her on a picnic up in the mountains at Cloudland Canyon.

I made some egg salad sandwiches and other picnic items and wrote on a paper plate, "I love you. Will you marry me?"

When we got to the planned picnic table, I laid out our lunch, put a sandwich on the plate, and sat next to her. She was taking her time eating chips and not getting to the sandwich so she could see my proposal message. I got down on my knees in the gravel and waited. I thought she would never get to the message. She finally did see it and then took her sweet time answering my question. I then asked if she would marry me. Finally, after what seemed an eternity, she said "yes."

We set a date for October 4, 2009 and proceeded to make plans for a small family and friends wedding in Lyerly, Georgia. We decided on getting married in her Uncle Paul's small Baptist Church so he could be there. In the meantime, before the wedding, Uncle Paul fell in his apartment and broke his big femur bone in the left leg. There were times that we were not sure he was going to be able to make it to give her away. On the appointed day, someone from the church fetched him in a van and wheelchair and brought him to the church. We had a beautiful wedding with about sixty friends and family in attendance.

After spending some time trying to live on Social Security, my rental income, and being Abe whenever I could, I got a call back in March of 2009 from Classic Manor Builders of Carrollton, Georgia that I had worked with several years ago. They offered me my old territory back. I was to be calling on twenty-six Home Depot stores all over northwest Georgia and into the Chattanooga, Tennessee area. I took the job and am bringing in some more bucks to pay the bills with.

Image in the Mirror

One day in May of 2009, Marti and I were going to one of my Home Depot stores to pick up some items we needed. We stopped in the parking lot to wait for a guy in a pickup about 100 feet in front of us to decide what he was going to do in his truck. As I watched in horror and laid on my horn, he proceeded to back up at high speed right into the front of my new truck. That slapped us both around a bit and Marti jammed her fingers on the dash as she tried to keep from hitting the windshield.

I am still trying to sell the house, barn, and 8.2 acres in Jasper, but with the market conditions where they are now, not much is moving in real estate.

I am still putting out twenty-four real estate directional signs on weekends and that makes some extra money to pay bills with.

On August 29, 2009, as Marti and I were driving her new Kia over to Rome, about thirty miles away, to visit her Uncle Paul in rehab, I was stopped at a traffic light in front of the Braves practice stadium. Another Kia slammed into the back of us at about fifty-five miles per hour. It surprised me how little damage was done to either car. I had Marti taken on a back board by ambulance to the local hospital. She was in a lot of neck and back pain and continues to be even as we go to press. So to say *we* have had our share of "driving accident experiences" in the last two years is an understatement for sure.

I recently went on an interview with Tom at the Booth Western Museum in Cartersville. He is in charge of development and fundraising at the museum and we had a nice visit for about an hour. Marti and I have performed at the museum for two events, including their big sixth birthday celebration on August 22, 2009. Our hopes are that Tom will find funding to pay for us to be there on a regular basis. I have always dreamed of having a fixed-base location where students and adults could come by to see me instead of having to be on the road as much as I have done in the past. Now that Marti is playing the part of Mary Todd Lincoln with me, we can have some fun and make some money at the same time.

Marti and I are living in Cartersville, Georgia, in her town home while we try to get my place in Jasper sold. If we could get hers and mine sold, she wants to move over to Egypt and live in the desert dry heat so her asthma wouldn't bother her as much as it does here. In the meantime, we keep plugging along and making the best of every day.

When the pain gets bad or things don't seem to be going the way we want them to, I always think of what an elderly gentleman told me a couple of years ago. I ran into him in a store somewhere and asked how he was doing? He said, "Homer, every day above ground is a great day!" And that is so true, isn't it? We need to thank God every day for all that *he* gives us and to continue to see what we can do to make the world a better place because *we* were here.

Please invite us to come visit you wherever you are or stop by to see us at the Booth Western Museum in Cartersville, Georgia... if we end up there. In the meantime, please check out my Web site at www.abeusa16.com to see over 200 pages all about what I've been doing since 1975 as Abe. There is some great Civil War music playing and a listing of all the places I have been. Perhaps by the time we get to press with this book, I will have gotten to my last four states for appearances: Louisiana, Montana, Hawaii, and Alaska.

Marti and I are very saddened to report that on March 5, 2010, after another bad fall, Uncle Paul passed away quietly while in a coma. We both miss him greatly. I had only known him for two years but he thought enough of me to call me "son." I took that as a great compliment coming from such a wonderful man of God.

In the early months of 2010 I heard that the Census was looking for folks to help with the 2010 counting of people all over the United States. I figured I could help out and make a little extra money at the same time. So I took the Enumerator test and the Supervisor test. I passed both and waited to hear from them about a job. In April I was offered a job. I went to the four days of training. On the second day I was offered a job to be a Crew Leader Assistant (CLA). I was to be helping my crew leader with his duties in making sure that our dozen Enumerators were doing their job accurately and in a timely fashion. The job will only last for a few weeks but while it lasts it is interesting and helps pay the bills.

Coincidences and Travel List

Coincidences between Abe Lincoln and John Kennedy

1. Both Lincoln and Kennedy were concerned with civil rights.
2. Lincoln was elected president in 1860. Kennedy in 1960.
3. Both were slain on a Friday in the presence of their wives.
4. Both were shot from behind and in the head.
5. Their successors, both named Johnson, were Southern Democrats and both were in the Senate.
6. Andrew Johnson was born in 1808. Lyndon Johnson in 1908.
7. John Wilkes Booth was born in 1839. Lee Harvey Oswald in 1939.
8. Booth and Oswald were southerners who favored unpopular ideas.

9. Both presidents lost children through death while in the White House.
10. Lincoln's secretary, whose name was Kennedy, advised him not to go to the theater.
11. Kennedy's secretary, whose name was Lincoln, advised him not to go to Dallas.
12. John Wilkes Booth shot Lincoln in a theater and ran to a warehouse.
13. Lee Harvey Oswald shot Kennedy from a warehouse and ran to a theater.
14. The names Lincoln and Kennedy each contain seven letters.
15. The names Andrew Johnson and Lyndon Johnson each contain 13 letters.
16. The names John Wilkes Booth and Lee Harvey Oswald each contain 15 letters.
17. Both assassins were killed before being brought to trial.
18. Lincoln was shot in the Ford's Theatre. Kennedy was shot in a Ford car. (And, as a matter of fact, it was a Lincoln.)

Coincidences between Abe Lincoln and Homer S. Sewell III

1. I delivered the Gettysburg Address on radio in Florida in sixth grade.
2. Exactly 100 years, to the minute, after Lincoln was shot, I was working for the White House Communications Agency (Switchboard operator).

3. The president I worked for was Lyndon Johnson. Lincoln's successor was Andrew Johnson.
4. The statue of Lincoln in the Lincoln Memorial was carved from marble taken from the county (Pickens) where I lived in North Georgia.
5. Lincoln's first election to public office (legislator) was 8/4/34. I was born 8/4/43.
6. Lincoln's hat size was seven and a quarter. So is mine.
7. Lincoln's boot size was twelve. So is mine.
8. Lincoln loved to read and needed glasses. So do I.
9. Lincoln had blue eyes. So do I.
10. Lincoln had long, black, unruly hair. So do I.
11. Our weight is about the same: 175 to 180 pounds.
12. Lincoln was raised in the Baptist Church. So was I.
13. I have a mole on my face in almost the same place Lincoln had one.
14. Lincoln was a storekeeper, and inventor, and a poet. So am I.
15. Both of us had a lot of store failures. I've probably had more than he did!
16. Lincoln was in the army in the Black Hawk Indian War for three months in '32. I was in the army in the Vietnam War for three years starting in '64.
17. Lincoln was a great public speaker. So am I.
18. My twins, Kimberly and Jason, were born in Macon County, North Carolina. When Lincoln first moved to Illinois, he lived in Macon County.

19. Lincoln's youngest son was born the day before my twins—April fourth.

20. Lincoln's oldest son was born the day before my oldest son, Chip—August 1.

21. Lincoln's oldest son, Robert, was born in August of 1843. I was born in August of 1943.

22. Lincoln's four sons were born during a ten year period. My three children were born during a ten year period.

23. Both of us built and lived in log cabins.

24. Both of us walked to school.

25. Both of us love people: any age, any color, anywhere!

26. Both of us had two mothers.

27. Lincoln was shot by John Wilkes Booth. I had some surgery done in 1989 by Dr. Arthur Booth of Atlanta.

28. Lincoln was chosen to be one of the four presidents carved onto Mount Rushmore. I was chosen by the National Park Service to be part of the Fiftieth Anniversary Celebration/Dedication during the week of July 4, 1991.

29. Neither of us ever drank any type of alcohol or smoked anything.

30. Right before his death, Lincoln told Mary he wanted to take a trip to the Holy Land. I spent two weeks in Israel in October of 1993 and again in 2008.

31. I recently found out I was born Jewish and have eighteen generations of Rabbis in my family. Lincoln loved Jews and had a lot of Rabbis for friends.

Image in the Mirror

32. My newly-found brother, Stuart, used to live in Hingham, Massachusetts, next door to a Lincoln descended from the Lincolns that settled there in 1636.

33. Lincoln stayed with families like Judge David Wills in Gettysburg. I stay with families in my travels around the country.

34. Lincoln had suits made by Brooks Brothers. I have a coat made by them.

35. Both of us were named after our grandfathers.

36. The names Abraham Lincoln & Homer Sewell III each contain 14 letters.

The following pages contain a listing of the places I've visited since 1975 and up until the time we went to press. I thought it might be interesting for you to see if you recognize any of these places.

	Date	Location Name	City	State	Numbers
1	Oct 00 75	Aloma Elem School	Winter Pk	FL	500
2	Oct 00 75	Lake Como Elem School	Orlando	FL	400
3	Jan 00 76	Joe B. McCawley Log Cabin 83rd Birth	Sanford	FL	250
4	Apr 00 76	Red Bug Elem School	Casselberry	FL	350
5	Jul 00 76	Winter Park Mall	Winter Pk	FL	300
6	Jul 00 76	Bicentennial Parade	Franklin	NC	9000
7	May 00 77	Cowee Elem School	Franklin	NC	400
8	Feb 00 78	Midfield Toyota Dealership	Birmingham	AL	100
9	July 4 78	Festival in the Park	Punta Gorda	FL	15000
10	Aug 00 78	Seminole County Library	Casselberry	FL	50
11	Jan 1 79	St. Mark AME Church Emancipation	Orlando	FL	1200
12	Feb 00 79	Dream Lake Elem School	Apopka	FL	400

13	Feb 00 79	Spring Lake Elem School	Altamonte Springs	FL	500
14	Feb 00 79	Apopka Jr. High School	Apopka	FL	500
15	Feb 00 79	Phyllis Wheatley Elem School	Apopka	FL	800
16	Feb 00 79	Boy Scout Eagle Court of Honor	Longwood	FL	100
17	Apr 00 79	Milwee Middle School	Longwood	FL	400
18	Jul 4 79	Republican Party Float in Parade	Maitland	FL	8000
19	Jul 4 79	Altamonte Mall Celebration	Altamonte Springs	FL	1000
20	Jul 4 79	2nd Annual Festival in the Park	Punta Gorda	FL	12000
21	Jul 00 79	Republican Party Dance	Altamonte Springs	FL	250
22	Sep 00 79	Republican Party Picnic for Candidates	Winter Pk	FL	500
23	Oct 00 79	Boy Scout Camporee	DeLand	FL	300
24	Nov 00 79	Veteran's Day Parade	Orlando	FL	3000
25	Feb 00 80	Lake Sybelia Elem School	Maitland	FL	500
26	Feb 00 80	Art Grindle for Senate Kickoff	Five Central	FL	2000
27	Feb 00 80	Reserve Officers' Assoc Dinner	Orlando	FL	500
28	Feb 00 80	Sweetwater Academy School	Longwood	FL	100
29	Feb 00 80	Conway Methodist Kindergarten School	Orlando	FL	100
30	Feb 12 80	Florida Festival, Sea World	Orlando	FL	20000
31	Mar 00 80	Shot TV Commercial- Don Reid Ford	Maitland	FL	10

32	Apr 00 80	"Stand Up for America" Celebration	Orlando	FL	5000
33	Apr 00 80	Church Convention	Williamsburg	VA	200
34	May 00 80	Lake Mary Day C of C Parade	Lake Mary	FL	1000
35	Jun 00 80	Real Estate Company Sales Meeting	Maitland	FL	100
36	Jun 00 80	Central Florida Zoo Fund Raising	Sanford	FL	250
37	July 27 80	CP Benefit at Civic Center	Altamonte Springs	FL	200
38	Aug 2 80	Benefit for MDA	Daytona Beach	FL	300
39	Aug 31 80	CP Telethon at Sheraton	Orlando	FL	500
40	Sep 12 80	Kiwanis Breakfast Meeting	Altamonte Springs	FL	50
41	Oct 30 80	Winter Springs Elem School	Winter Springs	FL	400
42	Jan 31 81	Reserve Officers' Assoc Dinner	Orlando	FL	250
43	Feb 9 81	Ferncreek Elem School	Orlando	FL	300
44	Feb 11 81	Woodlands Elem School	Longwood	FL	400
45	Feb 12 81	Pershing Elem School	Orlando	FL	350
46	Feb 12 81	St. Marks Kindergarten School	Altamonte Springs	FL	200
47	Feb 12 81	All American Skating Rink	Altamonte Springs	FL	500
48	Feb 20 81	Lincoln Day Dinner Republican Party	Altamonte Springs	FL	300
49	Feb 22 81	Humane Society Benefit	Longwood	FL	60
50	Mar 15 81	St. John's Missionary Baptist Church	Sanford	FL	150
51	Apr 4 81	"Stand Up for America" Celebration	Orlando	FL	8000

52	May 1 81	Good Shepherd Catholic Church School	Orlando	FL	500
53	May 5 81	South Seminole Middle School	Casselberry	FL	500
54	June 23 81	Cub Scouts at Naval Base	Orlando	FL	250
55	July 2 81	Seminole County Library	Casselberry	FL	100
56	Sep 9 81	Florida Assoc of Christian Schools Conv	Daytona Beach	FL	1000
57	Sep 10 81	Fire Prevention Week Celebration	Orlando	FL	300
58	Sep 15 81	Tom Skinner Club	Orlando	FL	50
59	Oct 19 81	Warner Christian School	South Daytona	FL	60
60	Oct 21 81	United Nations Day, Altamonte Mall	Altamonte Springs	FL	200
61	Nov 3 81	Women's Sorority	Lake Mary	FL	30
62	Nov 7 81	Bowl America Lanes	Sanford	FL	150
63	Nov 14 81	Sts. Peter & Paul Catholic Church Carn	Goldenrod	FL	1000
64	Nov 17 81	Ivey Lane Elem School	Orlando	FL	800
65	Nov 21 81	Travelers Protective Assn State Conv	Orlando	FL	50
66	Nov 21 81	Home Show at Fairgrounds	Orlando	FL	500
67	Dec 10 81	Sertoma Club	College Park	FL	30
68	Jan 9 82	Florida Music Ed Assn Conv	Daytona Beach	FL	2000
69	Jan 13 82	Colonial High School	Orlando	FL	2000
70	Jan 15 82	Lyman High School Civics Class	Longwood	FL	30
71	Jan 20 82	Rolling Hills Moravian Church Sr	Longwood	FL	50
72	Jan 24 82	Ronald McDonald's House Benefit	Orange City	FL	500

73	Jan 29 82	Charlotte County Republican Party LI	Punta Gorda	FL	400
74	Feb 4 82	Milwee Middle School	Longwood	FL	200
75	Feb 6 82	Private Birthday Party	Orlando	FL	25
76	Feb 7 82	Heritage Baptist Church	Forest City	FL	50
77	Feb 8 82	Pine Hills Christian Church School	Orlando	FL	50
78	Feb 8 82	Wheatley Elem School	Apopka	FL	900
79	Feb 9 82	Wekiva Elem School	Longwood	FL	350
80	Feb 10 82	St. Mark's Kindergarten School	Altamonte Springs	FL	200
81	Feb 10 82	Geneva Elem School	Oviedo	FL	300
82	Feb 10 82	Pace School	Forest City	FL	80
83	Feb 11 82	Audobon Park Elem School	Orlando	FL	500
84	Feb 11 82	Longwood Tourist Club	Longwood	FL	80
85	Feb 12 82	Cheney Elem School	Orlando	FL	500
86	Feb 12 82	Carole Nelson TV Show, Ch 9	Orlando	FL	NA
87	Feb 12 82	Osceola Cty Republican Party Dinner	Osceola	FL	200
88	Feb 12 82	Private Party for Nurses	Longwood	FL	30
89	Feb 22 82	Cub Scout Pack 540, Blue/Gold Banq	Casselberry	FL	300
90	Mar 3 82	Action Years Seniors	Maitland	FL	30
91	Mar 4 82	35-Live Show, TV Ch. 35	Orlando	FL	NA
92	Mar 6 82	Fourth Annual Goldenrod Parade	Goldenrod	FL	5000
93	Mar 13 82	Founder's Day Parade	Orange City	FL	6000
94	Mar 13 82	Lee Cty Republican Party Lincoln Day	Ft. Myers	FL	400
95	Mar 18 82	South Seminole Seniors	Casselberry	FL	80

96	Mar 24 82	Home Show Log Cabin Display	Tampa	FL	5000
97	Apr 2 82	Fla Real Estate Expo	Orlando	FL	3000
98	Apr 17 82	Historic Kingston Festival	Kingston	GA	3000
99	Apr 30 82	"I Love America Week" Celebration	Maitland	FL	500
100	May 17 82	Action Years Seniors Club	Orlando	FL	30
101	May 25 82	St. John Vianney Catholic School	Orlando	FL	400
102	May 27 82	Pine Hills Christian Church School	Orlando	FL	300
103	May 31 82	DeLand Jr. High School Memorial Day	DeLand	FL	800
104	June 13 82	"Stand Up For America," Third Annual	Orlando	FL	8000
105	July 4 82	Rolling Hills Moravian Church	Longwood	FL	200
106	July 17 82	"Here's To The Red, White, & Blue"	Titusville	FL	200
107	Aug 15 82	Orlando General Hospital Groundbreak	Orlando	FL	300
108	Aug 24 82	College Park Lions Club Dinner	Orlando	FL	30
109	Sep 24 82	First Pres. Church Senior's Group	Mt. Dora	FL	25
110	Nov 6 82	Old Time Musical Variety Show at Chu	Orlando	FL	100
111	Nov 18 82	Cub Scout Pack 629 Pioneers' Pageant	Maitland	FL	200
112	Nov 20 82	Holiday Parade	Winter Springs	FL	3000
113	Nov 29 82	World Book State Conv. Dinner	Orlando	FL	150

Image in the Mirror

114	Dec 14 82	Liberty National Bank Grand Opening	Longwood	FL	300
115	Dec 21 82	Kiwanis Breakfast Meeting	Ormond Beach	FL	40
116	Jan 26 83	Jackson Heights Middle School	Oviedo	FL	350
117	Feb 2 83	Cub Scout Pack 234	Longwood	FL	20
118	Feb 7 83	Phyllis Wheatley Elem School	Apopka	FL	500
119	Feb 8 83	Orlando Junior Academy School	Orlando	FL	300
120	Feb 8 83	Brownie Scout Troop 774	Altamonte Springs	FL	30
121	Feb 9 83	Apopka Elem School	Apopka	FL	700
122	Feb 9 83	St. Mark's Kindergarten School	Altamonte Springs	FL	200
123	Feb 9 83	Altamonte Elem School	Altamonte Springs	FL	100
124	Feb 10 83	Apopka Jr. High School	Apopka	FL	1000
125	Feb 10 83	Dream Lake Elem School	Apopka	FL	700
126	Feb 11 83	Southlake Elem School	Titusville	FL	700
127	Feb 12 83	All American Skating Rink	Altamonte Springs	FL	300
128	Feb 14 83	Sweetheart Banquet, First Baptist Ch	Ormond Beach	FL	60
129	Feb 24 83	Highlands Elem School PTA	Daytona Beach	FL	100
130	Feb 28 83	Newcomers & Social Club	Mt. Dora	FL	50
131	Mar 5 83	Frontier Day Parade, 25th Annual	Orange City	FL	5500
132	Mar 21 83	Apopka Elem School	Apopka	FL	700
133	Apr 15 83	Teague Middle School	Forest City	FL	400
134	May 25 83	LaPetite Academy School Grad	Maitland	FL	50

135	May 31 83	DeLand Jr. High School Memorial Day	DeLand	FL	1000
136	July 4 83	Patriotic Program at Resort	Big Canoe	GA	1000
137	Sep 17 83	Edwards Baking Company Picnic	Atlanta	GA	700
138	Feb 7 84	Cedardale Log Homes Dinner	Marietta	GA	10
139	Feb 10 84	Brockett Elem School	Atlanta	GA	500
140	Feb 10 84	Mountain Park Elem School	Atlanta	GA	500
141	Feb 12 84	Church St Station Antique Depot	Orlando	FL	2000
142	Feb 13 84	Altamonte Elem School	Altamonte Springs	FL	200
143	Feb 13 84	St. Mark's Kindergarten School	Altamonte Springs	FL	300
144	Mar 14 84	Wood Acres Country School	Roswell	GA	750
145	Mar 14 84	Cedardale Log Home Show	Atlanta	GA	10000
146	Dec 4 84	McEver Elem School	Gainesville	GA	750
147	Jan 16 85	Arts Council Meeting	Gainesville	GA	10
148	Feb 00 85	First Baptist Church	Jasper	GA	200
149	Feb 00 85	Jasper Elem School	Jasper	GA	110
150	Feb 00 85	Fair Street Elem School	Gainesville	GA	650
151	Feb 00 85	Enota Elem School	Gainesville	GA	800
152	Feb 00 85	Lanier Elem School	Gainesville	GA	650
153	Feb 00 85	Jones Elem School	Gainesville	GA	210
154	Feb 00 85	Tadmore Elem School	Gainesville	GA	500
155	Feb 00 85	Lochmar Elem School	Palm Bay	FL	900
156	Feb 00 85	Mountain Park Elem School	Stone Mtn.	GA	400
157	Feb 00 85	Marble Valley Historical Society	Jasper	GA	30
158	May 00 85	Warren Road Elem School	Augusta	GA	500

159	May 00 85	Visit with Base Commander Thomas	Ft. Gordon	GA	100
160	May 00 85	Lawrenceville Elem School	Lawrenceville	GA	1000
161	Jun 00 85	Bent Tree Resort Club Dinner	Jasper	GA	50
162	Jul 00 85	July 4 Celebration	Big Canoe	GA	1000
163	Oct 00 85	N.M.A. Conv, MGM Grand Hotel	Las Vegas	NV	5000
164	Nov 00 85	Pickens Tech College Real Estate Class	Jasper	GA	30
165	Nov 00 85	Lyndhurst Foundation	Chattanooga	TN	25
166	Dec 00 85	Lockheed Management Assn Christmas	Atlanta	GA	1000
167	Dec 00 85	Cain & Bultman-York A/C Sales Meet/D	Atlanta	GA	150
168	Feb 00 86	Riverside Elem School	Mableton	GA	500
169	Feb 00 86	Powder Springs Elem School	Powder Springs	GA	500
170	Feb 00 86	Sardis Elem School	Gainesville	GA	500
171	Feb 00 86	Oakwood Elem School	Gainesville	GA	700
172	Feb 00 86	Wauka Mt. Elem School	Gainesville	GA	550
173	Feb 00 86	Pine Street Elem School	Conyers	GA	750
174	Feb 00 86	Gwin Oaks Elem School	Lawrenceville	GA	200
175	Feb 00 86	Jasper Elem School	Jasper	GA	100
176	Feb 00 86	Seventh Day Adventist School	Ellijay	GA	100
177	Feb 00 86	Sarah Smith Elem School	Atlanta	GA	500
178	Feb 00 86	Cub Scout Pack 225 Blue/Gold Banq	Gainesville	GA	100
179	May 00 86	Pickens High School Band Concert	Jasper	GA	200
180	Jul 00 86	Lincoln Boyhood Drama Amphi Dedica	Lincoln City	IN	250

181	Jul 00 86	Community Care Center	Dale	IN	50
182	Aug 00 86	"Indiana Adventure '86" Tourism Prom	Indianapolis	IN	500
183	Sep 00 86	Nat. Conf. Editorial Writers, 40th C	Charleston	SC	500
184	Oct 00 86	Look-Alike Contest	Hodgenville	KY	1000
185	Dec 00 86	Pizza Expo, Lincoln Food Service Prod	Orlando	FL	5000
186	Feb 00 87	Annistown Elem School	Annistown	GA	1000
187	Feb 00 87	Mountain Park Elem School	Lilburn	GA	600
188	Feb 00 87	B. B. Harris Elem School	Duluth	GA	900
189	Feb 00 87	St. Matthews Catholic School	Mt. Vernon	IN	120
190	Feb 00 87	Mt. Vernon Jr. High School	Mt. Vernon	IN	400
191	Feb 00 87	Mt. Vernon High School	Mt. Vernon	IN	1100
192	Feb 00 87	Medco Center Nursing Home	Mt. Vernon	IN	150
193	Feb 00 87	Hedges Elem School	Mt. Vernon	IN	400
194	Feb 00 87	West Elem School	Mt. Vernon	IN	300
195	Feb 00 87	Marrs Elem School	Mt. Vernon	IN	300
196	Feb 00 87	Farmersville Elem School	Mt. Vernon	IN	300
197	Feb 00 87	General Electric "Elfun Society" Dinner	Evansville	IN	80
198	Feb 00 87	Seniors Luncheon	Freehome	GA	30
199	Feb 00 87	Flowery Branch Elem School	Gainesville	GA	500
200	Feb 00 87	St. John Newman Catholic School	Lawrenceville	GA	200
201	Feb 00 87	Lilburn Elem School	Lilburn	GA	800
202	Mar 00 87	Kennesaw College History Class	Kennesaw	GA	40
203	Apr 00 87	Jr. ROTC Drill meet	Marietta	GA	1000

204	May 00 87	Mt. Laurel Festival, 23rd Annual	Clarkesville	GA	5000
205	May 00 87	Southwest Atlanta Christian Academy	Atlanta	GA	100
206	Jun 00 87	United Methodist Church	Fields Chapel	GA	100
207	Sep 00 87	Riverside Elem School	Mableton	GA	500
208	Sep 00 87	Tadmore Elem School	Gainesville	GA	600
209	Sep 00 87	Credit Card Software Sales Meeting	Orlando	FL	200
210	Oct 00 87	Masonic Lodge 96	Atlanta	GA	50
211	Oct 00 87	Scottish Rite K.C.C.H. Meeting	Atlanta	GA	50
212	Feb 00 88	Jones Elem School	Gainesville	GA	330
213	Feb 00 88	Sugar Hill Elem School	Buford	GA	450
214	Feb 00 88	Harmony Elem School	Buford	GA	350
215	Mar 00 88	A Hike With Abe	Big Canoe	GA	25
216	Mar 00 88	Jasper Elem School	Jasper	GA	200
217	Aug 00 88	Jasper Lions Club	Jasper	GA	50
218	Oct 00 88	Marble Festival Parade	Jasper	GA	2000
219	Oct 00 88	Gold Rush Days Parade	Dahlonega	GA	50000
220	Oct 00 88	Royal Arch Masonic Meeting	Jasper	GA	15
221	Oct 00 88	Lions Club Ladies' Night	Canton	GA	100
222	Oct 00 88	Little Country Store Promo	Dahlonega	GA	210
223	Oct 00 88	"Stay in School" Program, Corps Eng.	Carter's Lake	GA	300
224	Oct 00 88	Little Country Store Promo	Dahlonega	GA	250
225	Feb 00 89	Marble Valley Historical Society	Jasper	GA	50
226	Feb 00 89	Berkeley Lake Elem School	Duluth	GA	1200
227	Feb 00 89	Electrolux Promo, Gwinnett Mall	Duluth	GA	5000
228	Feb 00 89	Arcado Elem School	Duluth	GA	950

229	Feb 00 89	Murdock Elem School	Marietta	GA	1300
230	Mar 31 89	Knollwood Elem School	Decator	GA	630
231	Mar 31 89	A. L. Williams Ins. Sales Rally	Atlanta	GA	2000
232	June 7 89	Pickens Middle School	Jasper	GA	250
233	June 15 89	Census Bureau Office	Marietta	GA	50
234	July 12 89	Pickens Star Masonic Lodge 220	Jasper	GA	25
235	July 17 89	Suwanee United Methodist Church Home	Suwanee	GA	100
236	Oct 5 89	American President Intermodal Confer	Atlanta	GA	250
237	Oct 26 89	"Stay in School" Program, Corps Eng.	Carter's Lake	GA	600
238	Nov 18 89	High Meadows School Caboose/Library	Roswell	GA	300
239	Feb 8 90	Winston Elem School	Winston	GA	500
240	Feb 8 90	Lanier Middle School	Buford	GA	1000
241	Feb 12 90	Rebecca Minor Elem School	Lilburn	GA	1400
242	Feb 13 90	Dacula Elem School	Dacula	GA	800
243	Feb 22 90	North Hall Middle School PTA Meet	Gainesville	GA	50
244	Feb 24 90	Smyrna Presbyterian Church Seniors	Smyrna	GA	50
245	Feb 28 90	First United Methodist Church	Marietta	GA	450
246	Mar 2 90	Jasper Elem School	Jasper	GA	1000
247	Apr 11 90	Bagley Middle School	Chatsworth	GA	750
248	Apr 24 90	R. D. Head Elem School	Lilburn	GA	950
249	May 9 90	Int'n Intermodal Expo & Int'n Read	Atlanta	GA	10000
250	May 15 90	Bells Ferry Elem School	Marietta	GA	750

251	May 26 90	Masonic District Deputies Meeting	Macon	GA	50
252	May 26 90	Masonic Children's Home	Macon	GA	50
253	May 28 90	Chambrel of Roswell Retirement Ctr	Roswell	GA	100
254	May 31 90	Knights of Mecca Masonic Dinner	Savannah	GA	50
255	June 5 90	Eastern Star 479 Meeting	Jasper	GA	50
256	July 4 90	Salute to America Parade	Atlanta	GA	450000
257	July 14 90	Woodruff Boy Scout Camp Parents' Ngt.	Blue Ridge	GA	400
258	July 21 90	Civil War Encampment, Atl. Historical	Atlanta	GA	2000
259	July 28 90	Masonic Lodge 154	Calhoun	GA	30
260	July 31 90	Life Chiropractic Class Video Project	Marietta	GA	50
261	Aug 2 90	Cohutta Masonic Lodge	Cohutta	GA	20
262	Aug 3 90	Palestine Masonic Lodge 486	Atlanta	GA	50
263	Aug 6 90	Super Singles Group, J.U.M.C.	Jasper	GA	20
264	Aug 11 90	Wing Ding Contest Judge	Stone Mtn.	GA	5000
265	Aug 16 90	Rabun Gap Masonic Lodge 265 Picnic	Lake Burton	GA	50
266	Sep 4 90	Mount Pleasant High School	Mt. Pleasant	TN	300
267	Sep 5 90	Waldron Middle School	Waldron	AR	600
268	Sep 6 90	Glover Elem School	Broken Bow	OK	100
269	Sep 7 90	Bowie Elem School	Ennis	TX	600
270	Sep 7 90	Cross Roads Isd School	Malakoff	TX	400
271	Sep 10 90	Burkeville Elem School	Burkeville	TX	300
272	Sep 10 90	Groves Elem School	Groves	TX	450
273	Sep 11 90	Laura Reeves Elem School	Silsbee	TX	640

274	Sep 11 90	Silsbee Middle School	Silsbee	TX	600
275	Sep 12 90	Read Turrentine Elem School	Silsbee	TX	650
276	Sep 13 90	Redd School	Houston	TX	200
277	Sep 14 90	Deep Wood Elem School	Round Rock	TX	650
278	Sep 17 90	Windcrest Elem School	San Antonio	TX	600
279	Sep 17 90	Jourdanton Jr. High School	Jourdanton	TX	1090
280	Sep 18 90	China Intermediate School	Brady	TX	300
281	Sep 19 90	Grandfalls School	Grandfalls	TX	250
282	Sep 20 90	Northridge Elem School	Lubbock	TX	650
283	Sep 20 90	Williams Elem School	Lubbock	TX	500
284	Sep 21 90	Estacado Jr High School	Plainview	TX	450
285	Sep 21 90	Maedgen Elem School	Lubbock	TX	500
286	Sep 22 90	Methodist Hospital Visits	Lubbock	TX	100
287	Sep 24 90	Childress Elem School	Childress	TX	600
288	Sep 25 90	Valley School	Turkey	TX	300
289	Sep 25 90	Notre Dame Elem School	Wichita Falls	TX	200
290	Sep 26 90	Ranchwood Elem School	Yukon	OK	400
291	Sep 26 90	Choctaw Elem School	Choctaw	OK	500
292	Sep 27 90	Justice School	Wewoka	OK	120
293	Sep 27 90	Wetumka School	Wetumka	OK	320
294	Sep 28 90	Lee Elem School	Tulsa	OK	400
295	Sep 28 90	J. F. Kennedy School	Oilton	OK	300
296	Oct 1 90	Fredonia High School	Fredonia	KS	250
297	Oct 1 90	Fredonia Elem School	Fredonia	KS	250
298	Oct 1 90	Arkansas City High School	Arkansas City	KS	600
299	Oct 2 90	Attica Public School	Attica	KS	250
300	Oct 2 90	South Haven School	South Haven	KS	250
301	Oct 3 90	Graber Elem School	Hutchinson	KS	350
302	Oct 3 90	Chase School	Chase	KS	200
303	Oct 4 90	Lyons Kiwanis Breakfast	Lyons	KS	25
304	Oct 4 90	Lyons High School	Lyons	KS	500
305	Oct 4 90	South Elem School	Lyons	KS	200

306	Oct 4 90	Lyons Seniors Center	Lyons	KS	50
307	Oct 4 90	Lyons Elem School	Lyons	KS	200
308	Oct 4 90	Rice County Hospital Visits	Lyons	KS	50
309	Oct 5 90	Ruppenthal Middle School	Russell	KS	250
310	Oct 5 90	Chaflin Elem School	Chaflin	KS	150
311	Oct 9 90	Norcross Elem School	Norcross	GA	1200
312	Oct 10 90	South Barber High School	Kiowa	KS	250
313	Oct 11 90	Mullinville Jr High School	Mullinville	KS	200
314	Oct 11 90	Meade Elem School	Meade	KS	300
315	Oct 12 90	Straight School	Straight	KS	40
316	Oct 12 90	Pritchett School	Pritchett	CO	100
317	Oct 15 90	Swink Elem School	Swink	CO	130
318	Oct 15 90	Swink High School	Swink	CO	200
319	Oct 15 90	Swink Community	Swink	CO	50
320	Oct 16 90	Colorado Boy's Ranch	Lajuanta	CO	50
321	Oct 17 90	East Middle School	Aurora	CO	750
322	Oct 17 90	South Elem School	Castle Rock	CO	600
323	Oct 18 90	Prospect Elem School	Keenesburg	CO	100
324	Oct 20 90	Pickens Cty Middle School Parade	Jasper	GA	3000
325	Oct 22 90	B. B. Harris Elem School	Duluth	GA	200
326	Oct 25 90	R. B. Stewart Elem School	Leoti	KS	400
327	Oct 25 90	Sharon Springs School	Sharon Springs	KS	400
328	Oct 26 90	Wakeeney Elem School	Wakeeney	KS	500
329	Oct 29 90	Phillipsburg Mid/ High School	Phillipsburg	KS	450
330	Oct 29 90	Callaway Public School	Callaway	NE	250
331	Oct 30 90	Chambers Public School	Chambers	NE	200
332	Oct 30 90	Spalding School	Spalding	NE	150
333	Oct 31 90	Norris Elem School	Omaha	NE	500
334	Oct 31 90	Northside Elem School	Nebraska City	NE	350
335	Nov 1 90	Skyline Elem School	Elkhorn	NE	400
336	Nov 1 90	Pawnee Elem School	Omaha	NE	500

337	Nov 2 90	St. Wenceslaus Catholic School	Omaha	NE	400
338	Nov 2 90	G. Stanley Hall Elem School	Lavista	NE	400
339	Nov 5 90	Grant City High School	Grant City	MO	200
340	Nov 5 90	Grant City Elem School	Grant City	MO	300
341	Nov 6 90	Cameron High School	Cameron	MO	500
342	Nov 6 90	Lathrop Elem School	Lathrop	MO	600
343	Nov 7 90	Spring Garden Middle School	St. Joseph	MO	400
344	Nov 7 90	Lucy Franklin Elem School	Blue Springs	MO	600
345	Nov 8 90	St. Regis Elem School	Kansas City	KS	400
346	Nov 8 90	Dobbs Elem School	Kansas City	KS	575
347	Nov 9 90	Louisburg Elem/ Jr High School	Louisburg	KS	850
348	Nov 9 90	Turner Elem School	Kansas City	KS	450
349	Nov 12 90	Sante Fe Trail Jr High School	Olathe	KS	200
350	Nov 12 90	Raymore Elem School	Raymore	MO	800
351	Nov 13 90	Osawatomie Middle School	Osawatomie	KS	300
352	Nov 13 90	Pleasonton Elem School	Pleasonton	KS	500
353	Nov 14 90	Prairie View Elem School	Parker	KS	150
354	Nov 14 90	Humboldt High School	Humboldt	KS	300
355	Nov 15 90	Yates Center Elem School	Yates Center	KS	450
356	Nov 15 90	Yates Center High School	Yates Center	KS	150
357	Nov 16 90	Florence Middle School	Florence	KS	100
358	Nov 16 90	Abilene Elem School	Valley Center	KS	500
359	Nov 19 90	St. Mary's School	Salina	KS	500
360	Nov 19 90	Dwight Elem School	Dwight	KS	300
361	Nov 20 90	Custer Hill Elem School	Ft. Riley	KS	250
362	Nov 20 90	Westmoreland High School	Westmoreland	KS	100
363	Nov 27 90	Riverbend Elem School	Gainesville	GA	400
364	Nov 28 90	Gladden Elem School	Belton	MO	550

365	Nov 29 90	Southwood Elem School	Raytown	MO	450
366	Nov 29 90	Robinson Elem School	Kansas City	MO	500
367	Nov 30 90	Butcher-Greene Elem School	Grandview	MO	450
368	Nov 30 90	Belvidere Elem School	Grandview	MO	400
369	Dec 3 90	McIntire Elem School	Fulton	MO	350
370	Dec 4 90	Cambridge Elem School	Belton	MO	650
371	Dec 4 90	Warford Elem School	Kansas City	MO	600
372	Dec 5 90	Lansing Middle School	Lansing	KS	400
373	Dec 5 90	Oskaloosa Elem School	Oskaloosa	KS	500
374	Dec 6 90	Potwin Elem School	Topeka	KS	300
375	Dec 6 90	McClure Elem School	Topeka	KS	350
376	Dec 7 90	Tecumseh South Elem School	Tecumseh	KS	450
377	Dec 7 90	Meadowmere Elem School	Grandview	MO	350
378	Dec 10 90	Waterville Elem School	Waterville	KS	450
379	Dec 10 90	Nemaha Valley School	Seneca	KS	380
380	Dec 11 90	St. Charles Catholic School	Kansas City	KS	350
381	Dec 11 90	Indian Trail Jr High School	Olathe	KS	500
382	Dec 12 90	Lebanon Jr High School	Lebanon	KS	850
383	Dec 12 90	Highlandville Elem School	Highlandville	MO	350
384	Dec 13 90	Mountain View Elem School	Mountain View	MO	750
385	Dec 13 90	Pleasant View Elem School	Springfield	MO	800
386	Dec 14 90	Dora School	Dora	MO	250
387	Dec 14 90	Gainesville Elem School	Gainesville	MO	400
388	Dec 17 90	St. Theresa Elem School	Glennonville	MO	70
389	Dec 17 90	Scott County Central Elem School	Sikeston	MO	250
390	Dec 18 90	Central Elem School	Harrisburg	AR	300
391	Jan 3 91	Snyder Park Elem School	Springfield	OH	350
392	Jan 3 91	Malinta Elem School	Malinta	OH	175
393	Jan 4 91	Eastwood Jr High School	Pemberville	OH	400

394	Jan 4 91	Longfellow Elem School	Fostoria	OH	350
395	Jan 7 91	East Palestine Middle School	East Palestine	OH	550
396	Jan 7 91	S.C. Dennis Elem School	Toronto	OH	280
397	Jan 8 91	Parkside Middle School	Westlake	OH	380
398	Jan 8 91	Cedarbrook Elem School	Painesville	OH	350
399	Jan 9 91	Holden Elem School	Kent	OH	350
400	Jan 9 91	Central Elem School	Kent	OH	400
401	Jan 10 91	Roosevelt Elem School	Akron	OH	400
402	Jan 10 91	Walls Elem School	Kent	OH	550
403	Jan 11 91	Hazel Harvey Elem Schol	Doylestown	OH	550
404	Jan 14 91	Liberty Elem School	North Ridgeville	OH	600
405	Jan 14 91	St. Mary's School	Avon	OH	200
406	Jan 15 91	Lakeview School	Lorain	OH	550
407	Jan 15 91	Mapleton Middle School	Nova	OH	200
408	Jan 16 91	Baker Middle School	Marion	OH	500
409	Jan 16 91	Clinton Middle School	Columbus	OH	550
410	Jan 17 91	McArthur Elem School	McArthur	OH	450
411	Jan 17 91	Meigs Jr High School	Middleport	OH	500
412	Jan 17 91	Meigs High School	Middleport	OH	500
413	Jan 18 91	Campbell Elem School	Ironton	OH	500
414	Jan 18 91	Hager Elem School	Ashland	KY	300
415	Jan 19 91	Boat/Sports Show	Cincinnati	OH	10000
416	Jan 21 91	Lexington Christian Academy School	Lexington	KY	275
417	Jan 21 91	Paint Lick Elem School	Paint Lick	KY	260
418	Jan 22 91	Meece Middle School	Somerset	KY	500
419	Jan 23 91	Munfordville Elem School	Munfordville	KY	550
420	Jan 23 91	Southern/Northern Jr High School	Somerset	KY	500
421	Jan 24 91	Morton's Gap School	Morton's Gap	KY	350
422	Jan 24 91	Clay Elem School	Clay	KY	530
423	Jan 25 91	Clark Elem School	Paducah	KY	750

Image in the Mirror

424	Jan 25 91	Harrisburg Jr High School	Harrisburg	IL	750
425	Jan 25 91	Franklin Park Elem School	Salem	IL	700
426	Jan 28 91	Altamont Elem School	Altamont	IL	600
427	Jan 28 91	Estelle Kampmeyer Elem School	O'Fallon	IL	700
428	Jan 29 91	Grant Elem School	Fairview Hgts	IL	400
429	Jan 30 91	Columbia Elem School	Columbia	IL	500
430	Jan 31 91	Festus Elem School	Festus	MO	1100
431	Jan 31 91	Lincoln Elem School	St. Charles	MO	250
432	Feb 1 91	Beirbaum Elem School	St. Louis	MO	800
433	Feb 1 91	Koch Elem School	St. Louis	MO	500
434	Feb 2 91	Mary Kay Cosmetics Sales Meeting	St. Louis	MO	300
435	Feb 4 91	Lewis & Clark Elem School	St. Louis	MO	500
436	Feb 4 91	Oakville Elem School	St. Louis	MO	500
437	Feb 5 91	Immaculate Conception School	Columbia	IL	300
438	Feb 5 91	Niedringhaus Elem School	Granite City	IL	500
439	Feb 6 91	St. Monica Catholic School	St. Louis	MO	480
440	Feb 6 91	Riverbend Elem School	Chesterfield	MO	450
441	Feb 7 91	Greenfield Elem School	Greenfield	MO	450
442	Feb 7 91	North Grade School	Mt. Sterling	IL	500
443	Feb 8 91	Macon Jr & Sr High	Macon	IL	450
444	Feb 8 91	Lincoln Elem School	Monticello	IL	450
445	Feb 11 91	Lanier Elem School	Gainesville	GA	750
446	Feb 11 91	North Hall Middle School	Gainesville	GA	750
447	Feb 13 91	Jefferson Park Elem School	El Paso	IL	450
448	Feb 13 91	Woodrow Wilson Primary School	Peoria	IL	600
449	Feb 14 91	Carrie Busey Elem School	Champaign	IL	500
450	Feb 14 91	John Greer Elem School	Hoopeston	IL	300
451	Feb 15 91	Robeson Elem School	Champaign	IL	700
452	Feb 15 91	Dr. Howard Elem School	Champaign	IL	550

453	Feb 18 91	Centennial School	El Paso	IL	300
454	Feb 18 91	Irving Elem School	Bloomington	IL	500
455	Feb 19 91	Granville Elem School	Granville	IL	250
456	Feb 19 91	Cornell Grade School	Cornell	IL	150
457	Feb 20 91	Hennepin Elem School	Hennepin	IL	150
458	Feb 20 91	Roosevelt Elem School	Peru	IL	330
459	Feb 21 91	Walnut Grade School	Walnut	IL	300
460	Feb 21 91	Northlawn Jr High School	Streator	IL	600
461	Feb 22 91	Kishwaukee Elem School	Garden Prairie	IL	220
462	Feb 22 91	Conklin Elem School	Rockford	IL	500
463	Feb 25 91	Longfellow Elem School	Clinton	IA	500
464	Feb 25 91	Lasalle High School	Cedar Rapids	IA	250
465	Feb 26 91	Eugene Field Elem School	Rock Island	IL	320
466	Feb 26 91	Silas Willard Elem School	Galesburg	IL	400
467	Feb 27 91	Van Allen Elem School	Chariton	IA	350
468	Feb 27 91	Hedrick Community School	Hedrick	IA	250
469	Feb 28 91	Carlisle Jr High School	Carlisle	IA	100
470	Mar 1 91	Collins-Maxwell Middle School	Collins	IA	300
471	Mar 1 91	Manson High School	Manson	IA	250
472	Mar 4 91	Smith Elem School	Sioux City	IA	300
473	Mar 4 91	Crescent Park Elem School	Sioux City	IA	430
474	Mar 4 91	Siouxland Seniors Center	Sioux City	IA	50
475	Mar 5 91	Everett Elem School	Sioux City	IA	300
476	Mar 5 91	Emerson Elem School	Sioux City	IA	250
477	Mar 6 91	Joy Elem School	Sioux City	IA	300
478	Mar 6 91	Morningside Christian School/Nursing	Sioux City	IA	250
479	Mar 7 91	St. Boniface Catholic School	Sioux City	IA	100
480	Mar 7 91	Roosevelt Elem School	Sioux City	IA	250
481	Mar 7 91	Westwood Nursing Home	Sioux City	IA	50
482	Mar 8 91	Lincoln Elem School	Sioux City	IA	400
483	Mar 8 91	Irving Elem School	Sioux City	IA	400

484	Mar 11 91	Whittier Elem School	Sioux City	IA	350
485	Mar 11 91	Akron Westfield Elem School	Akron	IA	500
486	Mar 12 91	Lynd School	Lynd	MN	200
487	Mar 12 91	Clarkfield Elem School	Clarkfield	MN	250
488	Mar 13 91	V. L. Reishus Middle School	Biwabik	MN	450
489	Mar 13 91	Chisholm Middle School	Chisholm	MN	500
490	Mar 14 91	St. Anthony Catholic School	Watkins	MN	100
491	Mar 14 91	St. Michael's School	West St. Paul	MN	250
492	Mar 15 91	Durand High School	Durand	WI	350
493	Mar 15 91	Howe Elem School	Wisconsin Ra	WI	500
494	Mar 18 91	Franklin Elem School	Lacrosse	WI	350
495	Mar 18 91	Lawrence-Lawson Elem School	Sparta	WI	350
496	Mar 19 91	Montello School	Montello	WI	800
497	Mar 19 91	Tri County Elem School	Plainfield	WI	550
498	Mar 20 91	Waupaca Elem School	Waupaca	WI	1000
499	Mar 20 91	Grant Elem School	Marshfield	WI	450
500	Mar 21 91	Sugar Camp Elem School	Sugar Camp	WI	130
501	Mar 21 91	Three Lakes Elem School	Three Lakes	WI	300
502	Mar 21 91	Three Lakes High School	Three Lakes	WI	250
503	Mar 22 91	Rothschild Elem School	Rothschild	WI	450
504	Mar 22 91	Northland Pines Middle School	Eagle River	WI	350
505	Mar 25 91	Wausaukee Elem School	Wausaukee	WI	450
506	Mar 25 91	McArthur Elem School	McArthur	WI	450
507	Mar 26 91	Washington Elem School	Stevens Point	WI	600
508	Mar 26 91	St. Paul Lutheran School	Stevens Point	WI	100
509	Mar 26 91	Ben Franklin Jr High School	Stevens Point	WI	500
510	Mar 27 91	Lincoln-Erdman Elem School	Sheboygan	WI	250
511	Mar 27 91	Lincoln Elem School	Hartford	WI	600

512	Mar 28 91	Traver School	Lake Geneva	WI	100
513	Mar 28 91	Edgewood Elem School	Greenfield	WI	300
514	Apr 4 91	Alice Callan Elem School	Ripon	WI	140
515	Apr 4 91	Central Elem School	Ripon	WI	250
516	Apr 5 91	Edgerton Middle School	Edgerton	WI	400
517	Apr 8 91	Kolmar Elem School	Oaklawn	IL	400
518	Apr 8 91	St. Margaret Mary School	Algonquin	IL	250
519	April 9 91	Williams Bay Elem School	Williams Bay	WI	250
520	Apr 9 91	Gifford Elem School	Elgin	IL	500
521	Apr 10 91	St. Walters School	Roselle	IL	450
522	Apr 10 91	St. Paul Lutheran School	Chicago	IL	150
523	Apr 10 91	Abe Lincoln Book Store	Chicago	IL	5
524	Apr 11 91	St. Monica Elem School	Chicago	IL	400
525	Apr 11 91	Hynes Elem School	Morton Grove	IL	250
526	Apr 12 91	Marion Hills Elem School	Darien	IL	250
527	Apr 12 91	Caroline Bentley Elem School	New Lenox	IL	650
528	Apr 12 91	Civil War Round Table Dinner Mtg	Chicago	IL	150
529	Apr 15 91	Whittier Elem School	Kenosha	WI	400
530	Apr 15 91	Johnson Elem School	Aurora	IL	350
531	Apr 16 91	Limestone-Walters School	Peoria	IL	125
532	Apr 17 91	Notre Dame School	Michigan City	IN	250
533	Apr 17 91	Crete Elem School	Crete	IL	700
534	Apr 18 91	Mt. Morris Elem School	Mt. Morris	IL	400
535	Apr 18 91	Wheatland Elem School	Naperville	IL	450
536	Apr 19 91	Jefferson Elem School	Kenosha	WI	450
537	Apr 19 91	Westview Elem School	Rockford	IL	500
538	Apr 22 91	Lincoln Jr High School	Plymouth	IN	800
539	Apr 22 91	Boone Grove Elem School	Boone Grove	IN	350
540	Apr 23 91	River Forest Elem School	Hobart	IN	350
541	Apr 23 91	Holy Trinity School	Gary	IN	250
542	Apr 24 91	Lake Prairie Elem School	Lowell	IN	375

543	Apr 25 91	Turkey Run Elem School	Marshall	IN	300
544	Apr 25 91	Shelburn School	Shelburn	IN	300
545	Apr 26 91	Clark Middle School	Vincennes	IN	800
546	Apr 26 91	Chandler Elem School	Chandler	IN	600
547	Apr 29 91	Southwestern Elem School	Shelbyville	IN	400
548	Apr 29 91	Shelbyville Jr High School	Shelbyville	IN	300
549	Apr 30 91	Webb Elem School	Franklin	IN	450
550	Apr 30 91	Eastside Elem School	Brazil	IN	400
551	Apr 30 91	Sheridan Rotary Dinner Mtg	Sheridan	IN	25
552	May 1 91	Marion-Adams Jr/Sr High School	Sheridan	IN	300
553	May 1 91	Lapel School	Lapel	IN	850
554	May 2 91	Hagerstown Elem School	Hagerstown	IN	700
555	May 2 91	Liberty Middle School	Liberty	IN	300
556	May 3 91	Fairview Elem School	Cincinnati	OH	650
557	May 6 91	Vail Middle School	Middletown	OH	600
558	May 6 91	Monroe Middle School	Monroe	OH	400
559	May 7 91	Onieda Elem School	Middletown	OH	300
560	May 7 91	Amanda Elem School	Middletown	OH	600
561	May 8 91	Roosevelt Elem School	Middletown	OH	800
562	May 8 91	Broadway Elem School	Tipp City	OH	700
563	May 9 91	Miami East Jr High School	Troy	OH	200
564	May 9 91	Ft. Loramie Elem/Jr High Schools	Ft. Loramie	OH	500
565	May 10 91	Verity Middle School	Middletown	OH	250
566	May 10 91	Ft. Recovery Elem School	Ft. Recovery	OH	400
567	May 11 91	Mayfest Parade	Sidney	OH	25000
568	May 13 91	Southeastern High School	South Charles	OH	250
569	May 13 91	New Knoxville School	New Knoxville	OH	450
570	May 14 91	St. Michael School	Sharonville	OH	400
571	May 15 91	Botkins Schools	Botkins	OH	700

572	May 15 91	Woodrow Wilson School, O.V.C.H.	Xenia	OH	200
573	May 17 91	Burneson Middle School	Westlake	OH	1000
574	May 20 91	Wyoming Middle School	Wyoming	OH	300
575	May 21 91	Ladyfield Elem School	Toledo	OH	250
576	May 22 91	Indian Hills Elem School	Rossford	OH	300
577	May 22 91	St. Catherine School	Toledo	OH	400
578	May 23 91	South View Elem School	Muncie	IN	650
579	May 23 91	College Corner Elem School	Anderson	IN	400
580	May 24 91	Zion-Immanuel Lutheran School	Matteson	IL	225
581	June 12 91	T.E.P.S.A. Convention	Austin	TX	2000
582	July 1 91	Mt. Rushmore National Memorial	Keystone	SD	2000
583	July 2 91	Mt. Rushmore National Memorial	Keystone	SD	2000
584	July 4 91	Mt. Rushmore National Memorial	Keystone	SD	2000
585	July 4 91	Mt. Rushmore National Memorial	Keystone	SD	2000
586	July 4 91	Independence Day Parade	Rapid City	SD	50000
587	July 5 91	Mt. Rushmore National Memorial	Keystone	SD	2000
588	July 5 91	West Hills Village Senior Center	Rapid City	SD	75
589	July 15 91	G.A.E.L., GA Assoc of Education	Jekyll Island	GA	1500
590	July 20 91	Civil War Encampment, Atl. Historical	Atlanta	GA	1500
591	July 21 91	Civil War Encampment, Atl. Historical	Atlanta	GA	1500

592	July 28 91	Little River United Methodist Church	Woodstock	GA	100
593	Aug 3 91	Stanford Center Retirement Home	Altamonte Springs	FL	100
594	Aug 4 91	Howell Place Retirement Center	Sanford	FL	150
595	Aug 14 91	Scottish Rite Assoc Dinner Mtg	Decatur	GA	30
596	Aug 19 91	Albany High School Staff Only	Albany	GA	100
597	Sep 7 91	Gwinnett Cultural Arts Workshop	Lawrenceville	GA	25
598	Oct 2 91	Annual School Superintendent's Seminar	Dawsonville	GA	50
599	Oct 3 91	Southland Academy School	Americus	GA	1000
600	Oct 4 91	Sumter County Elem School	Americus	GA	1400
601	Oct 5 91	Historic Andersonville Parade and Fest	Andersonville	GA	5000
602	Oct 6 91	Kansas School Food Service Assoc Con	Wichita	KS	400
603	Oct 16 91	Tate Elem School	Tate	GA	350
604	Oct 19 91	Jasper True Value Hardware Store	Jasper	GA	100
605	Oct 24 91	"Stay in School" Program, Corps Eng.	Carter's Lake	GA	1000
606	Nov 4 91	Fairwood Elem School	Berea	OH	350
607	Nov 5 91	Parknoll Elem School	Berea	OH	450
608	Nov 6 91	Smith Elem School	Berea	OH	300
609	Nov 6 91	Western Reserve Civil War Round Table	Berea	OH	50
610	Nov 7 91	Riveredge Elem School	Berea	OH	350
611	Nov 8 91	Perry Middle School	Perry	OH	450

612	Nov 8 91	Perry Elem School	Perry	OH	450
613	Nov 11 91	St. Mary of the Falls School	Olmstead Falls	OH	300
614	Nov 12 91	Falls Elem School	Olmstead Falls	OH	400
615	Nov 14 91	First Baptist Church "Lunch & Learn"	Roswell	GA	300
616	Dec 3 91	Lilburn Elem School	Lilburn	GA	1200
617	Dec 9 91	Mt. Vernon Elem School	Mt. Vernon	TX	800
618	Dec 10 91	Malta Elem School	Malta	TX	60
619	Dec 11 91	Queen City Elem School	Queen City	TX	450
620	Dec 12 91	Hooks Elem School	Hooks	TX	425
621	Dec 13 91	Avery Elem School	Avery	TX	200
622	Dec 13 91	Avery Jr & Sr High School	Avery	TX	200
623	Jan 8 92	Ellijay Elem School	Ellijay	GA	600
624	Jan 9 92	East Fannin Middle School	Morganton	GA	250
625	Jan 9 92	Epworth Mens Club	Epworth	GA	25
626	Jan 10 92	Compton Elem School	Powder Springs	GA	950
627	Jan 11 92	Taylorsville Library	Taylorsville	MS	25
628	Jan 13 92	Southside Elem School	Angleton	TX	600
629	Jan 13 92	Westside Elem School	Angleton	TX	500
630	Jan 14 92	Frontier Elem School	Angleton	TX	450
631	Jan 14 92	Rancho Isabella Elem School	Angleton	TX	550
632	Jan 15 92	Northside Elem School	Angleton	TX	600
633	Jan 16 92	Ferguson Elem School	League City	TX	950
634	Jan 17 92	Stewart Elem School	Kemah	TX	550
635	Jan 20 92	Pittsburg Intermediate School	Pittsburg	TX	500
636	Jan 21 92	Roxton School	Roxton	TX	200
637	Jan 21 92	Sulphur Springs Middle School	Sulphur Springs	TX	300
638	Jan 22 92	Bowie Elem School	Sulphur Springs	TX	450
639	Jan 22 92	Austin Elem School	Sulphur Springs	TX	250
640	Jan 23 92	Houston Elem School	Sulphur Springs	TX	300

641	Jan 23 92	Douglas Elem School	Sulphur Springs	TX	250
642	Jan 24 92	Lamar Elem School	Sulphur Springs	TX	300
643	Jan 24 92	Travis Elem School	Sulphur Springs	TX	450
644	Jan 27 92	Cimarron Elem School	Houston	TX	850
645	Jan 28 92	Holmsley Elem School	Houston	TX	1000
646	Jan 29 92	Sam Houston Elem School	Huntsville	TX	550
647	Jan 29 92	Scott Johnson Elem School	Huntsville	TX	700
648	Jan 30 92	Pleasonton Elem School	Pleasonton	TX	750
649	Jan 31 92	Rose Garden Elem School	Universal City	TX	460
650	Jan 31 92	Northview ECC School	Universal City	TX	450
651	Feb 3 92	Denver City Elem School	Denver City	TX	1300
652	Feb 4 92	Plum Creek Elem School	Lockhart	TX	600
653	Feb 5 92	Forestridge Ele School	Dallas	TX	750
654	Feb 6 92	Winnsboro Elem School	Winnsboro	TX	550
655	Feb 7 92	Braelinn Elem School	Peachtree City	GA	750
656	Feb 7 92	Big Canoe Homeowners	Big Canoe	GA	125
657	Feb 8 92	Masonic Lodge 228 & Rainbow Dinner	Norcross	GA	25
658	Feb 10 92	Camp Creek Elem School	Lilburn	GA	875
659	Feb 10 92	B.B. Harris Elem School	Duluth	GA	950
660	Feb 11 92	Hampton Elem School	Hampton	GA	550
661	Feb 11 92	Gwinnett Home Schoolers	Lilburn	GA	450
662	Feb 11 92	Clarkston Masonic Lodge 492	Clarkston	GA	100
663	Feb 12 92	Annistown Elem School	Annistown	GA	1000
664	Feb 13 92	Mountain Park Elem School	Lilburn	GA	600
665	Feb 13 92	Cedar Hill Elem School	Lawrenceville	GA	1650
666	Feb 14 92	T.G. Ritch Elem School	Jesup	GA	650
667	Feb 14 92	Jesup Middle Grade School	Jesup	GA	700
668	Feb 17 92	Como Pickton Elem School	Pickton	TX	300
669	Feb 18 92	Oakwood Terrace Elem School	Euless	TX	600
670	Feb 18 92	South Euless Elem School	Euless	TX	600

671	Feb 19 92	Midway Park Elem School	Euless	TX	700
672	Feb 19 92	North Euless Elem School	Euless	TX	550
673	Feb 20 92	Wilshire Elem School	Euless	TX	600
674	Feb 20 92	Lakewood Elem School	Euless	TX	650
675	Feb 21 92	Meadow Creek Elem School	Bedford	TX	850
676	Feb 21 92	Bell Manor Elem School	Bedford	TX	800
677	Feb 24 92	Shady Oaks Elem School	Hurst	TX	500
678	Feb 24 92	Donna Park Elem School	Hurst	TX	575
679	Feb 25 92	Bellaire Elem School	Hurst	TX	650
680	Feb 25 92	Harrison Lane Elem School	Bedford	TX	550
681	Feb 26 92	Hurst Hills Elem School	Hurst	TX	600
682	Feb 26 92	West Hurst Elem School	Hurst	TX	550
683	Feb 26 92	Masonic Home for Aged	Arlington	TX	50
684	Feb 27 92	Bedford Heights Elem School	Bedford	TX	850
685	Feb 27 92	Stonegate Elem School	Bedford	TX	550
686	Feb 28 92	Spring Garden Elem School	Bedford	TX	900
687	Feb 28 92	Shady Brook Elem Schol	Bedford	TX	600
688	Mar 2 92	Pleasant Grove Elem School	Texarkana	TX	650
689	Mar 3 92	Linden Kildare Jr High School	Kildare	TX	350
690	Mar 3 92	Linden Kildare Elem School	Kildare	TX	650
691	Mar 4 92	New Boston High School	New Boston	TX	300
692	Mar 5 92	Pewitt Jr High School	Omaha	TX	350
693	Mar 5 92	Atlanta Elem School	Atlanta	TX	500
694	Mar 6 92	New Boston Jr High School	New Boston	TX	150
695	Mar 9 92	Lamar Middle School	San Marcos	TX	475
696	Mar 10 92	Goodnight Jr High School	San Marcos	TX	1000
697	Mar 11 92	Crockett Elem School	San Marcos	TX	850
698	Mar 11 92	Bonham Pre-School	San Marcos	TX	300
699	Mar 11 92	Dezavala Elem School	San Marcos	TX	850
700	Mar 12 92	Bowie Elem School	San Marcos	TX	750

701	Mar 13 92	Travis Elem School	San Marcos	TX	800
702	Mar 26 92	Carden Academy	Park City	UT	60
703	Mar 26 92	Lubbock Arts Festival	Lubbock	TX	250
704	Mar 27 92	Lubbock Arts Festival	Lubbock	TX	5000
705	Mar 28 92	Lubbock Arts Festival	Lubbock	TX	3000
706	Mar 29 92	Lubbock Arts Festival	Lubbock	TX	3000
707	Mar 30 92	Austin Elem School	Slaton	TX	300
708	Mar 30 92	West Ward Elem School	Slaton	TX	600
709	Mar 30 92	Kappa Kappa Gamma Sorority	Lubbock	TX	100
710	Mar 31 92	Seagraves Elem School	Seagraves	TX	450
711	Mar 31 92	Ropes, Meadow & Wellman Elem Schs	Meadow	TX	500
712	Apr 1 92	Frenship Intermediate School	Lubbock	TX	800
713	Apr 1 92	Reese Elem School	Lubbock	TX	450
714	Apr 1 92	First Baptist Church	Meadow	TX	50
715	Apr 2 92	Sudan Elem School	Sudan	TX	250
716	Apr 2 92	Dillman ElemSchool	Muleshoe	TX	400
717	Apr 2 92	DeShazo Elem School	Muleshoe	TX	400
718	Apr 3 92	Lockney Elem School	Lockney	TX	450
719	Apr 3 92	Roosevelt Elem School	Lubbock	TX	750
720	Apr 17 92	Spring Place Elem School	Spring Place	GA	1200
721	Apr 28 92	TNN Live TV Show	Nashville	TN	1000
722	May 2 92	Snellville Days Festival & Parade	Snellville	GA	20000
723	May 8 92	Tryon Street Elem School	Greer	SC	550
724	May 9 92	Greer Family Festival	Greer	SC	1000
725	May 14 92	Dalton High Schools Honors Banquet	Dalton	GA	500
726	May 15 92	Cristy Lane Theater	Branson	MO	15
727	May18 92	Green Valley Elem School	Houston	TX	1000
728	May 24 91	Cristy Lane Theater	Branson	MO	18

729	May 25 92	Cristy Lane Theater	Branson	MO	17
730	May 27 92	Cristy Lane Theater	Branson	MO	24
731	May 28 92	Cristy Lane Theater	Branson	MO	34
732	Jul 4 92	Boone County Celebration	Harrison	AR	500
733	Jul 4 92	Lyric Theater	Harrison	AR	85
734	Jul 18 92	Lyric Theater	Harrison	AR	17
735	Jul 21 92	Lyric Theater	Harrison	AR	7
736	Jul 22 92	Lyric Theater	Harrison	AR	3
737	Jul 23 92	Lyric Theater	Harrison	AR	13
738	Jul 24 92	Lyric Theater	Harrison	AR	4
739	Jul 25 92	Lyric Theater	Harrison	AR	28
740	Jul 28 92	Lyric Theater	Harrison	AR	4
741	Jul 31 92	Lyric Theater	Harrison	AR	10
742	Aug 1 92	Lyric Theater	Harrison	AR	24
743	Aug 4 92	Lyric Theater B/D Party	Harrison	AR	100
744	Aug 7 92	Lyric Theater	Harrison	AR	6
745	Aug 8 92	Lyric Theater	Harrison	AR	7
746	Aug 10 92	Kiwanis Lunch Meeting	Harrison	AR	50
747	Aug 13 92	Lyric Theater	Harrison	AR	18
748	Aug 14 92	Lyric Theater	Harrison	AR	6
749	Aug 15 92	Lyric Theater	Harrison	AR	11
750	Aug 18 93	Lyric Theater	Harrison	AR	11
751	Aug 19 92	Lyric Theater	Harrison	AR	16
752	Aug 20 92	Lyric Theater	Harrison	AR	16
753	Aug 21 92	Lyric Theater	Harrison	AR	7
754	Aug 22 92	Lyric Theater	Harrison	AR	9
755	Aug 25 92	Lyric Theater	Harrison	AR	11
756	Aug 27 92	Lyric Theater	Harrison	AR	5
757	Aug 28 92	Lyric Theater	Harrison	AR	8
758	Aug 29 92	Lyric Theater	Harrison	AR	21
759	Sep 1 92	Lyric Theater	Harrison	AR	5
760	Sep 2 92	Lyric Theater	Harrison	AR	9
761	Sep 4 92	Lyric Theater	Harrison	AR	9

Image in the Mirror

762	Sep 5 92	Lyric Theater	Harrison	AR	7
763	Sep 8 92	Lyric Grand Opening	Harrison	AR	103
764	Sep 10 92	Lyric Theater	Harrison	AR	6
765	Sep 11 92	Lyric Theater	Harrison	AR	9
766	Sep 12 92	Lyric Woodmen of World	Harrison	AR	103
767	Sep 16 92	Lyric Theater	Harrison	AR	11
768	Sep 17 92	Lyric Theater	Harrison	AR	17
769	Sep 18 92	A.A.R.P. Meeting	Harrison	AR	20
770	Sep 18 92	Lyric Theater	Harrison	AR	17
771	Sep 19 92	Lyric Theater	Harrison	AR	23
772	Sep 22 92	Lyric Theater	Harrison	AR	15
773	Sep 24 92	Rodeo/Fair Parade	Harrison	AR	5000
774	Sep 26 92	Lyric Theater	Harrison	AR	10
775	Sep 29 92	Lyric Theater	Harrison	AR	5
776	Sep 30 92	Lyric Theater	Harrison	AR	7
777	Oct 1 92	Lyric Theater	Harrison	AR	10
778	Oct 3 92	Lyric Theater	Harrison	AR	8
779	Oct 7 92	Church Convention	St. Louis	MO	50
780	Oct 9 92	Lyric Theater	Harrison	AR	13
781	Oct 10 92	Lyric Theater	Harrison	AR	13
782	Oct 13 92	Parish Day School	Dallas	TX	400
783	Oct 14 92	Red Lick Elem School	Leary	TX	400
784	Oct 15 92	Winfield ISD School	Winfield	TX	100
785	Oct 15 92	Douglas Intermediate School	Sulphur Springs	TX	330
786	Oct 16 92	Daingerfield Jr High School	Daingerfield	TX	200
787	Oct 16 92	Liberty-Eylau Elem School	Texarkana	TX	200
788	Oct 17 92	Lyric Theater	Harrison	AR	19
789	Oct 22 92	Home Schoolers, Lyric	Harrison	AR	85
790	Oct 22 92	Lyric Theater	Harrison	AR	7
791	Oct 23 92	Lyric Theater	Harrison	AR	5
792	Oct 24 92	Girl Scouts, Lyric	Harrison	AR	150
793	Oct 26 92	Murfreesboro Elem School	Murfreesboro	AR	350

794	Oct 28 92	Lions Club Luncheon	Harrison	AR	40
795	Nov 5 92	N.A.C.C. Stay in School Program	Harrison	AR	100
796	Nov 5 92	Rotary Club Luncheon	Harrison	AR	50
797	Nov 14 92	Civil War Reenactment	Green Forest	AR	1000
798	Nov 16 92	Pleasant Hope Elem School	Pleasant Hope	MO	450
799	Nov 18 92	Dora School	Dora	MO	300
800	Nov 19 92	Riverview Bible School Honor Students	Harrison	AR	45
801	Dec 8 92	Green Forest School	Green Forest	AR	700
802	Dec 15 92	Alpena High School at Lyric Theater	Harrison	AR	55
803	Dec 30 92	Howell Place Retirement Center	Sanford	FL	80
804	Jan 13 93	Melaleuca Launch Convention	Tulsa	OK	2700
805	Jan 16 93	Photo Ops Downtwon	Washington	DC	1000
806	Jan 17 93	Capitol Mall Plus TV	Washington	DC	10000
807	Jan 18 93	Capitol Mall Area	Washington	DC	20000
808	Jan 19 93	Bureau of Engraving	Washington	DC	100
809	Jan 19 93	Kennedy Center Salute to Children	Washington	DC	10000
810	Jan 19 93	Kennedy Center Salute to Youth	Washington	DC	10000
811	Jan 19 93	Tour of USA Today/ Gannett Newsp	Washington	DC	50
812	Jan 20 93	Union Station	Washington	DC	1000
813	Jan 20 93	Inaugural Parade Route Photos	Washington	DC	10000
814	Jan 21 93	Capitol Mall "48 Hours" TV Appear.	Washington	DC	100
815	Jan 21 93	Lincoln Memorial	Washington	DC	50
816	Jan 22 93	Bureau of Engraving	Washington	DC	250

~ 248 ~

817	Jan 22 93	Lincoln Memorial	Washington	DC	100
818	Jan 23 93	Lyric Theater Special Show	Harrison	AR	25
819	Jan 25 93	West Side Elem School	Helena	AR	500
820	Jan 25 93	Woodruff Elem School	Helena	AR	400
821	Jan 26 93	Jefferson Elem SChool	Helena	AR	300
822	Jan 26 93	Helena Crossing Elem School	Helena	AR	175
823	Jan 27 93	J.F. Wahl Elem School	Helena	AR	600
824	Jan 28 93	Beech Crest Elem School	Helena	AR	550
825	Jan 28 93	Eliza Miller J.H. School	Helena	AR	200
826	Jan 29 93	Eliza Miller J.H. School	Helena	AR	500
827	Feb 9 93	Yale Elem School	Richardson	TX	850
828	Feb 10 93	Brentfield Elem School	Dallas	TX	750
829	Feb 12 93	Union County Elem School	Blairsville	GA	950
830	Feb 12 93	Peachtree Masonic Lodge #732	Atlanta	GA	60
831	Feb 14 93	70th Birthday Party - Rev. Willis Moor	Gainesville	GA	25
832	Feb 15 93	Jasper Elem School	Jasper	GA	1000
833	Feb 16 93	Hall County Home Schoolers	Gainesville	GA	225
834	Feb 17 93	Mineral Bluff Elem School	Mineral Bluff	GA	200
835	Feb 17 93	Fulton Masonic Lodge #216	Atlanta	GA	30
836	Feb 18 93	Huddleston Elem School	Peachtree City	GA	650
837	Feb 19 93	Rosemont Elem School	Lagrange	GA	600
838	Feb 20 93	Jasper Methodist Church Special Show	Jasper	GA	100
839	Feb 22 93	East Greer Elem School	Greer	SC	300
840	Feb 23 93	Shriner's Children's Hospital	Greenville	SC	50
841	Feb 24 93	Mitchell Road Elem School	Greenville	SC	670
842	Mar 2 93	Brushy Creek Elem School	Greenville	SC	750
843	Mar 3 93	Lake Forest Elem School	Greenville	SC	400
844	Mar 9 93	Kirby School	Kirby	AR	400

845	Mar 10 93	Glenwood Elem School	Glenwood	AR	200
846	Mar 10 93	Glenwood High School	Glenwood	AR	200
847	Mar 17 93	Rotary Club Luncheon	Jasper	GA	25
848	Mar 25 93	Braden River Elem School	Bradenton	FL	750
849	Apr 8 93	Summit Middle School	Edmund	OK	950
850	Apr 13 93	Dunwoody Kiwanis	Dunwoody	GA	50
851	Apr 21 93	Northeast Elem School	Arma	KS	300
852	Apr 22 93	Haderlein Elem School	Girard	KS	550
853	Apr 22 93	Melaleuca Meeting	Pittsburg	KS	30
854	Apr 26 93	Delight Schools	Delight	AR	400
855	May 25 93	Berkeley Lake Elem School	Duluth	GA	1200
856	May 27 93	Alan Laufman B/D Party	Dallas	TX	5
857	May 31 93	Masonic Wives Supper	Smyrna	GA	75
858	June 3 93	Good Old Days Shows	Ft. Scott	KS	80
859	Jun 4 93	Good Old Days Parade	Ft. Scott	KS	5000
860	Jun 12 93	Taste of Atlanta	Atlanta	GA	2000
861	Aug 7 93	Rose Creek Library	Woodstock	GA	25
862	Aug 7 93	Woodstock Library	Woodstock	GA	25
863	Sep 15 93	4th Annual Rotary Golf Tournament	Bent Tree	GA	150
864	Sep 25 93	Pioneer Days Celebration	Ft. Worth	TX	5000
865	Sep 26 93	Pioneer Days Celebration	Ft. Worth	TX	3000
866	Nov 8 93	Big Springs Elem School	Richardson	TX	700
867	Nov 9 93	Greenwood Hills Elem School	Richardson	TX	400
868	Nov 9 93	Greenwood Hills Elem School PTA Mtg	Richardson	TX	100
869	Nov 10 93	Northrich Elem School	Richardson	TX	450
870	Nov 10 93	Prestonwood Baptist Church	Richardson	TX	100
871	Nov 11 93	Canyon Creek Elem School	Richardson	TX	300
872	Nov 11 93	Canyon Creek Elem School PTA Mtg	Richardson	TX	100

873	Nov 12 93	Bowie Elem School	Richardson	TX	600
874	Nov 15 93	Lakeside Elem School	Irving	TX	25
875	Nov 16 93	Northlake Elem School	Richardson	TX	550
876	Nov 17 93	Terrace Elem School	Richardson	TX	650
877	Nov 19 93	Nannie Berry Elem School	Hendersonville	TN	600
878	Nov 22 93	Rotary Club Luncheon Mtg	Sandy Springs	GA	80
879	Jan 8 94	Give Kids the World	Kissimmee	FL	25
880	Jan 9 94	Give Kids the World	Kissimmee	FL	60
881	Jan 10 94	Fairglen Elem School	Cocoa	FL	1100
882	Jan 12 94	Talk of the Town TV Show	Melbourne	FL	10
883	Jan 12 94	Melaleuca Launch Mtg	Orlando	FL	2000
884	Jan 13 94	Challenger 7 Elem School	Port St. John	FL	1000
885	Jan 24 94	Milner Elem School	Hartford	CT	500
886	Jan 27 94	Ledyard Center School	Ledyard	CT	500
887	Jan 27 94	St. Joseph Catholic School	Baltic	CT	200
888	Jan 28 94	Gallup Hill Elem School	Ledyard	CT	450
889	Feb 1 94	Dalton J.H. School	Dalton	GA	500
890	Feb 2 94	Westwood Elem School	Dalton	GA	600
891	Feb 2 94	Roan Elem School	Dalton	GA	500
892	Feb 3 94	Ft. Hill Elem School	Dalton	GA	250
893	Feb 4 94	Compton Elem School	Powder Springs	GA	1000
894	Feb 8 94	Clarkdale Elem School	Austell	GA	500
895	Feb 10 94	Jasper Lions Club	Jasper	GA	60
896	Feb 11 94	Atherton Place for Seniors	Marietta	GA	100
897	Feb 16 94	Mustang Elem School	Mustang	OK	775
898	Feb 17 94	Mustang Valley Elem School	Mustang	OK	700
899	Feb 18 94	Mustang Trails Elem School	Mustang	OK	900
900	Feb 21 94	Stroud Elem School	Stroud	OK	350
901	Feb 22 94	Skyview Elem School	Yukon	OK	750
902	Feb 23 94	Parkland Elem School	Yukon	OK	600
903	Mar 10 94	Pickens High School	Jasper	GA	50
904	Mar 21 94	Grace Christian Academy	Ellijay	GA	35

905	Mar 27 94	Fairglen Elem Bus Tour	Washington	DC	40
906	Mar 28 94	Lincoln Memorial	Washington	DC	500
907	Mar 29 94	Ford's Theater	Washington	DC	500
908	Apr 7 94	Sasafrass Writing Club	Jasper	GA	50
909	May 2 94	Appalachian Home Schoolers	Jasper	GA	125
910	May 20 94	Battle Reenactment Encampment	Resaca	GA	300
911	May 21 94	130th Anniversary Reenactment	Resaca	GA	5000
912	May 22 94	130th Anniversary Reenactment	Resaca	GA	5000
913	Jun 1 94	XYZ Club	Ellijay	GA	50
914	Jun 4 94	Taste of Atlanta	Atlanta	GA	1000
915	Jun 4 94	Valujet Passengers	In the air	VA	125
916	Jun 5 94	Kick Off Meeting "Stop Youth Violence"	Chantilly	VA	20
917	Jun 16 94	Meet with Senators/ Congressmen	Washington	DC	50
918	Jun 17 94	Honda State Rally	Dalton	GA	200
919	Jun 25 94	Summerfest 94	Princeton	WV	1000
920	Jun 26 94	Summerfest 94	Princeton	WV	110
921	Jul 3 94	Mount Rushmore National Memorial	Keystone	SD	5000
922	Jul 4 94	Mount Rushmore National Memorial	Keystone	SD	10000
923	Jul 6 94	N.A.R.F.E. Luncheon Mtg	Marietta	GA	65
924	Jul 26 94	Kickoff Anti-Violence Program	Springfield	VA	500
925	Jul 30 94	Judge Hat Contest	Cape Cod	MA	500
926	Jul 31 94	Wigwam 100th Anniversary	Cape Cod	MA	200
927	Aug 13 94	AllPie Conference Book Signing	Brockport	NY	400

Image in the Mirror

928	Aug 14 94	AllPie Conference	Brockport	NY	400
929	Aug 18 94	Green Chimneys School	Brewster	NY	125
930	Aug 24 94	Vinings Rotary Luncheon	Atlanta	GA	50
931	Sep 12 94	Jasper Kiwanis Dinner Mtg	Jasper	GA	23
932	Sep 24 94	Library Book Signing	Jasper	GA	25
933	Oct 1 94	Marble Festival Parade	Jasper	GA	2500
934	Oct 1 94	True Value Hardware Book Signing	Jasper	GA	25
935	Oct 8 94	Eastern Star Dinner	Ellijay	GA	200
936	Oct 12 94	Briar Vista Elem School	Atlanta	GA	500
937	Oct 14 94	Dalton Jr High School	Dalton	GA	700
938	Oct 21 94	Aiken Elem School	Richardson	TX	800
939	Oct 23 94	Highland Park Methodist Church	Dallas	TX	50
940	Oct 24 94	Pleasonton Elem School	Pleasonton	TX	800
941	Oct 26 94	Somerset Elem School	Somerset	TX	1100
942	Oct 27 94	Somerset Middle School	Somerset	TX	500
943	Oct 27 94	Tiger Scout Meeting	Delight	TX	8
944	Oct 28 94	Natalia Elem School	Natalia	TX	500
945	Nov 1 94	Kingfisher Middle School	Kingfisher	OK	450
946	Nov 2 94	Hennessey Elem School	Hennessey	OK	600
947	Nov 3 94	Gilmour Elem School	Kingfisher	OK	600
948	Nov 3 94	Library Book Signing	Kingfisher	OK	32
949	Nov 4 94	Hennessey Elem School	Hennessey	OK	300
950	Nov 7 94	Bradford Elem School	Littleton	CO	1000
951	Nov 8 94	D'Evelyn Jr/Sr High School	Golden	CO	300
952	Nov 9 94	Colorow Elem School	Littleton	CO	700
953	Nov 9 94	Boy Scout Troop 47	Littleton	CO	25
954	Nov 10 94	Governor's Ranch Elem School	Littleton	CO	700
955	Nov 11 94	Schaffer Elem School	Littleton	CO	650
956	Nov 13 94	United Methodist Church	Raton	NM	25
957	Nov 17 94	Library Book Signing	Woodstock	GA	25

958	Nov 20 94	E.S.A. Benefit	Atlanta	GA	50
959	Jan 2 95	WOCA Radiuo Show	Ocala	FL	
960	Jan 10 95	WRXK Radio Show	Ft. Myers	FL	
961	Jan 11 95	WMBD Radio Show	Peoria	IL	
962	Jan 17 95	KUTI Radio Show	Yakama	WA	
963	Jan 17 95	WFAW Radio Show	Ft. Atkinson	WI	
964	Jan 20 95	Assoc. of Lincoln Presenters Conv.	Lexington	KY	50
965	Jan 21 95	Assoc. of Lincoln Presenters Conv.	Lexington	KY	100
966	Jan 22 95	Assoc. of Lincoln Presenters Conv.	Lexington	KY	50
967	Jan 27 95	Melissa Jones Elem School	Guilford	CT	450
968	Jan 30 95	Daisy Ingraham Elem School	Westbrook	CT	450
969	Jan 31 95	Southwest Elem School	Waterford	CT	350
970	Feb 1 95	Oakdale Elem School	Oakdale	CT	450
971	Feb 2 95	Mohegan Elem School	Uncasville	CT	480
972	Feb 3 95	Murphy Elem School	Oakdale	CT	650
973	Feb 6 95	Dartmouth Elem School	Richardson	TX	550
974	Feb 6 95	Dartmouth Elem School PTA Mtg	Richardson	TX	110
975	Feb 7 95	Prestonwood Elem School	Richardson	TX	485
976	Feb 7 95	Prestonwood Elem School PTA Mtg	Richardson	TX	100
977	Feb 8 95	Spring Valley Elem School	Richardson	TX	500
978	Feb 9 95	Mohawk Elem School	Richardson	TX	350
979	Feb 9 95	Mohawk Elem School PTA Mtg.	Richardson	TX	100
980	Feb 10 95	Northwood Hills Elem School	Richardson	TX	500
981	Feb 12 95	WFRL Radio Show	Freeport	IL	
982	Feb 13 95	WUSV Radio Show	Long Island	NY	

Image in the Mirror

983	Feb 14 95	Screven Elem School	Screven	GA	275
984	Feb 14 95	WHEN Radio Show	Syracuse	NY	
985	Feb 14 95	Optimist Club Dinner Mtg.	Jesup	GA	18
986	Feb 15 95	Jesup Elem School	Jesup	GA	650
987	Feb 15 95	James E. Bacon Elem School	Jesup	GA	675
988	Feb 15 95	Methodist Church Supper Mtg.	Jesup	GA	100
989	Feb 16 95	Oak Vista Elem School	Jesup	GA	600
990	Feb 16 95	GA State Prison	Jesup	GA	50
991	Feb 17 95	Odum Elem School	Odum	GA	300
992	Feb 20 95	America's Talking "What's New" TV	Ft. Lee	NJ	100
993	Feb 20 95	America's Talking "Break a Leg" TV	Ft. Lee	NJ	100
994	Feb 20 95	America's Talking "Pork" TV Show	Ft. Lee	NJ	100
995	Feb 20 95	Z104 Radio Show	Norfolk	VA	
996	Feb 20 95	WAAM Radio Show	Ann Arbor	MI	
997	Feb 20 95	WLTP Radio Show	Parkersburg	WV	
998	Feb 21 95	WTAR Radio Show	Norfolk	VA	
999	Feb 22 95	East Fannin Elem School	Morganton	GA	500
1000	Feb 27 95	Pre-Paid Legal Services Mtg.	Atlanta	GA	125
1001	Mar 3 95	Picken High School History Class	Jasper	GA	25
1002	Mar 10 95	Exchange Club	Rome	GA	80
1003	Mar 30 95	Antibellum Jubilee	Stone Mtn.	GA	5000
1004	Mar 31 95	Antibellum Jubilee	Stone Mtn.	GA	5000
1005	Apr 1 95	Antibellum Jubilee	Stone Mtn.	GA	5000
1006	Apr 2 95	Antibellum Jubilee	Stone Mtn.	GA	5000
1007	Apr 7 95	WGMD Radio Interview	Rehoboth Bea	DE	
1008	Apr 25 95	Enterprise Elem School	Port St. John	FL	800

1009	May 6 95	Optimist State Convention	Athens	GA	200
1010	May 7 95	Optimist State Convention	Athens	GA	200
1011	May 12 95	North Central Very Special Arts Fest	Ellijay	GA	1000
1012	May 19 95	Battle of Resaca	Resaca	GA	1000
1013	May 20 95	Battle of Resaca	Resaca	GA	2000
1014	May 21 95	Battle of Resaca	Resaca	GA	2000
1015	May 24 95	Kiwanis Breakfast Mtg.	Buckhead	GA	40
1016	May 24 95	Filming Promos	Norcross	GA	10
1017	Jun 15 95	KOA Campground Show	Hill City	SD	52
1018	Jun 16 95	KOA Campground Show	Hill City	SD	42
1019	Jun 17 95	KOA Campground Show	Hill City	SD	37
1020	Jun 20 95	Mount Rushmore Book Signing	Keystone	SD	500
1021	Jun 21 95	Mount Rushmore Book Signing	Keystone	SD	500
1022	Jun 22 95	Mount Rushmore Book Signing	Keystone	SD	500
1023	Jun 24 95	KOA Campground Show	Hill City	SD	57
1024	Jun 27 95	Mount Rushmore Book Signing	Keystone	SD	500
1025	Jun 28 95	Mount Rushmore Book Signing	Keystone	SD	500
1026	Jun 28 95	KOA Campground Show	Hill City	SD	32
1027	Jun 29 95	Mount Rushmore Book Signing	Keystone	SD	500
1028	Jun 29 95	Senior Citizens Show	Keystone	SD	30
1029	Jun 30 95	KOA Campground Show	Hill City	SD	35
1030	Jul 1 95	KOA Campground Show	Hill City	SD	53
1031	Jul 3 95	Mount Rushmore Book Signing	Keystone	SD	500
1032	Jul 4 95	Mount Rushmore Book Signing	Keystone	SD	1000

1033	Jul 5 95	KOA Campground Show	Hill City	SD	36
1034	Jul 6 95	Mount Rushmore Book Signing	Keystone	SD	1000
1035	Jul 7 95	KOA Campground Show	Hill City	SD	34
1036	Jul 9 95	Old School House Show	Keystone	SD	5
1037	Jul 10 95	Old School House Show	Keystone	SD	2
1038	Jul 11 95	Mount Rushmore Book Signing	Keystone	SD	500
1039	Jul 12 95	KOA Campground Show	Hill City	SD	34
1040	Jul 13 95	Mount Rushmore Book Signing	Keystone	SD	500
1041	Jul 13 95	Larry King's Dinner Theater	Keystone	SD	100
1042	Jul 14 95	Larry King's Dinner Theater	Keystone	SD	60
1043	Jul 14 95	KOA Campground Show	Hill City	SD	42
1044	Jul 15 95	Larry King's Dinner Theater	Keystone	SD	46
1045	Jul 15 95	KOA Campground Show	Hill City	SD	13
1046	Jul 16 95	Larry King's Dinner Theater	Keystone	SD	63
1047	Jul 17 95	Larry King's Dinner Theater	Keystone	SD	90
1048	Jul 18 95	Mount Rushmore Book Signing	Keystone	SD	500
1049	Jul 18 95	Larry King's Dinner Theater	Keystone	SD	90
1050	Jul 19 95	Larry King's Dinner Theater	Keystone	SD	100
1051	Jul 19 95	KOA Campground Show	Hill City	SD	65
1052	Jul 20 95	Mount Rushmore Book Signing	Keystone	SD	500
1053	Jul 20 95	Larry King's Dinner Theater	Keystone	SD	105
1054	Jul 21 95	Larry King's Dinner Theater	Keystone	SD	125
1055	Jul 21 95	KOA Campground Show	Hill City	SD	45
1056	Jul 22 95	Larry King's Dinner Theater	Keystone	SD	110
1057	Jul 22 95	KOA Campground Show	Hill City	SD	37
1058	Jul 23 95	Larry King's Dinner Theater	Keystone	SD	50
1059	Jul 24 95	Mount Rushmore Book Signing	Keystone	SD	500

1060	Jul 24 95	Larry King's Dinner Theater	Keystone	SD	125
1061	Jul 25 95	Larry King's Dinner Theater	Keystone	SD	80
1062	Jul 26 95	Mount Rushmore Book Signing	Keystone	SD	500
1063	Jul 26 95	Larry King's Dinner Theater	Keystone	SD	50
1064	Jul 26 95	KOA Campground Show	Hill City	SD	83
1065	Jul 27 95	Larry King's Dinner Theater	Keystone	SD	50
1066	Jul 28 95	Mount Rushmore Book Signing	Keystone	SD	500
1067	Jul 28 95	Larry King's Dinner Theater	Keystone	SD	75
1068	Jul 28 95	KOA Campground Show	Hill City	SD	35
1069	Jul 29 95	Larry King's Dinner Theater	Keystone	SD	50
1070	Jul 29 95	KOA Campground Show	Hill City	SD	20
1071	Jul 31 95	Larry King's Dinner Theater	Keystone	SD	75
1072	Aug 1 95	Mount Rushmore Book Signing	Keystone	SD	500
1073	Aug 1 95	Larry King's Dinner Theater	Keystone	SD	75
1074	Aug 2 95	Larry King's Dinner Theater	Keystone	SD	80
1075	Aug 2 95	KOA Campground Show	Hill City	SD	65
1076	Aug 3 95	Mount Rushmore Book Signing	Keystone	SD	500
1077	Aug 3 95	Larry King's Dinner Theater	Keystone	SD	40
1078	Aug 4 95	Larry King's Dinner Theater	Keystone	SD	50
1079	Aug 4 95	KOA Campground Show	Hill City	SD	25
1080	Aug 5 95	Larry King's Dinner Theater	Keystone	SD	25
1081	Aug 5 95	KOA Campground Show	Hill City	SD	25
1082	Aug 7 95	Larry King's Dinner Theater	Keystone	SD	50
1083	Aug 8 95	Mount Rushmore Book Signing	Keystone	SD	500
1084	Aug 9 95	Mount Rushmore Book Signing	Keystone	SD	1000
1085	Aug 9 95	KOA Campground Show	Hill City	SD	48

1086	Aug 10 95	Mount Rushmore Book Signing	Keystone	SD	500
1087	Aug 11 95	KOA Campground Show	Hill City	SD	20
1088	Aug 12 95	KOA Campground Show	Hill City	SD	15
1089	Aug 14 95	Rafter J Bar Ranch Campground Show	Hill City	SD	71
1090	Aug 16 95	Mount Rushmore Book Signing	Keystone	SD	500
1091	Aug 16 95	KOA Campground Show	Hill City	SD	31
1092	Aug 18 95	Mount Rushmore Book Signing	Keystone	SD	500
1093	Aug 18 95	KOA Campground Show	Hill City	SD	45
1094	Aug 19 95	KOA Campground Show	Hill City	SD	46
1095	Aug 21 95	Rafter J Bar Ranch Campground Show	Hill City	SD	46
1096	Aug 22 95	Mount Rushmore Book Signing	Keystone	SD	500
1097	Aug 23 95	Mount Rushmore Book Signing	Keystone	SD	500
1098	Aug 23 95	KOA Campground Show	Hill City	SD	50
1099	Aug 25 95	KOA Campground Show	Hill City	SD	31
1100	Aug 26 95	Holy Terror Days Parade	Keystone	SD	1000
1101	Aug 26 95	KOA Campground Show	Hill City	SD	30
1102	Aug 29 95	Mount Rushmore Book Signing	Keystone	SD	500
1103	Aug 30 95	Mount Rushmore Book Signing	Keystone	SD	500
1104	Sep 2 95	Benefit Show for town	Hill City	SD	65
1105	Sep 2 95	KOA Campground Show	Hill City	SD	35
1106	Sep 21 95	Ashville Elem School	Ashville	AL	400
1107	Sep 21 95	Ashville Middle School	Ashville	AL	300
1108	Sep 21 95	Reception at Roses & Lace B&B	Ashville	AL	50

1109	Sep 22 95	Reenactment at Armory	Ashville	AL	1100
1110	Sep 23 95	Show in Courtyard	Ashville	AL	125
1111	Sep 23 95	Battlefield Reenactment	Ashville	AL	2000
1112	Sep 23 95	Show in Courtyard	Ashville	AL	30
1113	Sep 23 95	Dance Ball in Armory	Ashville	AL	200
1114	Sep 24 95	Battlefield Reenactment	Ashville	AL	1500
1115	Sep 27 95	AIDS Walk Reception at Fernbank	Atlanta	GA	200
1116	Sep 28 95	Atlanta Project Mtg	Atlanta	GA	20
1117	Sep 29 95	Pine Ridge Elem School	Stone Mtn.	GA	1000
1118	Oct 5 95	Surprise Birthday Party	Stone Mtn.	GA	3
1119	Oct 17 95	Joelton Middle School	Joelton	TN	350
1120	Oct 19 95	"Stay in School" Program, Corps Eng.	Carter's Lake	GA	1300
1121	Oct 23 95	Nancy Creek Elem School	Atlanta	GA	450
1122	Oct 23 95	Buckhead Kiwanis	Atlanta	GA	50
1123	Nov 3 95	Powder Springs Elem School	Powder Springs	GA	950
1124	Nov 4 95	Kiwanis Youth Mtg.	Jasper	GA	75
1125	Nvo 8 95	Tate Elem School	Tate	GA	500
1126	Nov 8 95	Meet with Kroger Hdq people	Atlanta	GA	10
1127	Nov 28 95	Press Club Party	Atlanta	GA	300
1128	Nov 30 95	Chamber of Commerce After Hours Pty	Atlanta	GA	350
1129	Nov 30 95	Buckhead Lupus Fund Raiser	Atlanta	GA	50
1130	Dec 1 95	WSB TV "People to People" filming	Atlanta	GA	
1131	Dec 1 95	Lincoln Financial Group office visit	Atlanta	GA	60
1132	Dec 1 95	Peyton Forest Elem School	Atlanta	GA	125
1133	Dec 2 95	21st Ohio Christmas Dinner	Lawrenceville	GA	40

1134	Dec 5 95	Atlanta Cluster Mtg at Grove Park	Atlanta	GA	15
1135	Dec 6 95	Japan-American Society Dinner Party	Atlanta	GA	400
1136	Dec 12 95	Reading's Fun Book Fair	Atlanta	GA	200
1137	Dec 14 95	Marist High School	Atlanta	GA	300
1138	Dec 30 95	Peach Bowl Parade, "Another Way Out"	Atlanta	GA	5000
1139	Jan 3 96	Lincoln Financial Group Mtg.	Atlanta	GA	25
1140	Jan 17 96	Sarah Smith Elem School	Atlanta	GA	500
1141	Jan 19 96	Macedonia Elem School	Macedonia	GA	300
1142	Jan 24 96	Lincoln Financial Group Mtg.	Atlanta	GA	25
1143	Jan 26 96	Central Elem School	Carrollton	GA	1100
1144	Jan 29 96	Cottonwood Elem School	Omaha	NE	400
1145	Jan 29 96	LaVista Elem School	Omaha	NE	400
1146	Jan 30 96	Rumsey Station Elem School	Omaha	NE	400
1147	Jan 31 96	G. Stanley Hall Elem School	Omaha	NE	400
1148	Feb 1 96	Hitchcock Elem School	Omaha	NE	300
1149	Feb 2 96	Aldrich Elem School	Omaha	NE	500
1150	Feb 12 96	Trinity School	Atlanta	GA	200
1151	Feb 12 96	Lovett School	Atlanta	GA	200
1152	Feb 14 96	Northwest Kiwanis	Atlanta	GA	25
1153	Feb 19 96	King Springs Elem School	Smyrna	GA	600
1154	Feb 20 96	Grove Park Elem School	Atlanta	GA	600
1155	Feb 21 96	Pine Ridge Elem School	Stone Mtn.	GA	1000
1156	Feb 29 96	GPTV Mtg	Atlanta	GA	25
1157	Mar 6 96	First Board Meeting A.L.A.	Atlanta	GA	10
1158	Mar 7 96	Japan-American Society Dinner Party	Atlanta	GA	400

1159	Mar 12 96	Holy Innocents Episcopal School	Sandy Springs	GA	500
1160	Mar 13 96	Hightower Trail Middle School	Marietta	GA	300
1161	Mar 14 96	Esther Jackson Elem School	Roswell	GA	1300
1162	Mar 21 96	Emory Elderhostel Mtg	Atlanta	GA	40
1163	Mar 25 96	Kiwanis Mtg.	Atlanta	GA	50
1164	Mar 25 96	Austin Kelly PR Mtg	Atlanta	GA	10
1165	Mar 28 96	Antibellum Jubilee	Stone Mtn.	GA	2000
1166	Mar 29 96	Antibellum Jubilee	Stone Mtn.	GA	7000
1167	Mar 30 96	Antibellum Jubilee	Stone Mtn.	GA	1000
1168	Mar 31 96	Antibellum Jubilee	Stone Mtn.	GA	500
1169	Apr 2 96	Mimosa Elem School	Roswell	GA	1000
1170	Apr 3 96	"The Atlanta Project" Dinner	Atlanta	GA	25
1171	Apr 4 96	Debates for Lincoln Financial Group	Atlanta	GA	50
1172	Apr 5 96	Woodson Elem School	Atlanta	GA	500
1173	Apr 10 96	Several meetings around town	Rome	GA	100
1174	Apr 12 96	ALP Convention	Springfield	IL	100
1175	Apr 13 96	ALP Convention	Springfield	IL	100
1176	Apr 14 96	ALP Convention	Springfield	IL	100
1177	Apr 15 96	ALP Convention	Springfield	IL	75
1178	Apr 17 95	United Way Grants Mtg	Atlanta	GA	10
1179	Apr 18 96	Public Square Opra House	Adairsville	GA	25
1180	Apr 18 96	Shorter College Play	Rome	GA	100
1181	Apr 23 96	Dunleith Elem School	Marietta	GA	600
1182	Apr 23 96	Dunleith Elem School PTA Mtg	Marietta	GA	200
1183	Apr 27 96	Public Square Opra House	Adairsville	GA	25
1184	Apr 30 96	Brown Elem School	Smyrna	GA	400

1185	May 1 96	Seigakuin Atlanta Int'l School	Atlanta	GA	80
1186	May 3 96	T.A.P. Partners Mtg	Atlanta	GA	20
1187	May 4 96	"Stay & See Georgia" Show	Stone Mtn.	GA	5000
1188	May 5 96	"Stay & See Georgia" Show	Stone Mtn.	GA	5000
1189	May 13 96	Cook Elem School	Atlanta	GA	500
1190	May 17 96	Battle of Resaca	Resaca	GA	500
1191	May 17 96	"Little Women" Dinner Theater	Adairsville	GA	50
1192	May 18 96	"Little Women" Dinner Theater	Adairsville	GA	20
1193	May 19 96	Battle of Resaca	Resaca	GA	5000
1194	May 21 96	TV filming PSA Grove Park School	Atlanta	GA	50
1195	May 24 96	"Little Women" Dinner Theater	Adairsville	GA	35
1196	May 25 96	"Little Women" Dinner Theater	Adairsville	GA	55
1197	May 30 96	Dekalb PTA Assoc. Mtg	Duluth	GA	150
1198	Jun 14 96	"Good Day Atlanta" TV Show	Atlanta	GA	25
1199	Jul 3 96	Chastain Park Concert	Atlanta	GA	5000
1200	Jul 4 96	Salute to Honor America Concert	Rome	GA	25000
1201	Jul 5 96	Dinner Theater Show	Adairsville	GA	35
1202	Jul 7 96	Inn Scarlett's Footsteps Mtg	Concord	GA	30
1203	Jul 8 96	Rafter J Bar Ranch Campground Show	Hill City	SD	85
1204	Jul 9 96	Larry King's Dinner Theater	Keystone	SD	120
1205	Jul 10 96	Single Seniors Dinner Mtg	Rapid City	SD	30
1206	Jul 12 96	Rafter J Bar Ranch Campground Show	Hill City	SD	40

1207	Jul 14 96	White House Inn Fifth Anniver Celeb	Lead	SD	75
1208	Jul 15 96	Rafter J Bar Ranch Campground Show	Hill City	SD	60
1209	Jul 18 96	Rafter J Bar Ranch Campground Show	Hill City	SD	35
1210	Jul 20 96	I-75 Welcome Center	Ringgold	GA	100
1211	Jul 24 96	SKATE Rep Mtg	Atlanta	GA	10
1212	Jul 26 96	Wal-Mart	Newnan	GA	500
1213	Jul 27 96	Battle of Brown's Mill	Newnan	GA	1500
1214	Jul 28 96	Battle of Brown's Mill	Newnan	GA	1000
1215	Aug 1 96	Rome Auditorium	Rome	GA	35
1216	Aug 2 96	Rome Auditorium	Rome	GA	35
1217	Aug 9 96	N.A.C.A.C. Conference	Dallas	TX	1000
1218	Aug 10 96	N.A.C.A.C. Conference	Dallas	TX	500
1219	Aug 21 96	Film TV PSA for Adoptions	Dallas	TX	10
1220	Aug 28 96	Film video of show	Atlanta	GA	5
1221	Sep 7 96	MGM Grand Hotel	Las Vegas	NV	100
1222	Sep 16 96	Suder Elem School	Jonesboro	GA	900
1223	Sep 17 96	Rocky Mountain Elem School	Marietta	GA	800
1224	Sep 18 96	Moody Middle School	Moody	AL	700
1225	Sep 18 96	Springville Middle School	Springville	AL	700
1226	Sep 19 96	Morning Talk Show	Birmingham	AL	10
1227	Sep 20 96	Armory schools visiting	Ashville	AL	1000
1228	Sep 21 96	Battle Reenactment	Ashville	AL	100
1229	Sep 21 96	Show in Courthouse	Ashville	AL	150
1230	Sep 27 96	Dinner at Historic Site	Charleston	IL	50
1231	Sep 28 96	Debates at Fairgrounds	Charleston	IL	100
1232	Oct 2 96	Heiskell School	Atlanta	GA	200
1233	Oct 3 96	Chambrel Retirement Home	Roswell	GA	75
1234	Oct 5 96	Marble Festival Parade	Jasper	GA	5000

Image in the Mirror

1235	Oct 5 96	True Value Hardware Promo	Jasper	GA	50
1236	Oct 7 96	Harmony Leeland Elem School	Mableton	GA	500
1237	Oct 11 96	Heritage Festival	Decatur	GA	1000
1238	Oct 11 96	Rotary Club Luncheon	Decatur	GA	125
1239	Oct 17 96	Joelton Middle School	Joelton	TN	350
1240	Oct 28 96	Hightower Elem School	Doraville	GA	450
1241	Oct 29 96	Due West Elem School	Kennesaw	GA	500
1242	Oct 30 96	Ford Elem School	Acworth	GA	800
1243	Nov 4 96	Briarlake Elem School	Decatur	GA	450
1244	Nov 8 96	Shallowford Falls Elem School	Marietta	GA	650
1245	Nov 9 96	Arts/Craft Festival Civic Center	Gainesville	GA	250
1246	Nov 19 96	Tiger Creek Elem School	Tunnel Hill	GA	500
1247	Nov 20 96	Brilliant Elem School	Brilliant	AL	300
1248	Nov 27 96	Graves Memorial Library	Kennebunkport	ME	25
1249	Nov 27 96	Nashua Public Library	Nashua	NH	75
1250	Nov 29 96	Brooks Memorial Library	Brattleboro	VT	40
1251	Nov 29 96	Yankee Candle Factory visit	Deerfield	MA	1000
1252	Dec 1 96	Harris Public Library	Woonsocket	RI	10
1253	Dec 3 96	Woodstock Public Library	Woodstock	GA	20
1254	Dec 14 96	Georgia Speakers Assoc Mtg	Atlanta	GA	100
1255	Dec 17 96	Atlanta Conventions & Visitors Bureau	Atlanta	GA	75
1256	Jan 8 97	Cartersville Elem School	Cartersville	GA	800
1257	Jan 13 97	Brain Injury Assoc Mtg	Atlanta	GA	10
1258	Jan 15 97	Powder Springs Elem School	Powder Springs	GA	900
1259	Jan 28 97	Ellijay Elem School	Ellijay	GA	1600
1260	Jan 29 97	Hokes Bluff Elem School	Hokes Bluff	AL	500
1261	Feb 4 97	McEver Elem School	Gainesville	GA	500

1262	Feb 7 97	Westview Elem School	Spartanburg	SC	900
1263	Feb 11 97	Holly Springs Elem School	Holly Springs	GA	600
1264	Feb 12 97	Chambrel Retirement Home	Roswell	GA	100
1265	Feb 13 97	Schenck School	Atlanta	GA	200
1266	Feb 14 97	Brain Injury Assoc Fund Raiser	Atlanta	GA	100
1267	Feb 17 97	Bells Ferry Elem School	Marietta	GA	600
1268	Feb 18 97	Hickory Flat Elem School	McDonough	GA	715
1269	Feb 20 97	Upson-Lee North Elem School	Thomaston	GA	700
1270	Feb 21 97	Southside Elem School	Gadsden	AL	750
1271	Feb 24 97	Edison Park Elem School	Ft. Myers	FL	500
1272	Feb 25 97	Tice Elem School	Ft. Myers	FL	850
1273	Feb 26 97	Caloosa Elem School	Cape Coral	FL	850
1274	Feb 27 97	Pine Woods Elem School	Estero	FL	900
1275	Feb 28 97	Three Oaks Elem School	Ft. Myers	FL	980
1276	Mar 3 97	Spring Creek Elem School	Bonita Springs	FL	1000
1277	Mar 10 97	Redding Elem School	Lizella	GA	450
1278	Mar 15 97	Georgia Speakers Assoc Mtg	Atlanta	GA	150
1279	Mar 17 97	Woodland Heights Elem School	Spartanburg	SC	550
1280	Mar 18 97	Lone Oak Elem School	Spartanburg	SC	250
1281	Mar 18 97	Adult Ed Class at Arcadia Elem Sch	Spartanburg	SC	10
1282	Mar 18 97	Boy Scout Troop Mtg plus Cub Scouts	Spartanburg	SC	100
1283	Mar 19 97	Village School	Spartanburg	SC	120
1284	Mar 20 97	Buckhead Business Assoc Mtg	Atlanta	GA	150
1285	Mar 21 97	Nationwide Auto Club Mtg	Atlanta	GA	30

1286	Mar 28 97	Piedmont Baptist "XYZ" Club Lunch	Marietta	GA	90
1287	Apr 18 97	Fulton County PTA Vendor Fair	Roswell	GA	200
1288	Apr 18 97	C.H.A.T. American Girls Club	Blue Ridge	GA	60
1289	Apr 21 97	West Dekalb Rotary Club	Atlanta	GA	30
1290	Apr 25 97	A.L.P. Convention	Gettysburg	PA	100
1291	Apr 26 97	A.L.P. Convention	Gettysburg	PA	500
1292	Apr 30 97	Charlotte Elem School	Charlotte	TN	750
1293	May 9 97	Special Arts Fair	Ellijay	GA	600
1294	May 17 97	G/W Special Dinner Home of Dr. Van	Griffin	GA	15
1295	May 29 97	Photo Shoot at Carter Center Library	Atlanta	GA	15
1296	Jun 14 97	Wal-Mart Promo	Newnan	GA	300
1297	Jun 14 97	Battle of Brown's Mill	Newnan	GA	200
1298	Jun 15 97	Battle of Brown's Mill	Newnan	GA	300
1299	Jul 4 97	Beulah "World Record Parade"	Beulah	WY	2000
1300	Jul 4 97	Rafter J Bar Ranch Campground	Hill City	SD	75
1301	Jul 5 97	Advance Mobile Homes Promo	Rapid City	SD	25
1302	Jul 6 97	Rafter J Bar Ranch Campground	Hill City	SD	45
1303	Jul 8 97	Rafter J Bar Ranch Campground	Hill City	SD	45
1304	Jul 11 97	Rafter J Bar Ranch Campground	Hill City	SD	35
1305	Jul 12 97	Heart of the Hills Parade	Hill City	SD	2000
1306	Jul 13 97	Rafter J Bar Ranch Campground	Hill City	SD	40

1307	Jul 15 97	Rafter J Bar Ranch Campground	Hill City	SD	70
1308	Jul 17 97	Hart Ranch Breakfast	Rapid City	SD	25
1309	Jul 17 97	Hart Ranch Rodeo	Rapid City	SD	300
1310	Jul 18 97	Rafter J Bar Ranch Campground	Hill City	SD	40
1311	Jul 19 97	Family Birthday Party	Lead	SD	10
1312	Jul 20 97	Rafter J Bar Ranch Campground	Hill City	SD	83
1313	Jul 21 97	Mount Rushmore Gift Shop	Mt. Rushmore	SD	1000
1314	Jul 22 97	Mount Rushmore Gift Shop	Mt. Rushmore	SD	1000
1315	Jul 22 97	Rafter J Bar Ranch Campground	Hill City	SD	75
1316	Jul 25 97	Rafter J Bar Ranch Campground	Hill City	SD	50
1317	Jul 26 97	Gold Rush Days Parade	Custer	SD	3000
1318	Jul 26 97	American Legends Museum Show	Custer	SD	35
1319	Jul 27 97	Rafter J Bar Ranch Campground	Hill City	SD	55
1320	Jul 28 97	Mount Rushmore Gift Shop	Mt. Rushmore	SD	1000
1321	Jul 29 97	Mount Rushmore Gift Shop	Mt. Rushmore	SD	700
1322	Jul 29 97	Rafter J Bar Ranch Campground	Hill City	SD	103
1323	Jul 30 97	Mount Rushmore Gift Shop	Mt. Rushmore	SD	1000
1324	Aug 1 97	Rafter J Bar Ranch Campground	Hill City	SD	45
1325	Aug 2 97	Show at City Hall	Hill City	SD	35
1326	Aug 3 97	Rafter J Bar Ranch Campground	Hill City	SD	80
1327	Aug 4 97	Mount Rushmore Gift Shop	Mt. Rushmore	SD	1000
1328	Aug 5 97	Mount Rushmore Gift Shop	Mt. Rushmore	SD	1000

Image in the Mirror

1329	Aug 5 97	Rafter J Bar Ranch Campground	Hill City	SD	33
1330	Aug 6 97	Mount Rushmore Gift Shop	Mt. Rushmore	SD	1000
1331	Aug 7 97	Hart Ranch Show	Rapid City	SD	55
1332	Aug 8 97	Rafter J Bar Ranch Campground	Hill City	SD	40
1333	Aug 10 97	Rafter J Bar Ranch Campground	Hill City	SD	80
1334	Aug 11 97	Mount Rushmore Gift Shop	Mt. Rushmore	SD	1000
1335	Aug 12 97	Mount Rushmore Gift Shop	Mt. Rushmore	SD	2000
1336	Aug 12 97	Rafter J Bar Ranch Campground	Hill City	SD	80
1337	Aug 13 97	Mount Rushmore Gift Shop	Mt. Rushmore	SD	1000
1338	Aug 15 97	Rafter J Bar Ranch Campground	Hill City	SD	20
1339	Aug 17 97	Rafter J Bar Ranch Campground	Hill City	SD	20
1340	Aug 18 97	Mount Rushmore Gift Shop	Mt. Rushmore	SD	1000
1341	Aug 19 97	Mount Rushmore Gift Shop	Mt. Rushmore	SD	1000
1342	Aug 20 97	Mount Rushmore Gift Shop	Mt. Rushmore	SD	1000
1343	Aug 20 97	Rafter J Bar Ranch Campground	Hill City	SD	55
1344	Seo 27 97	True Value Hardware Grand Opening	Jasper	GA	200
1345	Sep 29 97	Harney Elem School	South Souix	NE	250
1346	Sep 29 97	E. N. Swett Elem School	South Souix	NE	250
1347	Sep 30 97	Cardinal Elem School	South Souix	NE	250
1348	Sep 30 97	Dakota City Elem School	Dakota City	NE	250
1349	Sep 30 97	Lewis & Clark Elem School	South Souix	NE	250
1350	Oct 1 97	BCLUW Elem School	Conrad	IA	230
1351	Oct 1 97	BCLUW High School	Conrad	IA	250
1352	Oct 7 97	Center High School	Center	TX	500
1353	Oct 7 97	Timpson School	Timpson	TX	150

1354	Oct 8 97	Timpson School	Timpson	TX	500
1355	Oct 9 97	Tenaha Elem School	Tenaha	TX	450
1356	Oct 10 97	Beckville Elem School	Beckville	TX	250
1357	Oct 21 97	Canton Elem School	Canton	GA	550
1358	Oct 23 97	Clarkdale Elem School	Austell	GA	450
1359	Oct 24 97	New Prospect Elem School	Alpharetta	GA	900
1360	Oct 27 97	Nancy Creek Elem School	Atlanta	GA	450
1361	Oct 28 97	Fayette Elem School	Fayette	AL	850
1362	Oct 29 97	Mountain Park Elem School	Roswell	GA	800
1363	Nov 10 97	Joelton Middle School	Joelton	TN	300
1364	Nov 11 97	Bell Aire Elem School	Tullahoma	TN	400
1365	Nov 11 97	Bell Aire Elem School PTA Mtg	Tullahoma	TN	300
1366	Nov 12 97	West Middle School	Tullahoma	TN	400
1367	Nov 13 97	Robert E. Lee Elem School	Tullahoma	TN	500
1368	Nov 14 97	Jolly Elem School	Clarkston	GA	700
1369	Nov 14 97	Glaxo Wellcome Mtg with doctors	Braselton	GA	20
1370	Nov 19 97	Glaxo Wellcome Sales Mtg	Atlanta	GA	20
1371	Dec 20 97	The Art Room	Jasper	GA	25
1372	Jan 15 98	Northwood Elem School	Roswell	GA	1000
1373	Jan 22 98	St. Joseph School	Marietta	GA	300
1374	Feb 4 98	State Bridge Crossing Elem School	Alpharetta	GA	1100
1375	Feb 4 98	Mt. Vernon Towers Seniors	Atlanta	GA	50
1376	Feb 9 98	Galloway School	Atlanta	GA	300
1377	Feb 9 98	Cobb Scottish Rite Dinner	Marietta	GA	30
1378	Feb 10 98	Atlanta Kiwanis Club Luncheon	Atlanta	GA	150
1379	Feb 10 98	Atherton Place Seniors	Marietta	GA	50
1380	Feb 11 98	Riverbend Elem School	Gainesville	GA	550
1381	Feb 12 98	Lakeview Academy	Gainesville	GA	400
1382	Feb 14 98	NSA Workshop	Norfolk	VA	400

1383	Feb 23 98	Lake Windward Elem School	Alpharetta	GA	1250
1384	Feb 26 98	Granada Upper Elem School	Granada	MS	700
1385	Mar 2 98	Canyon Lake Elem School	Rapid City	SD	300
1386	Mar 3 98	Meadowbrook Elem School	Rapid City	SD	600
1387	Mar 4 98	Beulah Elem School	Beulah	ND	800
1388	Mar 5 98	Center Elem School	Center	ND	200
1389	Mar 6 98	DeMore School	Medora	ND	200
1390	Mar 6 98	Prairie School	Prairie	ND	50
1391	Mar 9 98	Pinedale Elem School	Rapid City	SD	400
1392	Mar 19 98	Hammond Glenn Retirement Center	Atlanta	GA	100
1393	Mar 29 98	Shoot "Just for Feet" TV commercial	Birmingham	AL	5
1394	Mar 31 98	Weinstein Center Seniors	Atlanta	GA	20
1395	Apr 11 98	Lions Club Dinner Mtg	Jasper	GA	200
1396	Apr 17 98	Mark Twain Elem School	Charleston	IL	250
1397	Apr 17 98	Assoc of Lincoln Presenters Conv	Charleston	IL	150
1398	Apr 18 98	Assoc of Lincoln Presenters Conv	Charleston	IL	150
1399	Apr 20 98	Riley Elem School	Salt Lake City	UT	350
1400	Apr 21 98	Mountain View Elem School	Salt Lake City	UT	600
1401	Apr 22 98	Parkview Elem School	Salt Lake City	UT	800
1402	Apr 23 98	Franklin Elem School	Salt Lake City	UT	550
1403	Apr 23 98	L.D.S. Church supper	Salt Lake City	UT	200
1404	Apr 24 98	Edison Elem School	Salt Lake City	UT	600
1405	May 1 98	Lake Windward Elem School	Alpharetta	GA	1250
1406	May 4 98	Belfield Public School	Belfield	ND	225
1407	May 5 98	Lincoln Elem School	Beach	ND	175

1408	May 6 98	Taylor/Richardson Elem School	Taylor	ND	150
1409	May 13 98	Wall Schools	Wall	SD	400
1410	May 14 98	Mead Rural School	Union Center	SD	200
1411	May 21 98	Lk. Windward class climb Kennesaw Mt.	Kennesaw	GA	200
1412	June 10 98	Atlanta Masonic Club	Atlanta	GA	25
1413	June 10 98	First Church of the Nazarene	Atlanta	GA	50
1414	June 13 98	Rafter J Bar Ranch Campground	Hill City	SD	80
1415	June 15 98	Mount Rushmore Memorial	Keystone	SD	2500
1416	June 16 98	Mount Rushmore Memorial	Keystone	SD	2000
1417	June 16 98	Rafter J Bar Ranch Campground	Hill City	SD	40
1418	June 17 98	Mount Rushmore Memorial	Keystone	SD	1500
1419	June 18 98	Mount Rushmore Memorial	Keystone	SD	1000
1420	June 18 98	Rafter J Bar Ranch Campground	Hill City	SD	50
1421	June 19 98	Mount Rushmore Memorial	Keystone	SD	2000
1422	June 21 98	Rafter J Bar Ranch Campground	Hill City	SD	55
1423	June 22 98	Mount Rushmore Memorial	Keystone	SD	1500
1424	June 23 98	Mount Rushmore Memorial	Keystone	SD	1500
1425	June 23 98	Rafter J Bar Ranch Campground	Hill City	SD	36
1426	June 24 98	Mount Rushmore Memorial	Keystone	SD	1000
1427	June 25 98	Mount Rushmore Memorial	Keystone	SD	1000
1428	June 25 98	Rafter J Bar Ranch Campground	Hill City	SD	25
1429	June 26 98	Mount Rushmore Memorial	Keystone	SD	1000
1430	June 28 98	Rafter J Bar Ranch Campground	Hill City	SD	60

1431	June 29 98	Mount Rushmore Memorial	Keystone	SD	1000
1432	June 29 98	Chamber of Commerce	Hill City	SD	15
1433	June 30 98	Mount Rushmore Memorial	Keystone	SD	1000
1434	June 30 98	Rafter J Bar Ranch Campground	Hill City	SD	60
1435	July 1 98	Mount Rushmore Memorial	Keystone	SD	1000
1436	July 1 98	Flag Mountain Camp-Blind	Hill City	SD	30
1437	July 2 98	Mount Rushmore Memorial	Keystone	SD	1000
1438	July 2 98	Rafter J Bar Ranch Campground	Hill City	SD	35
1439	July 3 98	Mount Rushmore Memorial	Keystone	SD	1000
1440	July 4 98	Civic Center fund raiser	Rapid City	SD	500
1441	July 4 98	Chamber of Commerce	Hill City	SD	50
1442	July 5 98	Rafter J Bar Ranch Campground	Hill City	SD	30
1443	July 6 98	Mount Rushmore Memorial	Keystone	SD	1000
1444	July 7 98	Mount Rushmore Memorial	Keystone	SD	1000
1445	July 7 98	Rafter J Bar Ranch Campground	Hill City	SD	60
1446	July 8 98	Mount Rushmore Memorial	Keystone	SD	1000
1447	July 9 98	Mount Rushmore Memorial	Keystone	SD	1000
1448	July 9 98	Rafter J Bar Ranch Campground	Hill City	SD	30
1449	July 10 98	Mount Rushmore Memorial	Keystone	SD	1000
1450	July 11 98	Heritage Days Parade	Hill City	SD	1000
1451	July 11 98	With Native American "Spirit"	Hill City	SD	50
1452	July 12 98	Rafter J Bar Ranch Campground	Hill City	SD	17
1453	July 13 98	Mount Rushmore Memorial	Keystone	SD	1000
1454	July 14 98	Mount Rushmore Memorial	Keystone	SD	1000
1455	July 14 98	Rafter J Bar Ranch Campground	Hill City	SD	40

1456	July 15 98	Mount Rushmore Memorial	Keystone	SD	1000
1457	July 16 98	Mount Rushmore Memorial	Keystone	SD	1000
1458	July 16 98	Rafter J Bar Ranch Campground	Hill City	SD	40
1459	July 17 98	Mount Rushmore Memorial	Keystone	SD	1000
1460	July 17 98	Senior Center	Hill City	SD	5
1461	July 18 98	Jostens convention	Washington	DC	1000
1462	July 20 98	Mount Rushmore Memorial	Keystone	SD	1000
1463	July 21 98	Mount Rushmore Memorial	Keystone	SD	1000
1464	July 21 98	Rafter J Bar Ranch Campground	Hill City	SD	25
1465	July 22 98	Mount Rushmore Memorial	Keystone	SD	1000
1466	July 23 98	Mount Rushmore Memorial	Keystone	SD	1000
1467	July 23 98	Rafter J Bar Ranch Campground	Hill City	SD	20
1468	July 24 98	Mount Rushmore Memorial	Keystone	SD	1000
1469	July 25 98	McKey Family reunion	Rapid City	SD	35
1470	July 26 98	Rafter J Bar Ranch Campground	Hill City	SD	80
1471	July 27 98	Mount Rushmore Memorial	Keystone	SD	1000
1472	July 28 98	Mount Rushmore Memorial	Keystone	SD	1000
1473	July 28 98	Rafter J Bar Ranch Campground	Hill City	SD	20
1474	July 29 98	Mount Rushmore Memorial	Keystone	SD	1000
1475	July 30 98	Mount Rushmore Memorial	Keystone	SD	1000
1476	July 30 98	Rafter J Bar Ranch Campground	Hill City	SD	40
1477	July 31 98	Mount Rushmore Memorial	Keystone	SD	1000
1478	Aug 2 98	Rafter J Bar Ranch Campground	Hill City	SD	30
1479	Aug 3 98	Mount Rushmore Memorial	Keystone	SD	1000
1480	Aug 4 98	Mount Rushmore Memorial	Keystone	SD	1000

1481	Aug 4 98	Rafter J Bar Ranch Campground	Hill City	SD	60
1482	Aug 5 98	Mount Rushmore Memorial	Keystone	SD	1000
1483	Aug 6 98	Mount Rushmore Memorial	Keystone	SD	1000
1484	Aug 6 98	Rafter J Bar Ranch Campground	Hill City	SD	25
1485	Aug 7 98	Mount Rushmore Memorial	Keystone	SD	1000
1486	Aug 9 98	Rafter J Bar Ranch Campground	Hill City	SD	55
1487	Aug 10 98	Mount Rushmore Memorial	Keystone	SD	1000
1488	Aug 11 98	Mount Rushmore Memorial	Keystone	SD	1000
1489	Aug 11 98	Rafter J Bar Ranch Campground	Hill City	SD	30
1490	Aug 12 98	Mount Rushmore Memorial	Keystone	SD	1000
1491	Aug 13 98	Mount Rushmore Memorial	Keystone	SD	1000
1492	Aug 13 98	Rafter J Bar Ranch Campground	Hill City	SD	55
1493	Aug 14 98	Mount Rushmore Memorial	Keystone	SD	1000
1494	Aug 16 98	Rafter J Bar Ranch Campground	Hill City	SD	61
1495	Aug 17 98	Rotary Luncheon	Custer	SD	30
1496	Aug 17 98	Mount Rushmore Memorial	Keystone	SD	1000
1497	Aug 18 98	Mount Rushmore Memorial	Keystone	SD	1000
1498	Aug 18 98	Rafter J Bar Ranch Campground	Hill City	SD	30
1499	Aug 19 98	Mount Rushmore Memorial	Keystone	SD	1000
1500	Aug 20 98	Mount Rushmore Memorial	Keystone	SD	500
1501	Aug 21 98	Mount Rushmore Memorial	Keystone	SD	500
1502	Sept 2 98	Montessori Children's School	Omaha	NE	75
1503	Sept 9 98	Plantation School	Dunwoody	GA	20
1504	Sept 14 98	Allen W. Roberts Elem School	New Providence	NJ	550

1505	Sept 15 98	Trinity Lutheran School	Hicksville	NY	400
1506	Sept 16 98	Arlington Memorial High School	Arlington	VT	500
1507	Sept 17 98	Fisher Elem School	Arlington	VT	300
1508	Sept 18 98	Wyoming Seminary School	Wilkes Barre	PA	500
1509	Sept 21 98	Our Lady of Grace School	Penndel	PA	550
1510	Sept 23 98	Buckingham Friends School	Lahaska	PA	190
1511	Sept 24 98	Kmapp Elem School	Lansdale	PA	550
1512	Sept 25 98	Trinity Lutheran School	Joppatown	MD	350
1513	Sept 25 98	Edgewood Elem School	Edgewood	MD	400
1514	Sept 28 98	Arcola Elem School	Arcola	VA	500
1515	Sept 29 98	Huntingdon High School	Huntingdon	PA	800
1516	Sept 30 98	Central Elem School	New Paris	PA	550
1517	Oct 1 98	Moshannon Elem School	Houtzdale	PA	700
1518	Oct 2 98	East Union Elem School	Russellton	PA	350
1519	Oct 5 98	Hambden Elem School	Chardon	OH	300
1520	Oct 6 98	St. Thomas Lutheran School	Rocky River	OH	150
1521	Oct 6 98	Julie Billiart School	Lindhurst	OH	120
1522	Oct 7 98	Poland-Union Elem School	Poland	OH	350
1523	Oct 9 98	Richmond Elem School	Richmond	OH	400
1524	Oct 9 98	Our Lady of Peace School	Wheeling	WV	200
1525	Oct 12 98	Union County Middle School	Liberty	IN	350
1526	Oct 13 98	Hope Elem School	Hope	IN	400
1527	Oct 13 98	Granville-Wells Elem School	Jamestown	IN	500
1528	Oct 14 98	Nevin Coppock Elem School	Tipp City	OH	500
1529	Oct 14 98	Daleville Elem School	Daleville	IN	340
1530	Oct 15 98	Bethlehem Lutheran School	Ft. Wayne	IN	200
1531	Oct 15 98	Liberty School	Ohio City	OH	200
1532	Oct 16 98	Bingham Elem School	Lansing	MI	200

1533	Oct 19 98	Child of Christ Lutheran School	Hartland	MI	175
1534	Oct 20 98	Hampton Elem School	Rochester Hills	MI	600
1535	Oct 21 98	Thorne Elem School	Dearborn Heights	MI	800
1536	Oct 21 98	Brick Elem School	Ypsilanti	MI	800
1537	Oct 22 98	Ezra Eby Elem School	Napoleon	MI	800
1538	Oct 23 98	Edgerton Elem School	Clio	MI	500
1539	Oct 23 98	St. Mary Magdalen School	Hazel Park	MI	175
1540	Oct 26 98	Immaculate Heart of Mary School	Grand Rapids	MI	500
1541	Oct 27 98	Eugene Field Elem School	Chicago	IL	400
1542	Oct 28 98	Kingsford Heights Elem School	Kingsford Heights	IN	180
1543	Oct 29 98	Andrew Jackson Language Academy	Chicago	IL	600
1544	Oct 30 98	Roanoke-Benson Jr. High School	Benson	IL	200
1545	Oct 30 98	Eugene Field Elem School	Wheeling	IL	40
1546	Nov 2 98	River Forest Elem School	Hobart	IN	225
1547	Nov 2 98	Je-Neir Elem School	Momence	IL	400
1548	Nov 4 98	Cuba Elem School	Cuba	IL	200
1549	Nov 4 98	Gridley Elem School	Gridley	IL	270
1550	Nov 5 98	C.E.C. School	Chillicothe	IL	500
1551	Nov 5 98	South School	Chillicothe	IL	200
1552	Nov 6 98	Galena Primary School	Galena	IL	350
1553	Nov 9 98	North Freedom Elem School	North Freedom	WI	180
1554	Nov 9 98	Jefferson Elem School	Waupun	WI	290
1555	Nov 10 98	St. Patrick School	Mauston	WI	200
1556	Nov 11 98	St. John's Lutheran School	Two Rivers	WI	175
1557	Nov 11 98	Columbus Elem School	Kenosha	WI	200
1558	Nov 12 98	Whittier Elem School	Kenosha	WI	600

1559	Nov 13 98	St. Paul Lutheran School	Lake Mills	WI	230
1560	Nov 13 98	St. Paul Lutheran School	Stevens Point	WI	200
1561	Nov 16 98	Pittsville Elem School	Pittsville	WI	550
1562	Nov 17 98	Wyoming Elem School	Wyoming	MN	800
1563	Nov 18 98	Prairie Farm Elem School	Prairie Farm	WI	250
1564	Nov 18 98	Univ. of Wisconsin	Rice Lake	WI	360
1565	Nov 19 98	Longfellow Elem School	Eau Claire	WI	400
1566	Nov 19 98	Countryside School	Edina	MN	400
1567	Nov 20 98	Southview Elem School	Chippewa Falls	WI	260
1568	Nov 23 98	Irving School	Dubuque	IA	600
1569	Nov 24 98	Riverbend Middle School	Iowa Falls	IA	100
1570	Nov 24 98	Lincoln Elem School	Waterloo	IA	240
1571	Nov 25 98	Sacred Heart Catholic School	Adams	MN	130
1572	Nov 25 98	Lake Mills Elem School	Lake Mills	IA	300
1573	Nov 25 98	First Presbyterian Church	Albion	IA	20
1574	Nov 30 98	Franklin Elem School	Boone	IA	200
1575	Nov 30 98	Lincoln Elem School	Boone	IA	125
1576	Nov 30 98	Bryant Elem School	Boone	IA	200
1577	Dec 1 98	Adair-Casey Elem School	Adair	IA	225
1578	Dec 1 98	Van Allen Elem School	Chariton	IA	325
1579	Dec 2 98	Running Fox Elem School	Alexandria	MO	150
1580	Dec 2 98	Palmyra Elem School	Palmyra	MO	400
1581	Dec 3 98	Corse Elem School	Burlington	IA	270
1582	Dec 4 98	Green Forest Elem School	Salem	MO	250
1583	Dec 7 98	Highland Primary School	Highland	IL	600
1584	Dec 8 98	St. Clair Elem School	St. Clair	MO	600
1585	Dec 9 98	East Side Elem School	Edinburgh	IN	600
1586	Dec 9 98	North Davies Elem School	Elnora	IN	300
1587	Dec 10 98	Newman-May SCHOOL	Tell City	IN	350
1588	Dec 10 98	St. Paul School	Tell City	IN	450
1589	Dec 11 98	North Junior High School	Henderson	KY	300
1590	Dec 11 98	Oakland Elem School	Oakland	KY	280

1591	Dec 14 98	Clark Elem School	Prestonburg	KY	300
1592	Dec 14 98	Emmalena Elem School	Emmalena	KY	200
1593	Dec 15 98	Hindman Elem School	Hindman	KY	400
1594	Dec 15 98	Grassy Elem School	Inez	KY	140
1595	Dec 16 98	Barbourville Elem School	Barbourville	KY	300
1596	Dec 16 98	Beech Fork Elem School	Helton	KY	100
1597	Dec 17 98	Wellford Elem School	Wellford	SC	700
1598	Dec 18 98	Mt. Olive Middle School	Mt. Olive	NC	325
1599	Jan 5 99	Taylor Ranch Elem School	Venice	FL	800
1600	Jan 7 99	Reidville Elem School	Reidville	SC	360
1601	Jan 11 99	West Hills Elem School	Lewisburg	TN	600
1602	Jan 11 99	Mt. Pleasant High School	Mt. Pleasant	TN	400
1603	Jan 12 99	Michie Elem School	Michie	TN	400
1604	Jan 12 99	Medina School	Medina	TN	300
1605	Jan 13 99	Belmont Elem School	Hopkinsville	KY	350
1606	Jan 13 99	Cumberland Heights Elem School	Clarksville	TN	350
1607	Jan 14 99	Black Rock Elem School	Black Rock	AR	225
1608	Jan 14 99	Christ Lutheran School	Little Rock	AR	250
1609	Jan 15 99	Chocotah Intermediate School	Chocotah	OK	350
1610	Jan 15 99	North Ward Elem School	Hartshorne	OK	350
1611	Jan 18 99	R. V. Harderlein School	Girard	KS	500
1612	Jan 18 99	Will Rogers Middle School	Miami	OK	500
1613	Jan 19 99	Maynard Elem School	Emporia	KS	225
1614	Jan 19 99	Rochester Elem School	Topeka	KS	250
1615	Jan 20 99	Wellsville Elem School	Wellsville	KS	500
1616	Jan 21 99	Broken Arrow School	Shawnee	KS	700
1617	Jan 22 99	John Diemer Elem School	Overland Park	KS	260
1618	Jan 25 99	Dixon Middle School	Dixon	MO	300
1619	Jan 25 99	Hartville Elem School	Hartville	MO	350
1620	Jan 25 99	Grovespring Elem School	Grovespring	MO	125
1621	Jan 26 99	Rich Hill Elem School	Rich Hill	MO	300

1622	Jan 26 99	Rich Hill High School	Rich Hill	MO	300
1623	Jan 27 99	Roscoe Elem School	Roscoe	MO	100
1624	Jan 27 99	Hardin Central School	Hardin	MO	100
1625	Jan 28 99	Pauline South Intermediate School	Wakarusa	KS	300
1626	Jan 28 99	North Broadway Elem School	Leavenworth	KS	200
1627	Jan 29 99	North Platte Elem School	Camden Point	MO	300
1628	Jan 29 99	North Platte Intermediate School	Edgerton	MO	175
1629	Feb 1 99	South Park Elem School	Moberly	MO	300
1630	Feb 2 99	South Nodaway Elem School	Guilford	MO	125
1631	Feb 2 99	Hayward Elem School	Nebraska City	NE	300
1632	Feb 3 99	West Nodaway Elem School	Burlington Junction	MO	200
1633	Feb 3 99	Sunny Slope Elem School	Omaha	NE	500
1634	Feb 4 99	East Lincoln Center Elem School	Vinton	IA	350
1635	Feb 5 99	Lourdes Elem School	Nebraska City	NE	200
1636	Feb 5 99	Northside Elem School	Nebraska City	NE	300
1637	Feb 8 99	Polk-Hordville Elem School	Polk	NE	250
1638	Feb 8 99	Sutton Elem School	Sutton	NE	450
1639	Feb 9 99	Bellwood Elem School	Bellwood	NE	200
1640	Feb 10 99	Palmer Public School	Palmer	NE	300
1641	Feb 10 99	1 R School	Grand Island	NE	175
1642	Feb 11 99	Alma Elem School	Alma	KS	200
1643	Feb 11 99	Longford Elem School	Longford	KS	50
1644	Feb 12 99	Clay Center Middle School	Clay Center	KS	400
1645	Feb 12 99	Garfield School	Clay Center	KS	150
1646	Feb 15 99	Independence Middle School	Independence	KS	600
1647	Feb 15 99	Lincoln Elem School	Independence	KS	350

1648	Feb 16 99	Andale Elem School	Andale	KS	150
1649	Feb 16 99	Garfield Elem School	Augusta	KS	250
1650	Feb 17 99	Simpson Elem School	Russell	KS	200
1651	Feb 17 99	Southside Elem School	Kinsley	KS	100
1652	Feb 18 99	Lakin Grade School	Lakin	KS	450
1653	Feb 19 99	Gertrude Walker Elem School	Garden City	KS	250
1654	Feb 19 99	Stanton County Schools	Johnson	KS	300
1655	Feb 22 99	Wheatland Elem School	Grainfield	KS	100
1656	Feb 22 99	Brewster USD School	Brewster	KS	175
1657	Feb 23 99	Brush Middle School	Brush	CO	400
1658	Feb 23 99	Haxtun Elem/Jr.High School	Haxtun	CO	150
1659	Feb 24 99	Douglas Inter. School	Douglas	WY	400
1660	Feb 25 99	Shawsheen Elem School	Greeley	CO	600
1661	Feb 26 99	Karval School	Karval	CO	100
1662	Mar 1 99	Bennett Elem School	Bennett	CO	400
1663	Mar 2 99	North Mesa Elem School	Pueblo	CO	420
1664	Mar 3 99	Elizabeth Middle School	Elizabeth	CO	200
1665	Mar 4 99	Ibapah Elem School	Ibapah	UT	30
1666	Mar 5 99	Spring Creek Elem School	Spring Creek	NV	850
1667	Mar 8 99	Wilson Elem School	Spokane	WA	280
1668	Mar 8 99	Pasadena Park Elem School	Spokane	WA	250
1669	Mar 9 99	Roosevelt Elem School	Granger	WA	900
1670	Mar 9 99	Sunnyside Christian School	Sunnyside	WA	200
1671	Mar 10 99	Byrom Elem School	Tualatin	OR	640
1672	Mar 11 99	Park Place Elem School	Oregon City	OR	400
1673	Mar 11 99	Groner School	Hillsboro	OR	250
1674	Mar 12 99	Hazelgreen School	Salem	OR	200
1675	Mar 15 99	Hayfork Elem School	Hayfork	CA	325
1676	Mar 16 99	Pine Grove Elem School	Crescent City	CA	400
1677	Mar 16 99	Redwood Elem School	Ft. Dick	CA	500
1678	Mar 18 99	St. Victor's School	San Jose	CA	300

1679	Mar 19 99	Our Savior Lutheran School	Livermore	CA	400
1680	Mar 22 99	Nokomis Elem School	Ukiah	CA	650
1681	Mar 23 99	St. Vincents Elem School	Petaluma	CA	300
1682	Mar 24 99	E. I. Musick Elem School	Newark	CA	550
1683	Mar 25 99	Linden Elem School	Linden	CA	500
1684	Mar 25 99	Solano Christian Academy	Fairfield	CA	300
1685	Mar 26 99	Rancho Tehama Elem School	Corning	CA	90
1686	Mar 30 99	Bunker Elem School	Newark	CA	600
1687	Mar 31 99	Hopkins Jr. High School	Fremont	CA	800
1688	Apr 6 99	Oak Creek Inter. School	Oakhurst	CA	225
1689	Apr 9 99	Mountain View Middle School	Lamont	CA	600
1690	Apr 14 99	St. Michael Academy	San Diego	CA	350
1691	Apr 14 99	Show for relatives	Huntington Beach	CA	10
1692	Apr 16 99	Hermosa Valley School	Hermosa Beach	CA	300
1693	Apr 16 99	Hermosa View School	Hermosa Beach	CA	350
1694	Apr 16 99	ALP Convention	Burbank	CA	100
1695	Apr 17 99	Lincoln of the Year Award	Burbank	CA	100
1696	Apr 19 99	Frye Elem School	Chandler	AZ	800
1697	Apr 20 99	Casa Blanca Community School	Bapchule	AZ	300
1698	Apr 20 99	Gila Crossing Community School	Laveen	AZ	200
1699	Apr 22 99	Chinle Boarding School	Many Farms	AZ	475
1700	Apr 22 99	Wide Ruins Community School	Chambers	AZ	210
1701	Apr 23 99	Lukachukai Boarding School	Lukachukai	AZ	380
1702	Apr 23 99	Greasewood Springs School	Granado	AZ	350
1703	Apr 26 99	Lamerced Elem School	Belen	NM	600
1704	Apr 26 99	Gilsanchez Elem School	Belen	NM	200

1705	Apr 27 99	Rio Grande Elem School	Belen	NM	300
1706	Apr 27 99	Central Elem School	Belen	NM	300
1707	Apr 29 99	Smith Elem School	Frisco	TX	850
1708	Apr 30 99	Waurika Elem School	Waurika	OK	300
1709	May 5 99	W. C. Andrews Elem School	Portland	TX	550
1710	May 6 99	Clark Elem School	Portland	TX	600
1711	May 7 99	Robb Elem School	Uvalde	TX	600
1712	May 7 99	Benson Elem School	Uvalde	TX	350
1713	May 7 99	Anthon Elem School	Uvalde	TX	600
1714	May 7 99	Flores Elem School	Uvalde	TX	25
1715	May 10 99	St. Philip Episcopal School	Uvalde	TX	125
1716	May 11 99	Flores Elem School	Uvalde	TX	750
1717	May 17 99	North Georgetown Elem School	Georgetown	DE	500
1718	May 18 99	Annapolis Middle School	Annapolis	MD	160
1719	May 19 99	Selbyville Middle School	Selbyville	DE	700
1720	May 21 99	Elk Garden Elem School	Elk Garden	VA	110
1721	May 21 99	Belfast School	Rosedale	VA	100
1722	Jun 9 99	Dedication of Doctor's Office	Jasper	GA	15
1723	Jun 14 99	Community Christian School	Canton	GA	10
1724	Jul 1 99	Rafter J Bar Ranch Campground	Hill City	SD	40
1725	Jul 3 99	Heart Ranch Parade & talk	Rapid City	SD	100
1726	Jul 4 99	Rafter J Bar Ranch Campground	Hill City	SD	42
1727	Jul 6 99	Rafter J Bar Ranch Campground	Hill City	SD	35
1728	Jul 8 99	Rafter J Bar Ranch Campground	Hill City	SD	33

1729	Jul 11 99	Rafter J Bar Ranch Campground	Hill City	SD	30
1730	Jul 13 99	Rafter J Bar Ranch Campground	Hill City	SD	50
1731	Jul 15 99	Rafter J Bar Ranch Campground	Hill City	SD	30
1732	Jul 18 99	Rafter J Bar Ranch Campground	Hill City	SD	40
1733	Jul 20 99	Rafter J Bar Ranch Campground	Hill City	SD	70
1734	Jul 22 99	Rafter J Bar Ranch Campground	Hill City	SD	40
1735	Jul 25 99	Rafter J Bar Ranch Campground	Hill City	SD	45
1736	Jul 27 99	Rafter J Bar Ranch Campground	Hill City	SD	40
1737	Jul 29 99	Rafter J Bar Ranch Campground	Hill City	SD	22
1738	Aug 1 99	Rafter J Bar Ranch Campground	Hill City	SD	50
1739	Aug 3 99	Rafter J Bar Ranch Campground	Hill City	SD	40
1740	Aug 5 99	Rafter J Bar Ranch Campground	Hill City	SD	65
1741	Aug 8 99	Rafter J Bar Ranch Campground	Hill City	SD	50
1742	Aug 10 99	Rafter J Bar Ranch Campground	Hill City	SD	45
1743	Aug 12 99	Rafter J Bar Ranch Campground	Hill City	SD	40
1744	Aug 15 99	Rafter J Bar Ranch Campground	Hill City	SD	75

1745	Aug 17 99	Rafter J Bar Ranch Campground	Hill City	SD	45
1746	Aug 19 99	SD National Guard Recruiters Meeting	Lead	SD	250
1747	Aug 19 99	Rafter J Bar Ranch Campground	Hill City	SD	15
1748	Aug 22 99	Rafter J Bar Ranch Campground	Hill City	SD	45
1749	Sep 14 99	Joelton Middle School	Joelton	TN	500
1750	Sep 23 99	DeVeaux Jr. High School	Toledo	OH	150
1751	Sep 23 99	Larchmont Elem School	Toledo	OH	250
1752	Sep 24 99	Christian Sugar Grove Elem School	Dayton	OH	150
1753	Sep 25 99	River Fest for Medical Center	Canton	GA	500
1754	Sep 27 99	Market Street Elem School	Boardman	OH	450
1755	Sep 28 99	Dobbins Elem School	Poland	OH	260
1756	Sep 29 99	North Elem School	Poland	OH	280
1757	Sep 30 99	Maple Ridge Elem School	Alliance	OH	270
1758	Oct 1 99	C.H. Campbell Elem School	Canfield	OH	500
1759	Oct 4 99	IS77 School	Ridgewood	NY	1300
1760	Oct 5 99	Leptondale Elem School	Wallkill	NY	600
1761	Oct 7 99	Sully Elem School	Sterling	VA	500
1762	Oct 8 99	East High Elem School	Elizabethtown	PA	600
1763	Oct 11 99	St. Anselm School	Philadelphia	PA	900
1764	Oct 12 99	Ashkar Elem School	Hughesville	PA	600
1765	Oct 13 99	Woodhome Elem/ Middle Schools	Baltimore	MD	600
1766	Oct 13 99	Norrisville Elem School	Norrisville	MD	250
1767	Oct 15 99	Broad Street Elem School	Gibbstown	NJ	350
1768	Oct 18 99	Jouett Elem School	Mineral	VA	700
1769	Oct 20 99	Grandin Court Elem School	Roanoke	VA	300

1770	Oct 20 99	Sontag Elem School	Rocky Mount	VA	350
1771	Oct 21 99	Limestone-Central Elem School	Gaffney	SC	450
1772	Oct 21 99	Northwest Elem School	Gaffney	SC	250
1773	Oct 22 99	Banks County Middle School	Homer	GA	900
1774	Oct 23 99	Mousetail State Park, Landing State Park	Perryville	TN	100
1775	Oct 25 99	Lincoln Elem School	Bemidji	MN	325
1776	Oct 27 99	Hall Elem School	Grays Knob	KY	300
1777	Oct 28 99	Beaver Creek Elem School	Topmost	KY	350
1778	Oct 29 99	Rockcastle County Middle School	Mt. Vernon	KY	750
1779	Oct 29 99	Mt. Vernon Elem School	Mt. Vernon	KY	250
1780	Nov 1 99	Edna Tolliver School	Danville	KY	325
1781	Nov 1 99	Jennie Rogers Elem School	Danville	KY	310
1782	Nov 3 99	Hopkins Elem School	Somerset	KY	600
1783	Nov 3 99	North Metcalfe Elem School	Edmonton	KY	200
1784	Nov 4 99	Stevenson Elem School	Russellville	KY	650
1785	Nov 5 99	North Junior High School	Henderson	KY	300
1786	Nov 5 99	Niagara Elem School	Henderson	KY	375
1787	Nov 6 99	Catholic Mens Conference	Columbus	OH	800
1788	Nov 8 99	Brandeis Elem School	Louisville	KY	550
1789	Nov 8 99	St. Agnes School	Louisville	KY	450
1790	Nov 9 99	Bethany School	Glendale	OH	300
1791	Nov 10 99	Lapel Elem School	Lapel	IN	450
1792	Nov 11 99	Anna Middle School	Anna	OH	200
1793	Nov 12 99	Central Academy Elem School	Middletown	OH	300
1794	Nov 15 99	Parkwood Elem School	Sidney	OH	125
1795	Nov 15 99	Lowell Elem School	Sidney	OH	110
1796	Nov 15 99	Westwood Elem School	Lima	OH	230

1797	Nov 15 99	Avon Meeting	Columbus	OH	50
1798	Nov 16 99	Showcase with Thom	Columbus	OH	50
1799	Nov 16 99	South Main School	Clyde	OH	250
1800	Nov 17 99	Bronson Junior High School	Bronson	MI	200
1801	Nov 17 99	Chicago Street School	Bronson	MI	200
1802	Nov 18 99	Lynn-Kirk Elem School	Austintown	OH	400
1803	Nov 19 99	Apple Creek Elem School	Apple Creek	OH	500
1804	Nov 22 99	Norwin Middle School West	Irwin	PA	550
1805	Nov 23 99	Brookpark Memorial Elem School	Brook Park	OH	800
1806	Nov 24 99	Waterloo Primary School	Atwater	OH	550
1807	Nov 29 99	Rosedale Elem School	Rosedale	IN	300
1808	Nov 29 99	Meridian Elem School	Brazil	IN	225
1809	Nov 30 99	Warren Elem School	Terre Haute	IN	225
1810	Nov 30 99	Fayette Elem School	New Goshen	IN	300
1811	Dec 1 99	Newby Elem School	Mooresville	IN	300
1812	Dec 1 99	Hymera Elem/ Jr. High School	Hymera	IN	300
1813	Dec 2 99	Shelburn Elem School	Shelburn	IN	275
1814	Dec 2 99	Dixie Bee Elem School	Terra Haute	IN	600
1815	Dec 3 99	J. B. Nelson Elem School	Batavia	IL	650
1816	Dec 15 99	Clarkdale Elem School	Clarkdale	GA	800
1817	Jan 4 00	Daffron Elem School	Plano	TX	550
1818	Jan 5 00	Brady Elem School	Brady	TX	550
1819	Jan 6 00	Rogers Elem School	Rogers	TX	360
1820	Jan 6 00	Rogers Middle School	Rogers	TX	250
1821	Jan 10 00	Onsted Intermediate School	Onsted	MI	1000
1822	Jan 10 00	Herrick Park Elem School	Tecumseh	MI	275
1823	Jan 11 00	Palms Elem School	Fair Haven	MI	220
1824	Jan 11 00	Eddy Elem School	St. Clair	MI	450
1825	Jan 12 00	Hahn Intermediate School	Davison	MI	800
1826	Jan 12 00	Gearing Elem School	St. Clair	MI	550

1827	Jan 13 00	St. Paul the Apostle School	Grand Rapids	MI	260
1828	Jan 14 00	Central Elem School	Clinton	IN	400
1829	Jan 18 00	Maplewood Elem School	Beaver Lake	MN	450
1830	Jan 20 00	Holy Rosary School	Medford	WI	125
1831	Jan 21 00	Middleton Elem School	Woodbury	MN	1000
1832	Jan 21 00	Woodbury Lutheran Father/Son Banquet	Woodbury	MN	125
1833	Jan 24 00	G. D. Jones Elem School	Wausau	WI	425
1834	Jan 25 00	Merton Primary School	Merton	WI	330
1835	Jan 25 00	Merton Intermediate School	Merton	WI	440
1836	Jan 25 00	Randall School	Bassett	WI	725
1837	Jan 26 00	First German Lutheran School	Manitowoc	WI	100
1838	Jan 26 00	St. Paul Lutheran School	Appleton	WI	200
1839	Jan 27 00	Valley View Elem School	Green Bay	WI	700
1840	Jan 28 00	Red Smith Elem School	Green Bay	WI	600
1841	Jan 31 00	St. John's Lutheran School	Watertown	WI	200
1842	Feb 1 00	Nature Ridge Elem School	Bartlett	IL	525
1843	Feb 2 00	Dickinson Elem School	Depere	WI	600
1844	Feb 3 00	Prospect Elem School	Lake Mills	WI	550
1845	Feb 4 00	Southside Elem School	Sparta	WI	400
1846	Feb 6 00	Hoard Historical Museum & Indian Mounds	Lake Koshhonong	WI	100
1847	Feb 7 00	St. Joseph Catholic School	Ft. Atkinson	WI	135
1848	Feb 8 00	Somers Elem School	Kenosha	WI	650
1849	Feb 8 00	Salem Grade School	Salem	WI	1100
1850	Feb 9 00	Concordia Lutheran Schools	Racine	WI	130
1851	Feb 10 00	Elroy Primary School	Elroy	WI	260
1852	Feb 11 00	Apollo Elem School	Carbon Cliff	IL	175
1853	Feb 14 00	Northview School	Rantoul	IL	250
1854	Feb 15 00	Moweaqua Elem School	Moweaqua	IL	275
1855	Feb 15 00	Bond Elem School	Assumption	IL	200
1856	Feb 16 00	Clearview Elem School	Union	MO	300

Image in the Mirror

1857	Feb 17 00	Rossman School	St. Louis	MO	250
1858	Feb 17 00	Conway Elem School	St. Louis	MO	300
1859	Feb 18 00	St. Joseph Catholic School	Jefferson City	MO	450
1860	Feb 22 00	Alton Elem School	Alton	MO	410
1861	Feb 22 00	Campbell Elem School	Campbell	MO	400
1862	Feb 23 00	Dixon Elem School	Dixon	MO	500
1863	Feb 23 00	Dixon Middle School	Dixon	MO	300
1864	Feb 24 00	Camdenton Upper Elem School	Camdenton	MO	300
1865	Feb 25 00	Brookridge Day School	Overland Park	KS	300
1866	Feb 28 00	West Boubon Elem School	Uniontown	KS	300
1867	Feb 29 00	St. Elizabeth Ann Seton Catholic School	Wichita	KS	700
1868	Mar 1 00	Dale Elem School	Dale	OK	375
1869	Mar 1 00	Gatewood Elem School	Oklahoma City	OK	300
1870	Mar 2 00	Bennington Elem School	Bennington	KS	300
1871	Mar 3 00	Mill Creek Elem School	Independence	MO	400
1872	Mar 3 00	Ray Marsh Elem School	Shawnee	KS	375
1873	Mar 6 00	Corinth Elem School	Prairie Village	KS	350
1874	Mar 7 00	Leonard Lawrence Elem School	Bellevue	NE	600
1875	Mar 8 00	Garfield Elem School	Clarinda	IA	300
1876	Mar 9 00	Tara Heights Elem School	Papillion	NE	500
1877	Mar 10 00	Hiawatha Elem School	Hiawatha	KS	375
1878	Mar 14 00	Engleman Elem School	Grand Island	NE	340
1879	Mar 15 00	Decatur Community High School	Oberlin	KS	260
1880	Mar 15 00	Oberlin Elem School	Oberlin	KS	275
1881	Mar 16 00	Benkelman Elem School	Benkelman	NE	200
1882	Mar 17 00	Platte Valley Elem School	Sedgwick	CO	80
1883	Mar 22 00	Belleview Christian School	Westminster	CO	300
1884	Mar 27 00	Kayenta Community School	Kayenta	AZ	500
1885	Mar 28 00	Hotevilla-Bacavi Community School	Hotevilla	AZ	140

1886	Mar 31 00	Clyde Cox Elem School	Las Vegas	NV	750
1887	Apr 3 00	Northrup Elem School	Alhambra	CA	1000
1888	Apr 8 00	Show for relatives	Huntington Beach	CA	12
1889	Apr 10 00	Oak Creek Intermediate School	Oakhurst	CA	250
1890	Apr 11 00	Kennedy Elem School	San Jose	CA	750
1891	Apr 14 00	ALP Convention	Louisville	KY	100
1892	Apr 18 00	Emperor Elem School	San Gabriel	CA	500
1893	Apr 18 00	Jamie Harrison Elem School	San Gabriel	CA	500
1894	Apr 20 00	Loma Vista Intermediate School	Riverside	CA	700
1895	Apr 21 00	Grapevine Elem School	Vista	CA	1000
1896	Apr 28 00	Parkhill Jr. High School	Dallas	TX	400
1897	May 1 00	Manning Oaks Elem School	Alpharetta	GA	1000
1898	May 3 00	Broadway Elem School	Tipp City	OH	600
1899	May 4 00	South Range Elem School	Canfield	OH	400
1900	May 5 00	Beloit Elem School	Beloit	OH	180
1901	May 7 00	Loyalty Day Parade	Batavia	IL	15000
1902	May 17 00	WXIA TV Kids Show	Atlanta	GA	100
1903	May 22 00	Fairmount Kiwansis Dinner	Fairmount	GA	25
1904	Jun 6 00	Steele-Waseca EMC Annual Meeting	Owatonna	MN	1200
1905	Jun 11 00	Kids Talk TV Show	Atlanta	GA	100
1906	Jun 26 00	Classroom Connect Trade Show A.W.C.C.	Atlanta	GA	2000
1907	Jul 19 00	Kids Talk TV Show	Marietta	GA	100
1908	Sep 14 00	Fairmount Elem School	Fairmount	GA	500
1909	Oct 23 00	Wild Peach Elem School	Wild Peach	TX	375
1910	Oct 24 00	Brazosport Christian School	Lake Jackson	TX	300
1911	Oct 25 00	West Columbia Elem School	West Columbia	TX	500
1912	Oct 26 00	Charlie Brown Elem School	West Columbia	TX	200
1913	Oct 27 00	Brazoria Elem School	Brazoria	TX	400

1914	Nov 2 00	Briarcliff Elem School	Atlanta	GA	400
1915	Nov 3 00	Seniors Center	Marietta	GA	50
1916	Nov 9 00	Taylor Ranch Elem School	Venice	FL	900
1917	Nov 10 00	Masonic Patriotism Night	Pocatella	ID	200
1918	Feb 12 01	W.B. Redding Elem School	Lizella	GA	500
1919	Feb 19 01	First Presbyterian Church	Marietta	GA	75
1920	Mar 21 01	Venice Library	Venice	FL	100
1921	Apr 20 01	ALP Convention	Beckley	WV	125
1922	Apr 27 01	Oconee Country Club Luncheon	Oconee	GA	250
1923	Apr 28 01	Augusta Country Club for Rosewood Furn	Augusta	GA	400
1924	Jun 4 01	Technical College	Owatonna	MN	150
1925	Jun 5 01	McKinley Elem School	Owatonna	MN	500
1926	Jun 5 01	Steele-Waseca EMC Annual Meeting	Owatonna	MN	1200
1927	Jun 14 01	Hickory Flat Boy Scout Ceremony	Hickory Flat	GA	300
1928	Jun 24 01	Boy Scout Troop 641 Auction	Woodstock	GA	200
1929	Jul 4 01	Hammond Glen Seniors Center	Atlanta	GA	100
1930	Sep 5 01	Living Word Church	Jasper	GA	25
1931	Sep 29 01	Bent Tree Arts & Crafts Show	Bent Tree	GA	100
1932	Oct 6 01	Marble Festival Parade	Jasper	GA	3000
1933	Nov 12 01	Hitchcock Elem School	Omaha	NE	350
1934	Nov 13 01	Cottonwood Elem School	Omaha	NE	400
1935	Nov 14 01	Rockwell Elem School	Omaha	NE	400
1936	Nov 15 01	Black Elk Elem School	Omaha	NE	500
1937	Nov 15 01	Toys for Tots Fund Raiser	Omaha	NE	100
1938	Nov 16 01	Ackerman Elem School	Omaha	NE	500
1939	Jan 14 02	Vaughn Elem School	Powder Springs	GA	1100

1940	Jan 26 02	2nd Annual Cub Scout Fair	Canton	GA	400
1941	Jan 28 02	Eugene Field Elem School	Manhattan	KS	125
1942	Jan 29 02	Roosevelt Elem School	Manhattan	KS	375
1943	Jan 29 02	Boys & Girls Club of Manhattan	Manhattan	KS	50
1944	Feb 1 02	Woodrow Wilson Elem School	Manhattan	KS	450
1945	Feb 4 02	New Creation Log Homes Sales Meeting	Blue Ridge	GA	10
1946	Feb 6 02	N.A.R.F.E. Meeting	Marietta	GA	65
1947	Feb 12 02	Holcomb Bascomb UMC	Woodstock	GA	100
1948	Feb 17 02	Foothills Community Church	Marble Hill	GA	75
1949	Feb 18 02	Elderhostel Meeting	Dahlonega	GA	40
1950	Feb 21 02	Rotary Club Luncheon	Griffin	GA	150
1951	Feb 21 02	Hapeville Historical Society	Hapeville	GA	50
1952	Mar 5 02	West Fannin Elem School	Blue Ridge	GA	500
1953	Apr 8 02	Marlott Elem School	Manhattan	KS	450
1954	Apr 9 02	Amanda Arnold Elem School	Manhattan	KS	350
1955	Apr 10 02	Lee Elem School	Manhattan	KS	250
1956	Apr 11 02	Ft. Riley Elem School	Ft. Riley	KS	300
1957	Apr 12 02	Riley County Grade School	Ft. Riley	KS	400
1958	Apr 13 02	Charity Ball for St. Joseph's Hospital	Atlanta	GA	500
1959	Apr 19 02	ALP Convention	Ft. Wayne	IN	125
1960	May 11 02	Canton Alive Art Show	Canton	GA	500
1961	Jun 20 02	Ft. McPherseon Hospital Aux. Luncheon	Atlanta	GA	150
1962	Jul 3 02	Rotary Club Luncheon	Jasper	GA	30
1963	Jul 4 02	Parade in downtown	Nashville	GA	1000
1964	Jul 30 02	Rotary Club Luncheon	Blue Ridge	GA	20
1965	Aug 13 02	First Baptist Church	Marietta	GA	30

Image in the Mirror

1966	Aug 22 02	Kiwanis Luncheon	Marietta	GA	100
1967	Sep 10 02	Babcock for State House Rep.	Woodstock	GA	100
1968	Sep 10 02	Cub Scout Pack 670 Blue & Gold Banquet	Holly Springs	GA	100
1969	Sep 11 02	AARP Luncheon	Canton	GA	100
1970	Sep 27 02	Jimmy Carter Presidential Library/Museum	Atlanta	GA	200
1971	Sep 28 02	Jimmy Carter Presidential Library/Museum	Atlanta	GA	300
1972	Oct 18 02	Rome Middle School	Rome	GA	500
1973	Oct 19 02	Heritage Festival Parade	Rome	GA	2000
1974	Nov 11 02	Skaggs Elem School	Plano	TX	800
1975	Nov 12 02	Bettye Haun Elem School	Plano	TX	800
1976	Nov 13 02	Thomas Elem School	Plano	TX	850
1977	Nov 19 02	Holly Springs Elem School	Holly Springs	GA	1100
1978	Jan 31 03	CPAC Convention	Arlington	VA	500
1979	Feb 1 03	CPAC Convention	Arlington	VA	500
1980	Feb 12 03	Liberty Elem School	Woodstock	GA	650
1981	Feb 12 03	Cherry Log Church	Cherry Log	GA	75
1982	Mar 20 03	Young in Heart at Baptist Church	Sandy Plains	GA	50
1983	Apr 3 03	National Museum of Patriotism	Atlanta	GA	25
1984	Apr 11 03	ALP Convention	Lincoln City	IN	125
1985	May 8 03	Head Start kids	Canton	GA	50
1986	May 15 03	Optimist Club of Jasper dinner	Jasper	GA	50
1987	Jun 15 03	Confidence Methodist Church	Morganton	GA	100
1988	Jul 4 03	Parade in downtown	Nashville	GA	1000
1989	Jul 21 03	OPTASCO Conference	Traverse City	MI	500

~ 293 ~

1990	Jul 29 03	Travel Club of Community Bank	Jasper	GA	30
1991	Aug 19 03	Cherokee County Historical Society	Canton	GA	75
1992	Sep 9 03	Cub Scout Pack 670 Blue & Gold Banquet	Holly Springs	GA	50
1993	Sep 21 03	Liberty Hill Church	Canton	GA	100
1994	Sep 27 03	Community Bank Anniversary Party	Jasper	GA	150
1995	Nov 11 03	AOL "15 Hours of Fame" Contest Winner	Jasper	GA	5
1996	Nov 12 03	Hill City Elem School for contest video	Jasper	GA	50
1997	Nov 18 03	Masterson Academy Homeschoolers	Dawsonville	GA	75
1998	Nov 20 03	Travel Club of Bank of Gilmer County	Ellijay	GA	75
1999	Feb 9 04	Mountain View Elem School	Ellijay	GA	500
2000	Feb 12 04	Sabal Elem School	Melbourne	FL	750
2001	Feb 13 04	Sherwood Elem School	Melbourne	FL	850
2002	Feb 19 04	Izard Elem School	Izard	AR	350
2003	Feb 20 04	Mountainburg Elem School	Mountainburg	AR	300
2004	Feb 21 04	Crawford County Lincoln Day Dinner	Mountainburg	AR	100
2005	Feb 28 04	Seagraves Birthday party	Ila	GA	15
2006	Apr 12 04	Crossroads High School	Holly Springs	GA	200
2007	Apr 16 04	ALP Convention	Vandalia	IL	125
2008	Jun 15 04	Coca Cola Sales Meeting	Atlanta	GA	100
2009	Jun 30 04	Freedom Methodist Church	Chamblee	GA	100
2010	Aug 31 04	Birthday party for Barnes	Atlanta	GA	20
2011	Oct 2 04	Tate UMC at Marble Festival	Jasper	GA	250
2012	Oct 19 04	Johns Creek Baptist Church	Duluth	GA	75

2013	Nov 19 04	Windy Hill Senior Center	Smyrna	GA	75
2014	Jan 15 05	Bass Club dinner	Woodstock	GA	50
2015	Feb 14 05	Spaulding Drive Elem School	Atlanta	GA	600
2016	Apr 2 05	Tate UMC Dinner with ABE	Tate	GA	50
2017	Apr 15 05	ALP Convention	Detroit	MI	125
2018	Jun 30 05	Pickens Library	Jasper	GA	25
2019	Jul 3 05	Heritage United Methodist Church	Van Buren	AR	425
2020	Sep 12 05	R.T. Jones Memorial Library	Canton	GA	100
2021	Sep 26 05	Library	Ellijay	GA	40
2022	Nov 5 05	Tate UMC Breakfast with ABE	Tate	GA	30
2023	Nov 7 05	Hedge Home School Co-Op	Woodstock	GA	100
2024	Jan 10 06	Community Thrift Store Banquet	Jasper	GA	100
2025	Feb 6 06	Atherton Place Retirement Center	Marietta	GA	50
2026	Feb 20 06	Murphy-Harpst UMC School	Cedartown	GA	50
2027	Feb 27 06	National Museum of Patriotism	Atlanta	GA	100
2028	Apr 7 06	ALP Convention	Cincinnati	OH	100
2029	Jul 4 06	Parade in downtown	Woodstock	GA	5000
2030	Aug 1 06	River Explorer River Barge on Miss. River	St. Louis	MO	200
2031	Sep 5 06	River Explorer River Barge on Miss. River	St. Louis	MO	200
2032	Oct 6 06	Heritage Festival	Rome	GA	500
2033	Oct 7 06	Heritage Festival	Rome	GA	500

2034	Oct 19 06	American Legion Post 316 Dinner	Woodstock	GA	25
2035	Feb 12 07	Cumming UMC School	Cumming	GA	200
2036	Feb 12 07	Jasper Elem School	Jasper	GA	50
2037	Apr 13 07	ALP Convention	Mount Pleasant	IA	100
2038	Jun 10 07	American Legion Georgia Boys State	Statesboro	GA	400
2039	Jul 4 07	Freedom Festival & Parade	Woodstock	GA	5000
2040	Sep 18 07	River Explorer River Barge on Miss. River	St. Louis	MO	200
2041	Sep 25 07	River Explorer River Barge on Miss. River	St. Louis	MO	200
2042	Oct 23 07	Funk Heritage Museum Time Line	Waleska	GA	500
2043	Oct 24 07	Funk Heritage Museum Time Line	Waleska	GA	1000
2044	Oct 25 07	Funk Heritage Museum Time Line	Waleska	GA	1000
2045	Oct 26 07	Funk Heritage Museum Time Line	Waleska	GA	1000
2046	Feb 5 08	Cherokee Red Hat Ladies lunch at Funk Mus	Waleska	GA	50
2047	Feb 9 08	N.G.M.C.F. breakfast	Hill City	GA	50
2048	Feb 11 08	Cumming UMC School	Cumming	GA	200
2049	Feb 11 08	Atherton Place Retirement Center	Marietta	GA	50
2050	Feb 27 08	Excellence Academy School	Dawsonville	GA	300
2051	Apr 11 08	ALP Convention	Alton	IL	150
2052	Apr 12 08	ALP Convention	Alton	IL	150
2053	Apr 12 08	Shawn Olson run for ST. Senate Dinner	Valparaiso	IN	100
2054	May 16 08	Luncheon for Medal of Honor winners	Atlanta	GA	400

2055	Jul 4 08	Freedom Festival & Parade	Woodstock	GA	7500
2056	Jul 15 08	Help Larry Ray for Magistrate Judge	Jasper	GA	50
2057	Sep 10 08	Library of Canton	Canton	GA	75
2058	Oct 15 08	Bascomb UMC Seniors Lunch	Woodstock	GA	25
2059	Nov 4 08	Woodstock Library	Woodstock	GA	50
2060	Dec 4 08	T.A.P. Convention	Washington	DC	100
2061	Feb 5 09	Arbor Terrace Assisted Living Center	Austell	GA	50
2062	Feb 11 09	Cumming UMC School	Cumming	GA	250
2063	Feb 12 09	Kilough Elem School	Dawsonville	GA	500
2064	Feb 16 09	Carter Center Library & Museum	Atlanta	GA	250
2065	Feb 18 09	New Comer Club Luncheon	Alpharetta	GA	50
2066	Feb 19 09	Cub Scout Pack Blue & Gold Banquet	Cumming	GA	100
2067	Apr 17 09	ALP Convention	Washington	DC	100
2068	Apr 18 09	ALP Convention	Washington	DC	1000
2069	May 1 09	Law Day Celebration Luncheon	Cumming	GA	110
2070	May 21 09	Poetry Readings Fireside Café	Big Canoe	GA	10
2071	May 22 09	Poetry Readings Sharp Top Museum	Jasper	GA	25
2072	Jun 11 09	Fund Raiser 8th Regimental Band	Rome	GA	200
2073	Jun 15 09	CBPC Travel Club Dinner	Jasper	GA	35
2074	Jul 3 09	Hammond Glen Seniors Center	Roswell	GA	50
2075	Jul 4 09	Freedom Festival & Parade	Woodstock	GA	25000
2076	Jul 11 09	Booth Museum	Cartersville	GA	100
2077	Aug 12 09	Booth Museum	Cartersville	GA	25

2078	Aug 22 09	Booth Museum Anniversary Party	Cartersville	GA	400
2079	Sep 12 09	Old Milton Country Fair	Milton	GA	1000
2080	Sep 13 09	Old Milton Country Fair	Milton	GA	1000
2081	Oct 2 09	Westville Village	Lumpkin	GA	225
2082	Oct 3 09	Westville Village	Lumpkin	GA	400
2083	Oct 12 09	Golden Living Assisted Living	Rome	GA	50
2084	Oct 29 09	St. Joseph Catholic School	Macon	GA	400
2085	Oct 29 09	GA School Supply store	Macon	GA	50
2086	Nov 21 09	Barter Company annual trade show	Atlanta	GA	100
2087	Nov 22 09	Lyerly Baptist Church dinner	Lyerly	GA	60
2088	Feb 11 10	Florida State University Lincoln Day	Tallahassee	FL	500
2089	Apr 15 10	ALP Convention	Elizabethtown	KY	100
2090	Apr 16 10	ALP Convention	Hodgenville	KY	500
2091	Apr 17 10	ALP Convention	Elizabethtown	KY	500
2092	June 15 10	Fund Raiser 8th Regimental Band	Rome	GA	200
2093	June 23 10	Kennworth Golden Kiwanis	Acworth	GA	20
2094	Jul 4 10	Mount Olivet Baptist Church	Acworth	GA	100

For my students who are still in school, the list might become a fun geography lesson as you get a large United States map and try to locate all the places I've visited in the past thirty-five years.

P.S. My Suggestions for Change

I may make some enemies with this chapter, but I feel it needs to be said. I want to express my personal opinion about what needs to be done to take back our government from the politicians who are *trying* to run it now.

Our government has *not*, for many, many years, been a government of the people, by the people, and for the people, as Lincoln wrote in his famous speech. I feel our government is still the best anywhere in the world, but it needs to be as it was in Lincoln's time. It needs to run *of, by, and for the people*!

My solution would be for everyone to let their senators and congressmen know that they should either vote *now* to get rid of and abolish *all* Political Action Committees (P.A.C.s) or they will elect someone else who will! Our politicians are being controlled by these P.A.C.s and are not voting for the issues best for *us*, the people who elected them. They are taking a lot of expensive gifts and trips at the expense of these P.A.C.s. When the time comes to vote on an issue, their votes are controlled by which P.A.C. showed them the most personal gain!

Once these P.A.C.s are eliminated and the elected officials start voting the way *we* want them to vote, we will get some major changes in Washington. We will never get anything worthwhile accomplished as long as the P.A.C.s are running the country!

One of the first things they then need to vote for is to get rid of the I.R.S. and all of the billions of dollars they are wasting every year! They should then approve a *flat tax* for *everyone*! And I mean *everyone!* There should be no more exemptions for big or little businesses to lie about. Everyone—little or big—should pay the same *flat tax*.

I spoke to a young man a few years ago who had studied this matter pretty thoroughly for college and he said a flat tax of only 5% would give our government more money than they could ever spend. I think it could be somewhere between five and ten percent. There are a lot of big companies out there that haven't been paying anything and they would have to start paying their fair share.

One of the places where I want to see *more* of our dollars spent is on education. Our youth of today *are* tomorrow's leaders of this great nation and they are not getting the education they need! Part of the problem is our teachers are not being paid what they should *nor* are they allowed to discipline students when necessary. Teachers deserve more credit for the number of years they spent in college, their patience, and the amount of time and effort they put in every day and night at schools across this country.

Our teacher's salaries should be raised to be more in line with what private industry would pay someone as skilled and who puts in the number of hours teachers do. There are a lot of very dedicated men and women out there teaching *our* children and they deserve to be paid more than they are getting!

One place more dollars could be raised very easily and quickly and given to our teachers is to look at the school superintendents' salaries across the country. I have seen things in these past thirty-five years that amaze and astound me!

Every governor needs to look at his/her state educational systems *now*! What they will find is a lot of over-paid people out there with the title of "School Superintendent" or other positions we could do away with.

I have seen superintendents who had only one or two schools they were being paid $50,000 to $60,000 to supervise. What a waste of dollars! The principal of those little schools could just as easily do his/her own administrational duties. Instead of having a superintendent for each little town or district, why not do as they do in Florida and in Georgia and have a superintendent for the *whole* county.

When I asked one Texas superintendent about this, he said they might have to do too much driving to cover a large, spread-out area. Isn't that why he/she is earning those big bucks? And it's not as if they would have to drive the whole district every day!

I won't make any of my school superintendent friends very happy with what I've said here, but something needs to be done about this situation. That same superintendent in Texas told me a couple of years ago, "there was such a good-old-boy-network out there that you couldn't ever get them dislodged from these plush 'no-work' jobs!" Well! Governors...go for it! How many fat and happy superintendents do you have in your state that could be taken off those fat payrolls? The millions of dollars each state would save could be divided among the teachers who are doing the work in the classrooms.

Another place we could easily come up with more money to help education (without increasing our taxes) is to eliminate *all* subsidies the government is giving away to such industries as tobacco, cotton, corn, and many, many others they should get their hands out of. Let them survive or die on their own! Why should we subsidize the tobacco industry with our tax dollars on one hand and on the other hand tell us that tobacco is killing off Americans who smoke? This has got to rank as one of the worst government-give-aways *ever*! I say give our money to our educational systems instead. We need to *insist* that Washington look at *all* subsidies *now*!

Our teachers of today have to deal with more serious problems than years gone by: drugs and more and more violence in the classrooms. Youth violence needs to be stopped!

I met with a group of kids while I was in Washington who are trying to help curb youth violence. They are being guided by Jim Halley and call themselves and the news reports they handle, "US Kids TV." I was impressed with the job they are doing!

I told them I would do whatever I could to help curb youth violence. In 1994, we were trying to organize a "National Stop Youth Violence in America Week" and an essay writing contest. The winner from each state would be flown to Springfield, Illinois, and would ride the train to Washington to present the essay, "What I Think Needs to be Done to Stop Youth Violence in America," to President Obama on Abe's birthday in February 2011. I hope and pray we can get it all put together very soon.

I want to help kids however I can, and have told two other groups I would be glad to help in their efforts to raise money: Feed the Children and the Pediatric AIDS Foundation. Please do whatever you can to help these and other worthwhile youth organizations. I appreciate whatever you can do and I am sure they will also.

Lesson to be learned here is: Do what *you* can to help make our world a better place to live. Let's start with our government and our educational systems and stopping youth violence in America.

And in Conclusion

Let me leave you with these thoughts... sometime in your future, you may be having some difficult times and wondering how you could possibly make it through another day. When that happens, I want you to look back to today when you saw someone dressed up like Abraham Lincoln and this is what I want you to stop and think about...

If a big, tall, ugly fellow like me could make it past all of that sadness... from my mom dying, my sister dying, my girlfriend dying, my father dying, two sons dying... all of those store failures... one right after the other... all those political failures... one right after the other... Marfan's disease on top of all of that... without ever giving up... and going on to become president of this great country... the greatest country anywhere in the world... don't you ever give up in the pursuit of whatever it is you want to achieve with your lives. It can't possibly be as hard on you as it was on me! Be a dreamer, be a stargazer, be a rainbow chaser, and soar with the eagles. You can become and achieve anything you want with your lives. Just don't ever give up!

(And from the program I do for students) Now, students, let's go over the five main things I want you to remember from our little visit today...

1. Let's be sure we always tell the <u>truth</u>.
2. Every day, every chance we get, let's read lots of good <u>books</u>.
3. Let's be sure when we get older, we always say "no" to <u>drugs, alcohol, and tobacco</u>.
4. Let's be sure every day to give our teachers and all the staff at your school lots of <u>hugs or handshakes</u>.
5. I will do what I can not to be involved in <u>youth violence</u>.

I want to leave you with a little poem I wrote just for you. It's called, "The Creator."

<blockquote>
The Creator made a lot of things,
Some summers and a thousand springs.
The mornings and the afternoons,
The sky, the sea, the mist and moon.
The mountain winds and the new mown hay,
The little running brook and the oceans' spray.
And then there are some things you see
That HE made especially for me.
Red roses, yellow daffodils,
The sunlight on the purple hills,
Cobwebs pearled with morning dew,
A certain shining star...
And...YOU!
</blockquote>

I love you and thank you for coming. May God continue to bless you and your family. Keep reading lots of good books and I hope to see you again soon.

I hope you have enjoyed reading about my life and how Abe Lincoln has become intertwined with my personal life. My hopes and prayers are that whoever you are and wherever you are, your life will be changed for the better.

I hope each day from now on when you get up in the morning and are standing in front of the mirror primping or shaving and getting ready to go out to face the world, you will say to yourself, "Mirror, mirror on the wall, I know I am the very best at what I do! I know I can be number one! Today I will do something special for someone so that I, too, can help make this world a better place because *I* was here."

I hope you will never give up in the search for your dreams and *know* if you work at it hard enough, you can achieve anything you want with your life.

Don't ever forget tomorrow will *always* be a better day!

God loves you and Abe loves you, too.

Go tell someone how much you love them today. And hug a teacher every day. I firmly believe that if we have more hugging, there will be less mugging.

Have a great day and an even better tomorrow.

Be a dreamer, a stargazer, a rainbow chaser, and keep soaring with the eagles!

Remember, you can't soar with the eagles if you're still clucking around on the ground with the chickens.

As I was driving down the road recently God laid this message on my heart: Most of us know that "E.R." stands for the Emergency Room in a hospital, where we can get things fixed in or on our bodies. But, how many of us also know that "E.R." could stand for *Excuses* or *Results*? In our daily lives we can either make excuses for things that don't get done or we can make results happen. Which do YOU do? Do you have 100 excuses for why you didn't or can't do something? Or do you do as Lincoln would have done and go for the results? Give it your best each day and make things happen! You can do it if you put your mind to it.

If life ever starts to get you down and you think you need to get "high," please email me. You and I will get together and go climb one of my favorite mountains either here in North Georgia or up on the Blue Ridge Parkway in North Carolina. When we get up on that mountain, we will both be closer to God and that's one "high" you can't ever get from anything artificial.

My plans for the near future include getting to the remainder of the fifty states. I also want to take a trip to Japan, Australia, New Zealand, and England and take my shows to people in those countries. I have three more books I want to work on. One will be a book of letters I have received from students all over the country. It will be entitled, *Dear President Lincoln*. I want to put together a coffee table size book of photographs I've taken in my travels around our country. I also am working on a children's story and coloring book. Then I want to visit with my elderly friends and write a book about their lives.

Please take time to drop me a line and let me know what you thought about this book. Either via email at abeusa16@aol.com or snail mail at P.O. Box 13, Jasper, Georgia 30143. I would love to hear from you to let me know what is happening in your life.

God Bless You!

Please check out this high tech Lincoln at:
www.abeusa16.com or on Facebook.com,
YouTube.com or Twitter.com
and you can see my 3-minutes video
from the AOL 15 Hours of Fame Contest
You will be impressed!

PHOTO GALLERY

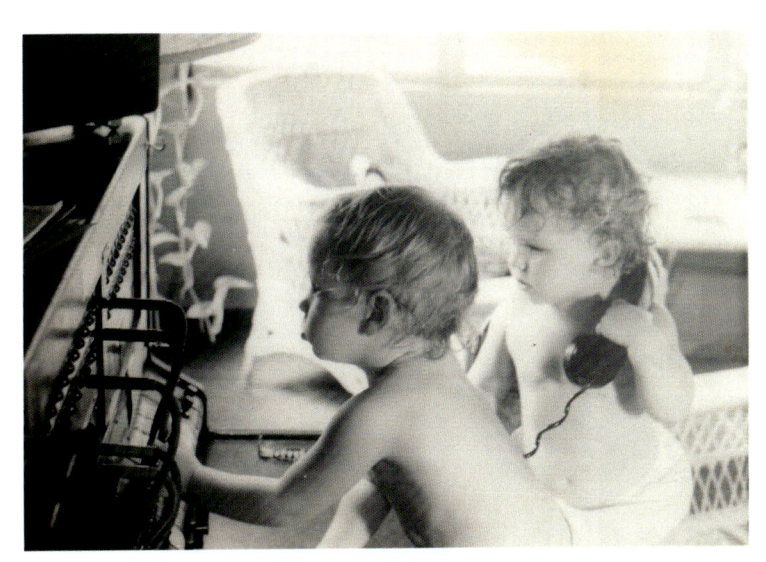

Jason & Kimberly on old Switchboard

Homer at 5 1/2 months old

Dad & Mom visiting at Ft. Gordon C-6-2

Image in the Mirror

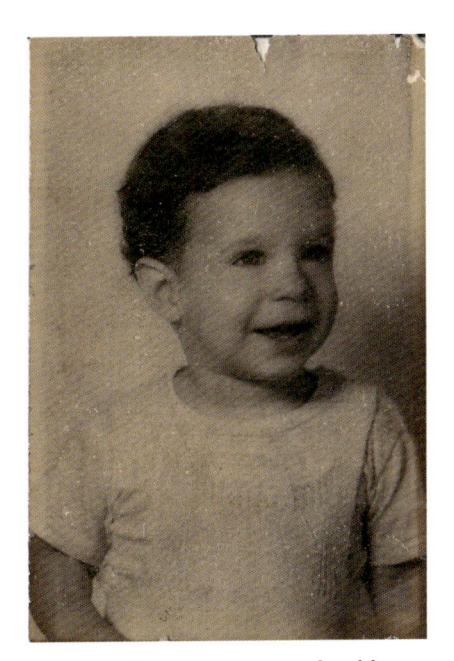

Homer at 15 months old

Homer, Mom, & D.A. at 5 & 3

Homer S. Sewell III

Homer at about 13 years old

Homer at Lincoln statue in Hingham, Mass. in 1992

Image in the Mirror

Homer, Dad, & wife, Susan—Thanksgiving 1992

Stuart, Homer, & Kimberly in 1992

Homer S. Sewell III

Barry, Dad, Homer & Susan in 1992

Birth Mother, Millie, upon Meeting Homer 1992

Image in the Mirror

Kimberly & Dad 1992

Homer, Kimberly & Dad in 1992

NYC Skyline from Hudson River in 1993—Notice Twin Towers

Image in the Mirror

Statue of Liberty before trip to Israel in 1993

Camels in Jerusalem

Twins, Jason & Kimberly

Image in the Mirror

Homer at Lincoln Street in Israel in 1993

Gershon, Barry, Homer & Stuart at Dead Sea in 1993

Kimberly, Jason, Homer & Chip

Image in the Mirror

2000 year old olive tree in Israel

Homer, Barry, Stuart, & Gershon in Israel in 1993

*Homer, Stuart, Gershon & Barry in Authentic
Biblical costumes in Israel in 1993*

Grandchildren Rylan, 5; Addie, 2

Image in the Mirror

Wedding October 4, 2009
Bride's matron of Honor, Laurie, Marti, Homer & Stuart, Best man

ABE & Marti the week we met at the Time Line Event.
I think she said "Mr. Lincoln, I've heard that line before!"